I0811740

FORT WORTH STORIES

FORT WORTH STORIES

by
Richard F. Selcer

Number 4 in the Texas Local Series

University of North Texas Press
Denton, Texas

Printed in the United States of America.

10 9 8 7 6 5 4 3 2 1

Permissions:
University of North Texas Press
1155 Union Circle #311336
Denton, TX 76203-5017

The paper used in this book meets the minimum requirements of the American National Standard for Permanence of Paper for Printed Library Materials, z39.48.1984. Binding materials have been chosen for durability.

Library of Congress Cataloging-in-Publication Data

Selcer, Richard F., author.
Fort Worth stories / by Richard F. Selcer. | "Book is collection of historical stories about Fort Worth, Texas, beginning in the 1840s and reaching the present day. Stories are chosen from typical events in Fort Worth that usually don't make it into traditional history books"—Provided by publisher.
Denton, Texas : University of North Texas Press, [2021]
pages cm
Includes bibliographical references and index.
ISBN-13 978-1-57441-830-9 (hardcover)
ISBN-13 978-1-57441-838-5 (ebook)
1. LCSH: Fort Worth (Tex.)—History.

F394.F7 S4486 2021
976.4/5315–dc23

2020042474

Fort Worth Stories is Number 4 in the Texas Local Series

The electronic edition of this book was made possible by the support of the Vick Family Foundation. Typeset by vPrompt eServices.

"A story told is a life lived."

—Chinese proverb

Contents

List of Illustrations

Acknowledgments

This, my thirteenth book, would not have been possible without the contributions of "the usual suspects" plus a few newcomers to the party. The list starts with Steve Coffman and Ron Chrisman. Steve is the editor of the *Fort Worth Star-Telegram* who first pitched the idea of a series of Sunday columns on Fort Worth history. Several of the chapters in this book started as columns in the Sunday newspaper in 2019. Second on the list is Ron Chrisman, director of the University of North Texas Press, who compressed the normal one-to-two-year timetable to publish a book into less than a year.

My biggest benefactors are Scott and Linda Jo Barker, who supported this latest Selcer project in so many ways: as IT experts, photo archivists, the occasional meal, and old-fashioned moral support. Scott created the photo array for the book, spending countless hours assembling, arranging, and photoshopping illustrations. This is the second book that he has filled this role for me.

I am also indebted to good friends and colleagues for putting me on the trail of many of these stories—and for helping fill in the gaps when my own research hit a dead-end. The "usual suspects" here are Carol Roark, Dalton Hoffman, Quentin McGown, Max Hill, John Roberts, Ruth Karbach, Clara Ruddell Holmes, Kevin Foster, Gayle Hanson, and Richard Gonzales. Without this support network, the book would not have been possible. Mike Nichols and Quentin McGown served as proof-readers *par excellence*, going through the manuscript with a fine-toothed comb uncovering errors that I'm sure I never wrote. Maybe gremlins?

Several libraries and archives contributed significantly to this book in both the research and illustrating stages: University of Texas at Arlington Special Collections (Sara Pezzoni, photo archivist and Brenda McClurkin, director); Tarrant County Archives (Dawn Youngblood, director, Lynn Spaulding, assistant archivist); the Fort Worth Library (Local History, Genealogy & Archives Unit, Linda Barrett, director), and Historic Fort Worth, Inc. (Jerre Tracy, president). Lisa Helbing also contributed illustrations out of her extensive personal collection of Fort Worth visual images.

I have to thank Randy Souders, a longtime friend and Fort Worth's most distinguished artist in residence, for allowing me to use his work, "Cattle Barons' Ball," as the cover. This is the second Souders painting I've used as a book cover. Keep painting 'em, Randy, and I'll keep writing 'em. I've said it before, but I'll say it again: a good book cover sells more books than all the glowing blurbs on the back ever did.

My sister Janet Lee Jones is an endless source of support and encouragement. I call her my "West Coast Agent" because she lives in San Jose, California, and she's always good for two or three sales.

Finally, I am indebted to the behind-the-scenes staff of the University of North Texas Press, starting with editor Karen DeVinney, for seeing this book through from rough manuscript to the final product you hold in your hands now. They did their usual fine job and in record time to make a 2021 release date.

—Richard Selcer
July 2020

Introduction

This book continues a journey I began more than a decade ago with *Fort Worth Characters* (UNT Press, 2009), namely, exploring the back roads of Fort Worth history. The stories told here are not part of the grand narrative of our city's history but throw more light on that narrative and hold some surprises for even the most knowledgeable of local historians. There is still a wealth of stories to be told buried in the old sources. They speak not just to those lucky enough to call Fort Worth home but to everyone interested in the life and times of bygone days.

This book began as a series of columns in the *Fort Worth Star-Telegram* in 2019 running once a month in the Sunday edition. (The "Fort Worth History" series rotated among this author, Mike Nichols, Carol Roark, and Richard Gonzales.) Some of the chapters here appeared in that column, but they have been fleshed out and annotated for readers who have a deeper interest in Fort Worth history than Sunday reading.

Basically, these are some of the stories Oliver Knight, the father of modern Fort Worth historians, did not tell, either because he did not know them or because he did not consider them worthy enough for the historical record. (Oliver Knight's 1953 book *Fort Worth, Outpost on the Trinity* is the Fort Worth historian's basic source.[1]) This book includes a lot of stories about blacks, women, Latinos, poor people—the kind of folks who slip between the cracks in traditional history—and a few stories about some famous folks who passed through Fort Worth to great or little fanfare at the time. Teddy Roosevelt, Harry Houdini, and Texas Guinan were never known for their visits to Fort Worth, but Fort Worthers got to see them up close and in the flesh and passed those memories down.

Some of the places and events described here did not seem important at the time. It is only looking back years later that their significance jumps out. Butch Cassidy and the Sundance Kid did stir a ripple of interest when they came to town in 1901; today we have a redeveloped section of downtown named for one of them. (They are not in this book because there's nothing new to say about them or their visit.) Others in this book were headline-worthy at the time but in the course of time were overwhelmed by more current events. Those old Fort Worth newspapers like the *Gazette*, the *Morning Register*, and the *Telegram* are gold mines of history that only recently have become accessible to the general public by being placed online. In the past they were not easy to navigate or to read. Even now they have to be used carefully because newspapers are only "the first edition of history." They were written in haste by men (yes, men) working under a deadline long before fact-checking became a standard in journalism.

Most of what we know about early Fort Worth history comes from three sources: Abraham Harris, Howard Peak, and B.B. Paddock. All three lived it and enjoyed long lives, which allowed them to tell their stories over and over to generations of Fort Worthers. In their final years they were honored as pioneer fathers or founding fathers. Fortunately for them all of their contemporaries died before they did, so there was no one around to contradict their stories. They outlived everybody! Many of their stories went into the 1949, 480-page Centennial Edition of the *Fort Worth Star-Telegram*, which was subsequently heavily mined by Oliver Knight for his 1953 book. Their names appear repeatedly in these stories, either because they were the source of the story or because they were personally involved. Either way, they cast a large, collective shadow over Fort Worth history.

Abe Harris was with Major Ripley Arnold when he established Fort Worth in 1849. He returned to Fort Worth after he left the army in 1852, went back into uniform for the Civil War, then settled in Fort Worth for good in 1865. In his sunset years he became a perennial favorite at Old Settlers' Reunions. Eventually he was crowned "the [unofficial] first settler of Fort Worth." By 1912 he was the last remaining member of the "pioneer" generation. B.B. Paddock tipped his hat to him when he wrote in 1906, "Col. Abe Harris, who recently celebrated his eightieth birthday, is the only man living of the volunteers and regulars who founded Fort Worth over fifty-six years ago." Always appearing in uniform, he regaled audiences with unflagging "interest and humor." When he died in 1915 the city lost its last living connection to its beginnings.[2]

B.B. Paddock was one of the men who helped forge the legend of "Col. Abe" in his newspaper columns and books. Paddock was the newspaper editor-turned-mayor-turned-author who ran two newspapers and wrote two books (1906 and 1922) in his lifetime. His newspaper columns and books contain a wealth of historic information—most of it factual. But not all of it. Like most people who rely on their memories, Paddock's stories in his later years sometimes differed from the original reports in his own newspapers. And like Forrest Gump, Paddock tended to place himself at the center of historic events like the coming of the railroad in 1876 when he said he was in the cab blowing the whistle as the first engine pulled into town.

His memory betrayed him in 1901 when he was pontificating on the city's early "street railways." Someone asked him when Fort Worth got its first streetcar line, and without hesitation he said "1875," which was actually a year before Fort Worth got its first rail line or streetcar (1876).[3]

More seriously, his version of historic events sometimes diverged significantly from the record. For instance, when he wrote about the Texas Spring Palace fire of 1890, he had hero Al Hayne leaping from a second-story window "holding a woman in his arms" and breaking both ankles when he hit the ground. Surprise: the newspapers of the day are very clear that Hayne collapsed exiting the building on the ground level and had to be dragged to safety. Paddock also says, "The officials of the company," which would have included himself, "directed the visitors to the various exits, and no Sunday School in the country was ever dismissed with more decorum and good order. Every person accepted the direction of those in charge as if they were on dress parade on a military plaza." Contemporary newspaper accounts tell a different story.[4]

Howard Peak, the third member of the troika who both lived and wrote our early history, was the first male child born in Fort Worth (1856), or at least that was the way he told it, and there are no medical records to say otherwise. A meeting of the Old Settlers' Association in 1899 confirmed his claim, which gave him all the license he needed to embellish the story further, claiming he was "the only boy born in the old military fort." He grew up to become a traveling salesman, which profession has always seemed to come with a gift for the blarney. By his sunset years he was not only a beloved guest of honor at public functions, he was also the oracle of Fort Worth whose recollections were serialized in the *Star-Telegram* starting in 1922 and delivered from the platform to generations of Fort Worth schoolchildren. He claimed that he got many of his stories from his father and mother,

The men who made Fort Worth history and wrote it, too: Abraham Harris (*ca.* 1892); Howard Peak (*ca.* 1929); and Boardman Buckley Paddock (*ca.* 1889). Harris courtesy of Genealogy, History & Archives Unit, Fort Worth Library, Historic Photographs Collection. Peak and Paddock from author's collection.

Dr. and Mrs. Carroll Peak, and from B.B. Paddock and Joseph C. Terrell, another couple of old-timers. It is ironic that Peak depended partly on Paddock who depended on his own faulty memory of events.[5]

Peak, Paddock, and Harris were all raconteurs *par excellence* as well as beloved senior citizens of Fort Worth. They were everyone's grandfather or favorite uncle. Who was going to question their version of things? And the next best thing to a good memory is outliving all your contemporaries.

These thirty-two chapters tell the stories behind the stories, or what Paul Harvey used to call, "the rest of the story," whether the broad strokes are about a well-known public building, famous person, or historic event. We may know about Theodore Roosevelt's visit to Fort Worth in 1905, but what photo-op act did he perform while he was here? We've heard about the Texas Spring Palace fire and Al Hayne, but was he really the only "hero" of the tragedy?

In other cases, we remember some of the famous persons who visited Fort Worth, like Quanah Parker and Will Rogers and John F. Kennedy, because we have statues that commemorate their visits. But what about other celebrities whose visits to Fort Worth have been completely forgotten, like Harry Houdini, who played our fair city not once but twice, or Vernon Castle? These might be called "The Stories Oliver Knight Never Told," or just "Fort Worth Stories." If nothing else, these stories remind us that the final version of history can never be written. We are constantly rewriting it with new information and new interpretation. Yesterday's hero becomes today's scamp, and yesterday's nobody becomes today's hero. That is the way of things, always has been, always will be.

Chapter 1

The Comanche Raid that Never Happened

It was another Howard Peak story that fit Fort Worth's frontier image of itself, so no one questioned it. Besides, by the time he got around to telling it, none of Peak's contemporaries were alive to challenge it.

Howard Peak was the son of Dr. Carroll M. Peak, the town's first doctor, and Howard claimed to be the first (white) male child born in Fort Worth, on June 14, 1856. That claim was certified, as it were, by the Old Settlers' Association in 1899 by a vote of all those present at their regular meeting. In the telling of his life Peak later tweaked the story to say he was the only male child born on the post, but there was no military post when he born; the Army closed Fort Worth down in 1853.[1] After getting an education at the U.S. Naval Academy and University of Kentucky, he became a traveling salesman, peddling hardware to merchants across west Texas. In those years traveling salesmen traveled by horse-drawn wagon along marked trails and back roads from community to community. He eventually retired to become the oracle of Fort Worth history. That position made him a regular lecturer on early Fort Worth history in the schools and the guest of honor at many a public gathering. It also got him a regular column in the *Fort Worth Star-Telegram* in the 1920s. In 1929 he published *A Ranger of Commerce OR 52 Years on the Road*, which gathered and expanded upon many of the stories he had told over the years. Among those stories was "A Fight with the Comanches in 1850," one of his most popular.

For the first time Peak revealed the source of the story, an important fact to know since obviously he had not been around to witness events personally. He said he got the story from "an old file of my father," who died in 1885. According to this story, the Comanche were a threat to Fort Worth from their "stronghold" in the area of Palo Pinto County. Chief Jim Ned, the purported leader of the tribe, was determined to "wipe [Fort Worth] out of existence," and prepared his warriors after first engaging in the usual "war dance." He divided his forces into two bands of

(a) Steel engraving of Dr. Carroll Peak, original source of Comanche raid story. (b) Historic marker put up in the 1920s on Summit Ave. memorializing a raid that never happened. Both from author's collection.

roughly 100 warriors each to approach Fort Worth from two directions and meet up a few miles from the post.[2]

When the raiding parties rendezvoused at the meeting place, they were spotted by a fur trapper "by the name of Cockerell," who hurried to Fort Worth to alert the garrison. In an hour's time, the full garrison of forty men had turned out and readied to march out. Besides the mounted dragoons, the command included "ambulances and equipment wagons." They reached the Indians' camping ground late at night and surrounded it quietly. Major Arnold divided his troops up into three groups under himself, Captain Robert Maclay, and Lt. Washington Street to charge the camp from three directions. At a given signal the mounted dragoons charged the camp and wreaked havoc among the sleeping Comanche, killing thirty-seven and severely wounding another fifteen. On Arnold's orders the wounded Indians were "dispatched" because it was "imperative under the circumstances." Not a soldier was wounded in the engagement.[3]

The troops then set out to locate the other band of Indians under Chief Feathertail who had not linked up with Jim Ned yet. Scouts located them and reported they had been joined by Jim Ned and were in full retreat back to "the Palo Pinto mountains." By forced march they reached the Comanche war village but stopped to rest and regroup before attacking. Arnold called a council of war of his officers and ordered a dawn attack on foot. At the designated hour the next morning, they advanced through a canyon on the village only to be ambushed themselves by their foe. All that saved them from massacre was their "repeating carbines." The battle raged for several hours. According to Howard Peak, "The deafening peal of firearms, the groans of the wounded, and the wailing of squaws and children was awful." When Chief Feathertail was downed, his followers fell back, forcing Chief Jim Ned to do likewise. Maj. Arnold ordered his men to advance and "annihilate the wavering opponents," and the Indians fled "into the mountains." It was over.[4]

In the aftermath, Arnold took stock of his losses and prepared to return to Fort Worth. Five dragoons were dead and another fifteen wounded. (He also counted forty-five Indians on the ground.) "Surgeons Halliday and Standifer" treated the wounded and loaded them into the "ambulances" The dead were buried "where they had fallen."[5]

The story did not end there. According to Peak, Chief Jim Ned was bent on revenge and "some six months later" mounted another attack on Fort Worth. He approached from the southwest under cover of night, pausing on a hillside. But Maj. Arnold was not caught napping. Advised by scouts of the approaching war party, he unlimbered his six-pound howitzer and dropped a round in the middle of the war party. The explosion scattered them and sent them running. Arnold ordered a pursuit that killed a number of the war party and chased the rest back to their home territory. "They never attempted a repetition of such bold hostility" again. Chief Jim Ned came in and accepted amnesty and lived peacefully until his death some years later.[6]

That's the story of the only engagement the Fort Worth garrison ever had against hostile natives during its four-year existence (1849–1853). It's what reviewer Mary Daggett Lake called one "thrilling story" among the many told by Howard Peak. Thrilling indeed, but there are so many historical problems with the story it's hard to know where to begin.

One might begin with the fact that another go-to source for early Fort Worth history, Abe Harris, told B. B. Paddock "The Indians never attacked Fort Worth." Howard Peak's own father, Dr. Carroll M. Peak, also told a different story at the ceremony laying the cornerstone for the 1877 courthouse. As he told it, a report reached Lancaster (sixteen miles south of Dallas) on one occasion that that Fort Worth was "beleaguered" by Indians and "the situation was extreme." A 60-man party mounted up and raced to the rescue only to be greeted upon arrival by a puzzled Maj. Arnold who told them everything was fine.[7]

The story's details are equally problematical, starting with the fact that "fur trapping" on the north Texas plains would have been meager at best considering the local fauna. Fur trappers stuck to the mountains, not the plains. Then there is the fact that Jim Ned was no Comanche; in fact, he was only half Native American. He was mixed blood, Delaware Indian and negro. He was never known to have ridden with the Comanche, much less as a warrior chief. When he was not stealing horses, he worked for whites as an interpreter and scout. In 1853, Maj. Hamilton Merrill, Ripley Arnold's successor at Fort Worth, asked his superiors for authorization to pay Jim Ned to serve as a "guide, etc." It hardly makes sense that Merrill would hire as a scout the selfsame Indian who just three years previously had tried to wipe out his garrison. The real Jim Ned would go down in Texas history as one of the "good Indians," honored by Taylor County naming their consolidated school district for him. It seems likely Jim Ned was the only "Chief" that Howard Peak, or his father, knew by name, thus he became the leader of a war party of Comanche.[8]

The names of the officers cited by Howard Peak also do not match up with the time and the place. Captain Robert Maclay was an 8th Infantry officer, not a 2nd Dragoons officer. It is Maclay who brought infantry reinforcements to Fort Worth in October 1849. Neither he nor his men would have ridden out on Maj. Arnold's sweep against the Indians as they were not mounted troops. Lt. Washington Street was also 8th Infantry and not at Fort Worth at the same time as Arnold. While Arnold was in command, he only had one lieutenant, Jonas P. Holliday, who was away on sick leave most of the time. Peak gives the names of two post surgeons connected to the action, which in itself is another clue he does not know what he's talking about. No frontier post ever had more than one assigned medical officer. In the case of Fort Worth, Dr. Jesse M. Standifer was a civilian, contract physician who was at the post only from June through October 1849. In the case of "Halliday" Peak may have been confusing a surgeon in his story with Lt. Jonas Holliday who was never a medical officer, or just a name made up out of whole cloth. In any case, the names of the principals in Peak's story do not match up with the known personnel at the post.

The arms that Peak describes either were not part of the arsenal at Fort Worth or they had not yet been invented in 1850. The artillery piece that Arnold used to scatter the Indian attack is described by Peak as a six-pounder (meaning it fired a six-pound shell). The garrison had a gun, but it was a twelve-pounder, not a six-pounder, and there is no record of it ever being fired in anger. As for Peak's "repeating carbines" that saved the day during the Indian ambush, there was no such weapon in 1850. The first repeating rifle used by the U.S. Army was the Spencer, 7-shot carbine, which was developed between 1854 and 1860 and adopted in 1863. In 1850 the dragoons would have been as amazed as the Indians at the presence of a repeating carbine.

The clincher is the complete lack of any mention in the official record of an engagement with the Comanche. Maj. William G. Freeman, on an official inspection of Fort Worth in September 1853, reported, "No Indians have visited the post … except a small party of Caddoes and Ionies," both of whom were peaceful tribes. The same report includes a letter from Maj. H.W. Merrill, the last commander at Fort Worth, who enumerates all the Indian tribes in the state, including "5 to 600 Comanche" in far west Texas, and says only about 250 "are capable of bearing arms." This was just two to three years after Howard Peak's phantom attack, so it is doubtful if the situation had changed that much. Plus, nowhere in the monthly post returns is there any mention of five soldiers being killed in action. Such a report would have been an absolute requirement for any officer commanding a military post. The post returns for Fort Worth, 1849–1853, make no mention of hostile action, much less casualties incurred in same. And those same returns also do not show that Fort Worth ever had an ambulance. That was a luxury that no frontier outpost would have possessed. The nearest army ambulance would have been at San Antonio.[9]

Peak's story bears a suspicious resemblance to one told by Abe Harris, likewise a beloved raconteur of frontier stories. His bona fides come from the fact that he was not just an old-timer but that he had been an original member of the garrison at Fort Worth. In Harris's story it was a war party of 300 Comanche and Caddo Indians led by Chief Towash that threatened the post, also in 1850. They were chasing a band of Tonkawas who sought the garrison's protection. When Towash sent a messenger to demand the garrison turn over the Tonkawas, Maj. Arnold replied he was "not in the habit of serving up his guests for breakfast," which is as thrilling as Xerxes' reply to the Persians at Thermopylae and Travis' reply to the Mexicans at the Alamo. Arnold punctuated his reply by ordering his howitzer to fire a shot "grazing the heads" of the war party "without hitting them," and a well-placed shell sent them running. According to Harris, this was the only time the garrison ever experienced a serious Indian threat. Like Peak's story, it has several historical problems, but the important thing is that the two old-timers told similar stories not borne out in the historical record, and the Army kept fairly complete records back then even for frontier posts.[10]

Finally, there is the comment of B.B. Paddock, himself no mean raconteur, of the believability of traveling salesmen. For his own writings he had interviewed many old-timers over the years. He may have had Howard Peak in mind when he wrote in his last work (1922) that practical jokes and tall tales were a way of life in Texas, especially among "traveling men." He goes on to relate a story about a group of such men who had great fun regaling a bunch of "tender-foot" visitors about wild Indians roaming west Texas. Paddock enjoyed a tall Texas tale as much as anyone.[11]

A popular legend is hard to kill. It gets embellished and the details are altered, but it lives on, to be told and retold. Variations on the phantom Comanche attack were recounted by other old-timers (AKA, "pioneers") six decades later. In 1913, E.B. "Bud" Daggett, scion of another distinguished family, gave an interview in which he "graphically described an Indian massacre, the last at Fort Worth." As he told a *Fort Worth Record* reporter, it had occurred just west of the North Side stockyards sometime "in the '50s." Mrs. Margaret Ann Holloway, who had been here since 1849, told a similar story to the *Record*, also about 1913. As she told it, the Comanche chased a band of Tonkaway Indians to the fort where they took shelter under the protection of the garrison. When Ripley Arnold arranged a peace conference, the Comanche fell upon the peaceful Tonkaway with knives. They were only driven off after Arnold fired the fort's cannon in their general direction. The common denominators in the Holloway and Peak stories are the hostile Comanche and the cannon shot. Peak's story loses out in credibility to both the Daggett and Holloway stories because of all the unsupported details. The moral is to maintain credibility it pays to keep the details skimpy. Thus, in one form or another the Comanche attack was passed down from one generation to another. No one could challenge the memories of old-timers because there were no archival records or visual proof saying otherwise, and who was going to call a beloved senior citizen a liar?[12]

The most repeated versions of the story remain Abe Harris's and Howard Peak's. The former's version never got the traction of Peak's because Harris never published his in book form, and he died before Peak. Howard Peak's longevity—he lived until 1939—and the publication of *A Ranger of Commerce* cemented his place in Fort Worth history as a gold-standard primary source. Two generations of Fort Worth schoolchildren grew up hearing his stories in the flesh in their classrooms where he spoke often, and their parents read his book. That was enough to get a memorial put up to the Comanche raid that never happened: a small concrete obelisk put up in 1923 by the Diamond Jubilee Committee on a shaded lawn on Summit Ave., just west of downtown. The marker stood there until just a few years ago when it was taken down to make way for new construction. It was saved from landfill by the quick action of a local historian and is currently in his garage awaiting a new home. It deserves to be saved not so much for the history it purports to remember as for what it says about the vagaries of public memory.[13]

Chapter 2

Longhair Jim Courtright, Legendary Marshal, Terrible Witness

Much has been written about Timothy Isaiah "Longhair Jim" Courtright over the years. He is Fort Worth's only claim to gunfighter fame. Tombstone, AZ, has the Earps; Abilene, Kansas, has Wild Bill Hickok; Fort Worth has Longhair Jim. He ended up on the wrong side of the law and the wrong side of a gunfight, but he is still ours.[1]

He had been on the lam for more than a year from a murder charge in New Mexico when he came back to Fort Worth in January 1886. The charges against him in New Mexico were still pending as he resumed his life in Fort Worth. He had already dodged an extradition warrant once with help from his pals in the police department. He was no longer city marshal, having been voted out of office in 1879, but he was still a force to be reckoned with. He put his guns and his reputation to work by opening a private detective agency that worked for whoever would hire him, supplementing his income by running what amounted to an extortion racket selling "protection" to saloon owners. Mostly, he drank heavily and spent his time at the gambling tables. When he drank, he was a belligerent drunk.

Timothy Isaiah "Longhair Jim" Courtright, legendary "two-gun marshal" of Fort Worth. His only known picture. Author's collection.

Whatever skills he once had with a gun eroded over the years. He got by on his reputation and bullying ways. His date with destiny came on February 8, 1887, when he called out Luke Short. The two stepped out onto the sidewalk from the White Elephant Saloon. They exchanged words, and the next thing anyone knew, ex-Marshal Courtright lay dead on the sidewalk, dispatched by the dapper gambler known as "Little Luke."[2]

Courtright's last hurrah as a lawman came ten months earlier during the Great Southwest Railroad Strike of 1886, which involved the Buttermilk Junction ambush of a Texas & Pacific train and led to a Congressional investigation. Courtright was a star witness in that investigation, a role none of his experiences in life to date prepared him for.

The labor strike had begun in Marshall, Texas, in February 1886, with a wildcat strike against Jay Gould's Texas & Pacific line. The strike pitted the biggest labor union in the nation (Knights of Labor) against one of the biggest railroads in the nation and was fought out in the biggest state in the nation. What began as a localized action in Marshall quickly spread throughout the entire Missouri Pacific network (the T&P was part of the Missouri Pacific system). Fort Worth was a major rail center and a strong union town with nearly a thousand residents working for the T&P. The *Fort Worth Gazette* editorialized that the Knights of Labor "seem to be stronger than the law in Fort Worth."[3]

History would dub it the Great Southwest Railroad Strike of 1886. The ex-marshal was pressed into service by Mayor John Peter Smith as a special deputy acting under the orders of City Marshal and old Courtright pal William Rea. He also had the added authority of holding a deputy U.S. marshal's commission. His job was not so much to be a peacekeeper as to guard Texas & Pacific property. Courtright, exercising his new authority, issued "bullying threats" against the strikers that was typical of the way he had always done things, but alienated the strikers. They felt the law was in cahoots with the railroad and against them. Mayor Smith defended the appointment by stating that "people who violated the law had no right to choose who should arrest them." Cattleman Will Lake supposed that Courtright had been appointed because "he was competent to exercise the duties to which he was assigned." As a former town marshal who had held office during some of the wildest times in Fort Worth history, he knew how to handle hard cases with either fists or guns. In retrospect, Courtright was a man who only knew one way of handling things; he always brought a hammer where sometimes a scalpel was better.[4]

Courtright tapped seven deputies whose only qualification was being "friends of Jim." Together they formed an escort for a strike-busting train dispatched by T&P authorities in Fort Worth on April 3 to Alvarado, 27 miles south of Fort Worth. When the train got to Buttermilk Junction, two miles outside of town, it was ambushed by a group of eight or nine men armed with Winchesters. Courtright and his crew were only armed with six-shooters, a serious oversight under the circumstances. Three of his men went down in the gun battle. Courtright himself received two bullets through his hat but otherwise escaped unscathed. He ordered his wounded loaded onto the train which then backed all the way back to town. One of the wounded deputies, Dick Townsend, died that night, and the other two were in serious condition.[5]

Courtright's reputation took a beating because he had been in charge, and it was he who ordered the precipitous retreat. The *San Antonio Light* laid the blame for what it called the "Fort Worth massacre" squarely on his shoulders. He did not wear it well though he continued to wear a badge and work with Sheriff Walter Maddox and Marshal William Rea searching the countryside for the bushwhackers.[6]

Fort Worth authorities locked the city down. Heavily armed police and special deputies patrolled the streets. They called on the governor to send in the Texas Rangers and state militia to help restore order. Fort Worth was literally under martial law. The federal government was involved but only peripherally. The trains carried the U.S. mail, and the strike had stopped the trains. The fact that the strikers had resorted to violence raised the stakes, persuading Congress to take a direct interest in what was happening in Texas. The House of Representatives formed a subcommittee chaired by Texas Congressman W.H. Crain to go to Texas and investigate on the ground. They arrived in Fort Worth by special train on Thursday morning, May 6, to be met by the mayor and other dignitaries. The opera house had been suggested as the best site to hold the hearings, but they wound up "in a dingy room on the ground floor" of a newspaper office on the square. They got down to work that same afternoon around two o'clock, conducting two grueling sessions over the next two days. They were more interested in the "railroad troubles" than in the Buttermilk Junction ambush specifically, a focus that was reflected in their list of witnesses, which consisted mostly of businessmen who denounced the labor union and the strike.[7]

Among those called on the first day was Deputy James [*sic*] Courtright. (No one called him "Longhair Jim" anymore.) When asked to describe the fight he emphasized that he and his men had been fired on by the strikers without provocation. He did not mention that at the time the firing started he was arresting Charles Dalton, one of the strikers who had obstructed the tracks and brought the train to a halt. When bullets started flying Dalton got away. After that, he said, they had defended themselves. Under cross-examination, however, some witnesses were not so sure which side fired first. What was clear was that Special Officer Courtright got back to Fort Worth with three wounded men and no prisoner. On Saturday, the Congressmen packed up and headed back to Washington. Nothing ever came of their investigation except a general government campaign to break the Knights of Labor. The Great Southwest Strike was resolved peaceably a few days later, but the consequences of the Buttermilk Junction ambush kept Fort Worth authorities busy for a long time.[8]

They continued to scour the countryside and raid the homes of known Knights of Labor members and sympathizers. When Charles Dalton was brought in under arrest a couple of weeks after Buttermilk Junction, Courtright went down to the jail to identify him, which was important because none of the other bushwhackers had shown themselves. In what passed for a line-up in those days, Courtright stood at Dalton's cell and identified him. "I cannot be mistaken in the man," he told a reporter who was there. Still a sworn officer of the law, Courtright's identification should have carried a lot of weight, but Dalton would be acquitted on all charges when eventually brought to trial. A few days later Courtright was called to Parsons, Kansas, where another accused bushwhacker, Tom Low, was being held by the authorities. Courtright dutifully went to Parsons and identified the prisoner even though he could not honestly say he had seen him at the scene of the bushwhacking. Low was just another Fort Worth strike leader the authorities were rounding up.[9]

Though Courtright was no longer a special deputy, the Buttermilk Junction ambush still hung over him. He managed to stay sober and step away from the gaming tables long enough to testify in the habeas corpus hearing of accused bushwhacker Henry Henning on January 15, 1887. He was called as a witness for the state who wanted to keep Henning locked up until his trial. Courtright's testimony was unenlightening when it came to describing the particulars of the attack. He would only say he "believed" Henning was one of the bushwhackers but could not "swear positively" to it, which was not what prosecutors wanted to hear and was at variance with what Courtright had said eight months earlier.

He also testified that Deputy Dick Townsend had been shot in the back at point-blank range, contrary to the evidence and to the testimony of other witnesses. Witnesses for the defense, who could only have been either other train guards or T&P crew, testified that Courtright had spent most of the gun battle hugging the ground more concerned with his own safety than with organizing his men. Henning was denied bail, no thanks to Courtright. Still another accused bushwhacker captured sometime later told officers that Courtright had been their primary target. The fact that he had escaped without a scratch suggested to some that Courtright may have been present, but he was not in the fight, a damning reflection on the personal courage of the ex-marshal.[10]

Henry Henning did not come to trial until June 1887, four months after Luke Short had removed Longhair Jim Courtright from the scene. The defense made good use of Courtright's subcommittee testimony to poke holes in the state's case. On top of that, defense witness O.F. Darby, who had been a train guard at Buttermilk Junction, testified that Courtright deputy James Thompson had fired the first shots. Henning was convicted nonetheless and sentenced to life in prison, but Courtright's reputation had taken another beating.[11]

When John R. Hardin, the accused leader of the bushwhackers, was brought to trial, six years after the battle of Buttermilk Junction, he was acquitted. The *Dallas Morning News* blamed the prosecution's failure to secure a conviction largely on Courtright. They did not find a pinch of difference between the two parties in the affair, saying, "This verdict is in a great degree attributable to the reputation of Jim Courtright, a local desperado who was in charge of the party of guards on the train on which Hardin and his crowd made the attack." By then Jim Courtright was no longer around to defend himself with his fists or anything else. He had always been a man of action, not words anyway. That was why he made such a terrible witness. The man once lauded as the marshal who brought law and order to Fort Worth had outlived his legend. The day after he met his end, the *Dallas Morning News* summed up his life this way: "With Courtright's death a character prominent in the history of Fort Worth passes away … He was game to the backbone."[12]

Chapter 3

Hogs Rule in Cowtown

Everyone loves it when the little guy takes on powerful special interests and wins. If the little guy happens to be a hog farmer and the special interests are the city and a national hotel chain, so much the better. It happened in 1973, but Fort Worth's love for porcine animals goes back to the city's beginning. Everybody kept hogs and had a smokehouse, including the soldiers at Fort Worth, 1849–1853. What was not turned into meat was turned into soap. They were the easiest form of livestock to keep for meat; they could eat anything, required minimal oversight, and bred like rats, meaning a steady supply of meat or a steady income from marketing them. For these reasons, hogs were the most numerous of all livestock on the frontier, even more than horses or cattle. In 1860 Texas had 2.37 hogs per capita; that is 2.37 hogs for every man, woman and child.[1]

According to Fort Worth's first city engineer, I.C. Terry, feral hogs had the complete run of the town in the early years. When R.E. Beckham became mayor in 1878 he vowed to get the animals off the streets and keep them off. The city council approved a hog ordinance that was then referred to the voters in a referendum election. It passed but by the slim margin of 377 to 344. But the animals continued to be a "major nuisance" because old habits are hard to change (the voters', not the hogs').[2]

There was another "hog election" seven years later to address the same problem: whether hogs and other livestock should be allowed to run "at large" on the streets. Since most of the city's streets were still unpaved, and there was no Sanitation Department to keep the streets clean, the animals could make a mess of things. They also posed a physical danger to people trying to walk the streets. Fort Worth liked to think it was civilized in 1885, but the truth was something else. County Judge Sam Furman ordered the election after a citizens' petition was submitted to him demanding city fathers do something. The proposed ordinance was not equally popular with everyone. Since so many residents owned the little critters, they did not want to see their livestock impounded by the police, and they sure did not want to pay a fine. After six days, the election was still too close to call, but eventually, it was declared to have passed. Thereafter, city police maintained a "holding pen" (pound) for stray hogs at the corner of Ninth and Throckmorton, on the future site of Fort Worth's first public library (1901).[3]

Hogs roaming the streets may have been a nuisance, but the local economy needed hogs as much as it did cattle. While longhorns merely passed through town on the way up to Kansas railheads, hog processing was an early industrial enterprise. In 1875 a Dallas-based hog processing venture was in the works. John Peter Smith even donated six acres on the south end of town to build it. The plant was never built, and meat processing had to wait until Swift and Armour came to town thirty years later. And Swift and Armour meatpackers' part in creating the popular image of the Fort Worth Stockyards as a cattle kingdom ignores the fact that they slaughtered and processed more hogs every day than cattle. Moreover, the critters were never the exclusive province of dirt farmers and slaughterhouses. Khleber Van Zandt, remembered as Fort Worth's first banker and a town builder, kept pigs on his Main-and-Sixth-St. property until selling it to State National Bank in 1884. Hogs were still part of the political culture in 1926 when First Baptist preacher J. Frank Norris thundered from the pulpit that Mayor H.C. Meacham was not fit to be "mayor of a hog pen." The mayor's good friend Dexter E. Chipps subsequently took up the matter with the preacher, much to Chipps's regret.[4]

Hogs were such an important part of Fort Worth history, Howard Peak devoted a whole chapter on them in his first book of memoirs, *My Recollections of Fort Worth.* He referred to them all as "razor-back hogs" before the University of Arkansas practically patented the name.[5]

As Fort Worth grew into a 20th -century metropolis, hogs and hog farms seemed a thing of the past—until hog farmer A.L. Miner went to war with city fathers in 1970. Even while he worked for the Texas & Pacific, Miner had kept a hog farm in Sycamore Creek bottom on the eastern edge of downtown, sharing the 3.6-acre piece of land with his son. They continued to raise hogs even as the city built out to them after the Dallas-Fort Worth turnpike (I-30 today) was completed in 1957 and Beach St. intersected it nearby. Then in December 1970 the city council amended the animal control ordinance to make it unlawful "to keep or permit to be kept any swine … within the city limits" not counting slaughterhouses (Swift and Armour) or livestock expositions (the annual Fat Stock Show). A month later Miner got his first citation and was fined $100 in municipal court. He appealed to county court, and in the meantime, police kept issuing citations and he came to trial in municipal court. It came out during the legal fight that the Ramada Inn chain was planning to build a hotel on Beach St. right above Miner's farm. The developers offered to buy him out for $50,000, which he refused. At the time the two pieces of property together were

A.L. Miner and four-legged friend. Courtesy *Fort Worth Star-Telegram* Collection, Special Collections, University of Texas at Arlington Library, Arlington, TX.

appraised at approximately $10,000. The Miners offered to sell for $95,000 and vowed to take their fight to the Supreme Court if necessary.

It was a David-vs.-Goliath story—if David had been a pig farmer. Goliath was the city of Fort Worth led by Mayor R.M. "Sharkey" Stovall and the H.A.T. company, a Dallas hotel developer. Miner posed for newspaper photographers holding one of his animals, and nearby residents, when interviewed, said Miner was a good neighbor, and they had no objection to his farm. Several even offered to testify for him.

Miner's stubbornness seemed to have been a big mistake when his citations came to trial in municipal court in 1973. A jury with not a single farmer on it found him guilty and ordered him to pay his fines, but on appeal to county court he was found not guilty of violating city ordinance. Having won in court, later that year Miner and son sold their property to H.A.T. for a cool $102,000. He also got the final laugh by moving his hog operation across the highway to land he leased until 1979. Miner died in 1989. The retired railroad man lived his final years in comfort thanks to winning his legal fight with the city and developers.[6]

The little porkers continued to have a place in the hearts (and arteries) of Fort Worthers long after they disappeared off the city's streets and out of residents' backyards. In 1921 the first Pig Stand restaurant was launched by Jesse G. Kirby in Tarrant County, the first of what eventually became a national chain. It was the Pig Stand that introduced the concept of the drive-in restaurant so ubiquitous today. The last Fort Worth Pig Stand on W. Seventh closed in the 1970s. The last Pig Stand nationally closed in 2006.[7]

Served on a bun smothered with BBQ sauce, pigs were everyone's favorite. On the hoof was another matter. In the 1990s, however, a stomach-churning civic debate arose over keeping pot-bellied pigs as pets. When the city council outlawed them, the owners banded together to petition the council to treat the

(a) A.L. Miner's hog farm just east of downtown (I–30 at Beach). Courtesy *Fort Worth Star-Telegram* Collection, Special Collections, University of Texas at Arlington Library, Arlington, TX. (b) Ramada Inn Central where once hogs roamed free. Author's collection.

cute little critters the same as dogs and cats. Pot-bellied pigs even found their way into the Southwestern Exposition and Fat Stock Show, that Cowtown celebration of bronc-bustin' cowboys and bull-riders. When traditionalists complained about showing the animals, pig owners retorted, "If you can't ride it, eat it, or rope it," they're against it.[8]

In recent years, not all the pigs found in Fort Worth could be classified as cute, cuddly pets or show animals. The city's parks and recreation department has been waging an ongoing war against feral hogs for decades. The animals live in the Trinity River bottoms, coming out to devour backyard gardens and destroy landscaping and scare joggers all over the Metroplex. They started turning up in significant numbers about 1999 and have grown more numerous and more aggressive ever since.[9]

Pioneer fathers like Joseph C. Terrell and K.M. Van Zandt might wonder what all the fuss is about over a very useful, nutritious, and profitable animal, but 21st century Fort Worthers are not in the habit of slaughtering a few hogs every fall to lay in meat for the winter and make soap. Pigs are now considered "exotic animals." Unfortunately, no one told the critters they no longer have any place in our town except on a bun or as spareribs.

Chapter 4

Fort Worth Learns to Bathe

Today we consider bathing to be part of our daily routine, and every home has bathroom facilities that include hot-and-cold running water. But it has not always been so. People in the 19th century did not bathe every day or even every week, and when they did it was usually just a dip in the nearest lake or river with or without clothes. Regular bathing and the facilities for same were part of becoming urbanized. Still, bathing was considered such a luxury that many cities taxed bathtubs in homes at $8 per annum and public baths at $6 per tub per annum.[1]

Fort Worth's early bathing facilities—besides a dip in the nearby Trinity—were connected to barber shops. Phil Decker's barber shop at 703 Main was such a place. A man or woman could get a bath there for $1. The Mansion Hotel, which opened in 1878, was the first public accommodation to offer guests the chance to take a bath—an additional 25¢ on top of the 25¢ room charge. The wooden tub sat on the back porch sheltered from prying eyes by walls on two sides and grapevine-covered trellises on the other two. It was filled from a pump in the alley next to the hotel that connected via a V-shaped trough. The water was unheated. When a guest wanted a bath, he had to ask the porter to fill the tub and give him a bar of soap. Those were first-class accommodations![2]

There were other bathtubs in town, but they were not for just anybody. The Texas & Pacific railroad had a tub in the roundhouse for its conductors and engineers to use after coming off hot, sooty journeys. It was especially appreciated in the summer months by the engineers who rode in the engine next to the boiler and by conductors who had to wear ties and coats regardless of the weather. This was one of the privileges of "railroad men" at a time when private bathtubs in the home were practically unheard of. Another class of persons who were anything but privileged also had access to a bathtub. These were long-term prisoners in the county jail for whom a bath if not a change of clothes was part of their weekly routine. The tub, which was also used by the jailers, had an important secondary use on occasion. It was available for baptisms, which came in handy in particular for men facing execution who underwent a late spiritual conversion. The Tarrant County jail in this regard was nothing special. Every county jail had a bathtub, which was something every hotel could not say.[3]

The city's first public bath house that did not require renting a room or working for the T&P was W.R. Haymaker's Artesian Bath House on the northwest corner of the public square. It opened in 1884 to serve both "gentlemen and ladies." It had "first-class attendants" and "hot and cold water at all hours." Though located practically on the river it got its water from a deep well on-site, ensuring purity and allowing the owner to brag that he had "the best bathing water in the state." Artesian water was notably "soft," which made it easy to work up a good, soapy lather that left the skin feeling "velvety" afterwards. It cost the same as a bath at the Mansion Hotel.[4]

When the Natatorium opened in 1890 (Third and Rusk/ Commerce), it was not so much for recreational swimming, which few people did, as for bathing, which was finally catching on in Fort Worth. The Natatorium put Haymaker's Artesian Bath House out of business. Both boasted of using pure, artesian well water, not "river water or surface water." At four stories and costing $150,000, it was more than just a bath house. It offered Fort Worthers a level of luxury they had never experienced before: a 50 × 90-foot public swimming pool, Turkish and Russian steam baths, and rooms to rent for longer stays like a hotel. All this was in addition to a barbershop and old-fashioned "tub baths." The Turkish and Russian facilities were the biggest novelty, so much so that the *Gazette* published the name of the first person to try the Turkish bath, Col. J.K. Ashby, who declared that it "excelled anything of the kind he had ever taken." And, he added, he had taken such baths "in all of the larger cities of the country." There were no subsequent reports of how many persons tried the novelty of the Russian and Turkish baths, but business in general went up in the summer months, suggesting that most folks wanted just a simple soap-and-water bath, not the exotic steam-room experience. Catering to that audience, management reached out to those "determined to go through the summer clean, cool, and healthy."[5]

But it was treating bathing as part of one's personal routine that represented the biggest step forward for Fort Worthers. Historically, bathing at home was difficult; it required setting up the tub and heating the water even before one got naked and leaped in. The usual lye soap was hard on the skin, and in winter weather bathing was believed to cause colds.

Fort Worth's first bathtub of record belonged to J.Y. Hogsett, a prominent lawyer who came to town in 1872 and was well-regarded enough to get the job of writing the city's charter in 1873. Hogsett was a man of "strict sobriety" and a fastidious dresser who paid a lot of attention to personal hygiene. No one knows exactly when, but sometime before 1876, he ordered his bathtub by mail from St. Louis and had it shipped by rail to Dallas. It was hauled the last thirty-five miles to Fort Worth by wagon. Reportedly the whole town celebrated its arrival as a mark of advancing civilization on the Trinity. It was made of iron and shaped like "an old-fashioned coffin," two feet wide at the upper end, tapering to a foot wide at the lower end. It sat on four stubby legs. Someone dubbed it "Old Ironsides," and the name stuck. It was still the only bathtub in town a few years later when merchant B.C. Evans came down with a dangerously high fever. Dr. W.P. Burts prescribed cooling baths, so Old Ironsides was loaded onto a wagon and hauled to Evans' residence for his use. About 1904 the historic tub passed into the hands of Ballard Ice and Fuel Co. who used it to water the horses and mules that pulled their wagons. It was still in the family, however, because Joseph J. Ballard was Judge Hogsett's son-in-law.[6]

Private bathtubs remained luxury items owned only by the privileged few. Another early bathtub owner was Ed Farmer, one of Fort Worth's pioneer businessmen and biggest real estate developers. As a "capitalist" and distinguished member of the Board of Trade, Farmer had to maintain a certain image. He also lived in one of the mansions that had room for a bathroom with bathtub and hot-and-cold running water. No more hauling hot water in from the kitchen stove on Saturday nights.

Inmates of the jail were not always willing bathers; some of them had to be persuaded. This was the job of a prisoner "kangaroo court" that forced every inmate to take twice-weekly baths (Wednesdays and Saturdays). The jailers backed the kangaroo court, not for the benefit of the prisoners but to keep down the stench and help prevent disease. Woe be unto any prisoner who resisted his required bath. Eventually the city jail also installed a bathtub for the same reasons as the county jail only with more of a sense of urgency. Since the city lockup

Famous moments in Fort Worth bathing history: (a) The county jail's bathtub kept the jail population reasonably clean. (b) The Mansion was Fort Worth's first hotel with a bathtub. Sketches from 1915 *Star-Telegram* series. Author's collection.

was in the basement of city hall, the need to keep a certain level of cleanliness was an important consideration for those who had business at city hall.[7]

Even after Fort Worth became a civilized metropolis, the finer points of bathing were still foreign to some citizens. In 1911 James Ellis proposed turning the burned-out shell of the high school building into "a public bath house." He argued, "There is but one public bath house in Texas, I understand, and that is inferior. Why shouldn't Fort Worth take the lead instead of following other Teas cities." He added anachronistically, "the public bath house is inevitable."[8]

A year later the city had two public swimming pools, the Natatorium and the YMCA. As the park board considered building the first outdoor pool in Trinity Park, a number of things had to be considered: Should the pool be drained and refilled periodically? What about mixed swimming? And what sort of bathing attire should be allowed? But the clincher concerned what to do about swimmers who treated the pool like their own private bathtub. As the *Star-Telegram* pointed out in an editorial, "The great trouble lies in the fact that nearly everyone looks upon the swimming pool as a place where they may wash as well as swim." Some persons would inevitably show up with soap and a towel and proceed to scrub down in the midst of their fellow swimmers. One possible solution to the sanitation problem was suggested by the Physical Director of the YMCA who pointed out that many public pools across the nation were experimenting with chemically treating the water (with chlorine).[9]

Fort Worth had come a long way since the good people of the town had come out to gawk at J.Y. Hogsett's new bathtub and wonder what he was going to do with it. In a few short years every new house built would have indoor plumbing including a bathtub. Daily ablutions would become a civilized routine.

Chapter 5

"Sign Us Up!" Fort Worthers Dig Deep to Support Their Town

Fort Worthers have always shown a willingness to dig deep when asked to support worthy projects, anything that would make Fort Worth bigger and better. Today when taking on a big project, we look to Uncle Sam for financing, but back in the 1880s the *City Directory* bragged, "Everything in Fort Worth is done by private subscription, and her citizens are public spirited beyond parallel." Even the name for it, "subscribing," transformed the simple act of contributing when the hat was passed into an investment in the future. Fort Worth had an enviable reputation from the very beginning as a community of movers and shakers. In 1887 the *Quanah Advance* said, "It only takes a little time, money and Fort Worth pluck to do anything." About the same time, the *Houston Post* put it this way: "Fort Worth owes no man anything for what it has accomplished. This town is self-made." It was not the Fort Worth way to beg for a legislative appropriation or federal grant before moving on a big project. Until well into the 20th century aggressive fund-raising drives paid for big-dollar projects like the Texas Spring Palace, Swift and Armour meatpacking plants, Camp Bowie, and the General

Motors assembly plant. There were plenty of other examples where citizens signed on with no promise of ever receiving a dime back in dividends. The future was what mattered.[1]

It started with thinking BIG, which means taking on near-impossible projects with an enthusiasm both admirable and risky. In 1890 the *Fort Worth Gazette* proudly dubbed Fort Worth "the pluckiest city in Texas." Forty-six years later Will Rogers echoed those same sentiments, saying, "Fort Worth never turned down a good cause because Fort Worth possesses both a heart as well as a head." Howard Peak called it "the Fort Worth spirit."[2]

"Public subscription" meant in effect passing the hat collecting contributions small and large; the size of the contribution was not what mattered. Every citizen was asked to be part of the worthy project. Fort Worthers were united in their desire to see their town grow up to be a big city. Typically, the call went out in a series of public meetings where boosters announced the goal and beat the drum for the project. Some subscribers actually put up money at these meetings. Others pledged substantial donations to come in later. While the drive was underway, the money was held by the town's leading newspaper, one of the principal banks, or the Board of Trade (Chamber of Commerce). For subscribers there was no promise of repayment if the project fell through. They subscribed on faith and the promise that good things would surely follow. They were betting on the future of Fort Worth. As little old Fort Worth became a metropolis and the cost of public works increased exponentially, subscription drives took the form of bond issues, usually handled by a New York firm. Bonds guaranteed a return on the investment but had to be approved by the voters and depended on local investors, which in the end was the same thing as the old town-meeting subscription drives.

Town boosterism was typically spearheaded by one of those legendary figures in Fort Worth history: B.B. Paddock in the late 19th century, Amon G. Carter for much of the 20th century, and Bob Bolen in the modern era. Paddock set the standard, using his newspapers, the *Democrat* and *Gazette,* to beat the drum for bringing railroads and industry to town. One Texas editor grumped, "Hell is full of newspapermen who killed themselves blowing for some little one-horse town … without enough support to fatten a grasshopper." Fort Worth was not such a town. Paddock and other city fathers were determined to put Fort Worth on the map—and make it bigger than Dallas. Paddock's career overlapped that of his successor, Amon Carter. In 1912 they were both members of the Chamber of Commerce trying to bring new industry to Fort Worth. They came up with the slogan, "We're for smoke," to get their message out that a little air pollution was a good thing. In 2006 mayor emeritus Bob Bolen said, "Cowtown remains a can-do town.... May we never lose that spirit." Of course, the major newspapers flogged the boomer spirit tirelessly by contributing generously themselves and running subscription drives in their pages. B.B. Paddock's *Gazette* and Amon Carter's *Star-Telegram* were always willing to get behind a big subscription drive.[3]

Fort Worthers' enthusiasm for big public works projects was almost boundless. At some mass meetings in the 1880s when railroads were being enticed to town, a packing plant was in the works, and a waterworks was being built, boosters collected pledges at the rate of a thousand dollars a minute. On one occasion, B.B. Paddock, John Peter Smith, and their pals raised $100,000 in a single evening. Of course, pledging was one thing; coming through with the money was something else. Some pledges required a little subsequent arm-twisting.[4]

The first subscription drive in Fort Worth history was for a county courthouse. After stealing the county-seat title from Birdville, Fort Worth set about building an appropriate place to conduct the county's business. Col. Middleton Tate Johnson donated a piece of prime real estate atop the bluff, and forty-one citizens kicked in $2,700. Construction got underway in 1860 only to be delayed by the Civil War. Finally completed after the war, it burned in 1876. A population that numbered only about 2,000 dug deep again to come up with the $60,000 needed to build another courthouse.[5]

Citizens turned out again in the spring of 1876 to bring the railroad to town. Without that lifeline to civilization the town was likely to dry up and blow away. At a series of well-attended public meetings, citizens subscribed $25,000 and chartered the Tarrant County Construction Company to lay the last few miles of track into town. In the years to follow, bringing in additional railroads was the No. 1 cause for town boosters. The money raised went to stock companies with the magic word ("railroad") in their name and promises of future wealth for all concerned. Boosters termed the money "a bonus" to the railroad; critics called it extortion. Years later, the Chamber of Commerce conceded that Fort Worth had literally "bought all the railroads she ever secured." That generosity included "subscribing" $75,000 in 1880 to entice the Gulf, Colorado & Santa Fe to town. It took only three days to raise the full amount. John Peter Smith alone kicked in $5,200. B.B. Paddock later told how he and Khleber Van Zandt had called a public meeting and locked the doors until the money was raised. Paddock, of course, had a good story for every history-making event, usually with himself at the center. Another subscription drive in April 1881 raised $25,000 for the Fort Worth & Denver City spearheaded by the usual cast of characters: Paddock, Ephraim Daggett, Walter A. Huffman, Joseph C. Terrell, and Carroll M. Peak. When they reached their goal, a Dallas newspaper reported, "The people [of Fort Worth] are jubilant." They were at it again in the next year or two, coming up with $40,000 to bring the Fort Worth & Rio Grande to town and $75,000 for the Cotton Belt. Fully $27,000 of the FW&RG's bonus was subscribed in just the first four hours. As far as city fathers were concerned, no price was too high to pay, no railroad demand too extravagant. It was in 1881 that the *Fort Worth Democrat* reported, "In the past six months Fort Worth has contributed by public subscription to various enterprises nearly $200,000," a truly remarkable sum by a town with a population of only about 7,000. Sometimes, the less affluent required a little cajoling, but civic pride was a hot button not just for rail lines but also for a hospital or a public library. In 1883, a group raised $14,000 in three hours to build an infirmary specifically for Texas & Pacific workers (what eventually became St. Joseph's Catholic Hospital). Fort Worth railroad baron S.B. Hovey once said if there was a political party "For the Good of Fort Worth" he would be a charter member. He would have had a lot of company.[6]

Other worthy causes in these same years persuaded Fort Worthers to dig deep. In 1878 the first "free bridge" across the Trinity was built with one-half of the $6,000 cost coming from subscriptions. Among subscribers, John Peter Smith led the way with $300. Another sixty-nine businesses and individuals pitched in with amounts ranging from $5 to $100.[7]

A booming economy in the 1880s made raising money through subscription drives easy. The true test of public spirit came with the bad times. When the 1890s brought a national economic downturn ("Panic"), the people of Fort Worth still raised the money to land a packing plant, a brewery, and a cotton mill. Let others retrench in hard times; Fort Worth citizens went full throttle. They sniffed at Dallas's timidity, comparing themselves to Chicago as a great regional metropolis.[8]

Fort Worth's penchant for calling fund-raising meetings led the *Dallas Herald* to sneer, "The citizens of Fort Worth never do anything without a public meeting." It was not just the rich who answered the call; farmers and shopkeepers rubbed elbows with bankers and "capitalists." Someone such as Robert McCart or B.B. Paddock always opened the meeting with a rousing speech touting the "invincible spirit of Fort Worth." Then came the call for citizens to "subscribe." In 1890, $125,000 was raised to build a new city hall. Major contributors included cattleman Jake Johnson; General R.A. Cameron of the Fort Worth & Denver City Railway; real estate developer Humphrey Barker Chamberlin; banker Michael C. Hurley; and Sallie Huffman, the widow of Walter Huffman. No one said subscribers had to be men. Each gave at least $1,000.[9]

The proudest moment may have been building the Texas Spring Palace in 1889. From start to finish it was a hometown project. Even before 1889 Fort Worth viewed itself as a regional metropolis, which Howard Peak called "putting on metropolitan airs," but it was one thing to put on airs; putting on an exhibition on the scale of the New Orleans Cotton Palace (1884) or Sioux City Corn Palace (1887) was a breathtaking challenge. The closest thing to it held in Texas up to that time was the annual State Fair in Dallas, and that enjoyed the backing of the state legislature. A Fort Worth Spring Palace was guaranteed of no such official endorsement. The idea that took shape in the winter of 1889 envisioned a grand display of Texas' natural resources with exhibitors coming from across the state. The first meeting to gauge interest was held on January 16. Two hundred men and women showed up to hear the sales pitch. The organizers explained their idea, estimating the cost at $50,000 and promising it would be bigger and better than the Corn Palace, which had cost $30,000. The dramatic moment came when they asked all those in favor to signify by standing. To a man (and woman) everyone in the room stood.[10]

A Committee of Fifty was formed that drew up a charter for a private corporation to be known as the Texas Spring Palace Company. It would then issue $100,000 in stock at $10 a share. A "soliciting committee" of ten was appointed to fan out across town and sell stock. They put the squeeze on every private citizen and business. Even saloon owners were "solicited" and contributed generously. The Committee of Ten raised $8,800 in just the first day. After subscriptions reached $25,000 the stockholders selected a board of directors headed by B.B. Paddock, chosen partly because he was the First Citizen of Fort Worth and partly because he had kicked off the drive with a donation of $800. Paddock appealed to his fellow citizens by telling them not to think of the money as "a gift or donation but as in investment" in Fort Worth's future. While funding was also solicited from residents of Tarrant and other counties across the state, and even the railroads kicked in, most of it came from a town that at the time numbered barely 23,000. More amazing still is the fact that Fort Worth at the same time was putting together pots for the Union Stockyards and two railroads (the Fort Worth & Rio Grande and Fort Worth & Northwestern). "Soliciting committees" worked the population for each of those drives, raising more than $40,000 for the Northwestern road alone. Fort Worthers were in danger of becoming subscription-poor![11]

A local contractor, Thomas J. Hurley & Co., got the construction contract with a bid of $26,000. They even promised to rebate $2,000 of that amount by purchasing that much stock. The Texas Spring Palace opened as promised on May 10, 1889, and enjoyed a successful run (an average of 3,000 visitors a day) until it closed on June 27. When the books were balanced it ended $40,000 in the red, which did not deter the directors from committing to a second season. The call to action went out again in 1890, raising $50,000 to renovate and enlarge the building. Although the Spring Palace closed in the red again after a fiery ending on May 31, 1890, boosters immediately began talking about rebuilding "bigger and better than ever," and there is little doubt Fort Worthers would have stepped up again.[12]

The Spring Palace proved to doubters that Fort Worth was a city of BIG thinkers ***and*** BIG doers. More than one visitor had been heard to remark "What infinite faith the people of Fort Worth have in their city!" or something similar.

The Texas Spring Palace, a Fort Worth triumph! A broadside published in glorious living color. Author's collection.

President John F. Kennedy said it a little differently in November 1963: "There are no faint hearts in Fort Worth." The Spring Palace put Fort Worth on the national map and furthered the city's desire to be the regional capital of "West Texas." It also pioneered marketing techniques that became standard practice for future expositions: nation-wide advertising, advance ticket sales, excursion rates on the railroads, blanket newspaper coverage, playing on historic rivalries to boost attendance, and signing top-drawer acts as entertainment. Investors in the Spring Palace may have lost their shirts, but the popular feeling at the end of the day was that the benefits for Fort Worth were well worth the cost.[13]

Three years later another subscription drive raised $1,437 to put up a memorial to Al Hayne, the hero of the Spring Palace fire. The Woman's Humane Association spearheaded the drive to build the twenty-six-foot-tall monument, which has stood for more than 130 years.[14]

It took another subscription drive to make "Cowtown" the permanent nickname of Fort Worth. Going back to the beginning, citizens had been willing to dig deep to bring the cattle drives through town. In time that came to include rail connections for shipping the animals to market and eventually slaughterhouses to process the beef right here. In 1882 the Fort Worth Packing Co. was built with $6,000 raised in another subscription drive, leading the city directory to boast, "Everything in Fort Worth is done by private subscription." Twenty years later, Swift and Armour were enticed to town in the same way, making what B.B. Paddock called the "cornerstones of [future] greatness." The cost of doing business had gone up substantially since the first packing plant was built. The city promised Armour $200,000, and the Fort Worth Stockyards kicked in another $400,000. When Swift showed an interest, the city persuaded the two friendly rivals to split a $100,000 subsidy between them. The Stockyards and North Fort Worth then sweetened the pot.[15]

Before the deal was sealed, something like subscription fatigue had set in. Citizens were still paying for the 1895 courthouse, and the economy was just emerging from the worst downturn in the nation's history. For the packing-plant subscription drive, the first four days brought in nearly $41,000, but donations slowed to a trickle after that, leading the head of the drive, Judge G.W. Armstrong, to grumble that in the old days the goal would have been met in the first hour. The city's leading newspapers did their part by spreading the rumor that Dallas was going to snatch the prize away. The Board of Trade finally took over the drive, bringing organization to it and twisting the arm of every labor and trade group in town. On October 7, 1901, the Board made a desperate appeal to all public-spirited citizens, warning of Fort Worth sinking back into irrelevance if the necessary money were not raised. That did the trick, bringing in the final $15,000. The *Fort Worth Register* put a nice spin on this latest subscription drive with the headline, "Fort Worth Never Failed."[16]

Other projects would come along in the years that followed, but nothing to rival the packing-plant drive until 1910, the year city fathers set their sights on bringing Texas Christian University "home" to the town where it had started in 1873 as Add-Ran College. Waco had the school, but it had recently burned, so the school's board was open to relocating, which was all the opening Fort Worth needed. A hard-sell subscription drive raised $200,000 in eleven weeks from churches, business, and private citizens. Leaders of the drive resorted to the usual tactics of shaming the wealthy and raising the specter of Dallas stealing the prize. Mayor W.D. Davis called donating "a civic duty." It was another mass movement. Big land-owners southwest of town promised the land, and the Northern Texas Traction Company promised to build a streetcar line out to the campus. On June 30, 1910, Fort Worth closed the deal with Texas Christian University.[17]

Over the years, as the projects got bigger along with the money required, Fort Worthers were also willing to take on bond debt. In 1884 the city issued $200,000 in bonds to buy the municipal waterworks followed by a $320,000 bond issue for street-improvements. In 1891 Tarrant County launched a $400,000 bond drive to pay for a new courthouse, and in 1915, city and county joined forces to build a new county jail. Bond drives were not as emotion-driven as passing the hat at a public meeting and listing contributors in the newspaper, but they were just as dependent on the public buying in.[18]

When World War I came along in 1917, Fort Worth stepped up to the plate again. City fathers led by B.B. Paddock, Robert McCart, Ben E. Keith, and Mayor Elisha T. Tyra offered the U.S. Army more than 1,000 acres on the heights west of town virtually for free. In return for putting a training camp on the land, Fort Worth would build all the necessary infrastructure out to the camp—a streetcar line, sewage and electrical connections. Fort Worth's gift became Camp Bowie. The Government spent $1,953,000 building it and subsequently spent an average of $1,150,000 daily to operate it. The spike in population from adding 46,000 new residents caused some social disruption, but virtually everyone thought the benefits outweighed the costs.[19]

Patriotism and civic mindedness came into play again in 1918 in a government-sponsored Liberty Loan drive supporting the war effort. Many of the same people who had already dug deep to bring Camp Bowie to town bought war bonds. Their ranks included the Texas & Pacific Coal Co. ($100,000), Sheriff Sterling Clark ($300), and Bewley Mills employees ($3,000).[20]

As the 20th century progressed, Fort Worthers retained their willingness to contribute during good times and bad. Amon Carter rallied citizens in 1936 to create a "Frontier Centennial" celebrating Texas independence. He was determined that Fort Worth put on a bigger, splashier celebration than Dallas, and he got what he wanted. Two million visitors came through the Frontier Centennial before it closed on November 15. Despite impressive attendance, producer, Billy Rose went extravagantly over budget. Investors, not all of them as deep-pocketed as Amon Carter and his pals, lost their shirts. Still, Fort Worth opened its wallets again in 1937 to have a second season.[21]

Today they are called "public-private ventures," but the pitch is the same: subscribe and everyone wins. This is how we still fund massive projects with huge price tags, like Alliance Airport or the Texas Motor Speedway. It is how we do things on this side of the Trinity. In the local mythology, Fort Worth has always followed a different path than our sister city to the east, which grew largely by using public monies and eminent domain. This "Dallas Way" is part of their "can-do" mythology. Fort Worth's mythology says we have always been willing to dig deep for worthy projects. The coming of the New Deal in the 1930s, which opened the federal spigot, may have changed the reality, but it did not change the mythology. Only the name has changed. A *Star-Telegram* columnist a few years ago gave it a new name: "The city that runs on pro bono."[22]

Chapter 6

Forgotten Hero of the Texas Spring Palace Fire

If you grew up in Fort Worth or have lived in our fair city for more than five minutes, you have heard of Al Hayne, the hero of the 1890 Texas Spring Palace Fire. If not, you can drive down Lancaster and see his memorial standing near the intersection of Lancaster and Commerce. Poor Al is a little weather-beaten after more than a hundred years but still recognizable.

He should forever be remembered for his self-sacrificing actions on the night of May 30, 1890. It was the last night of the Texas Spring Palace's second season when the building erupted into flames. At the time the place was crammed with visitors, perhaps as many as seven thousand, enjoying the last night of the grand exhibition. It was about 10:00 PM and the Elgin Watch Band had just concluded their concert. The Cotillion Ball was about to begin on the second floor, so many people were making their way there. Elsewhere in the building people milled around taking a final look at the exhibits under the electric lights. The next thing anyone knew, the place was on fire. Exactly how it started was in dispute afterwards, but everyone agreed it started on the east end of the second floor. The jangling of the fire alarm in the northeast corner of the building got everyone's attention. There was a "great rush" for the exits, but the structure had not been designed for a swift evacuation. While there were ten "large" exits on the first floor, there were only two narrow staircases from the second floor to the ground, both on the south side of the building. Apparently, the designers felt additional staircases would have marred the imposing beauty of the exterior. So now the entire crowd on the second floor was funneled to these two staircases.[1]

Al Hayne, an English-born civil engineer who had called Fort Worth home for ten years, was there that night. He sprang into action finding a rope somewhere that he used to lower women and children to safety from the west tower. He also helped reunite frantic mothers and crying children and point them towards the stairs. With the building beginning to collapse in upon itself, he raced back into the inferno one last time to see if anyone was left. Instead, the rescuer became another victim. Too weak to save himself he leaned against an outside wall barely able to stand. With fiery embers falling all around him, he was just moments away from death when another hero sprang into action.[2]

Jesse Williams had been standing on the grounds watching the festivities when the fire started. He could not join in those festivities because he was black and racial segregation was a fact of life, but he had a hero's heart. In 1890 he was twenty-six years old, born into slavery in Virginia. Sometime after 1870 he left Virginia and found his way to Fort Worth. In 1880 he was working as the porter in an uptown boarding house on Houston. One of the residents of that house was Fort Worth Mayor John J. Brown. Jesse's circumstances had not notably improved ten years later. In the summer of 1890, he was an out-of-work "hostler" (stableman) looking for a job, any kind of job. He had what he described as "good recommendations," which may have

(a) Al Hayne Memorial, *ca.* 1893; (b) Al Hayne the man; and (c) Oran McCormick's painting of the Spring Palace fire of May 30, 1890. Courtesy Scott and Linda Jo Barker.

included former Mayor Brown, and felt he was qualified to be a "general utility man," which meant glorified porter. He had no known family in town.[3]

Jesse could have stood by at a safe distance and watched the Spring Palace burn as thousands of others did that night. But something drove him to jump in and help save people he did not know and who would not have given him the time of day under normal circumstances. He caught one lady being lowered by a rope from the second floor then when Al Hayne appeared in a doorway, he rushed forward to save him. It is hard to imagine the two knew each other.[4]

By the time Jesse got to the Englishman, Hayne was lying on the ground in an agony of pain. Williams picked him bodily and carried him to safety. He carefully laid the grievously injured Hayne on the ground where others ministered to him. Only then did he notice his own coat was on fire. He put it out with some help then disappeared into the crowd. Hardly anyone noticed. They were focused on getting Hayne to the city's only hospital, St. Joseph's Infirmary, where he died within the hour.[5]

From the first cries of "Fire" it took just four minutes for the entire building to be ablaze and another eleven minutes for it to be reduced to a pile of smoldering embers. It is amazing that only one person died. Thirty were injured in the rush from the building. A few were singed by the flames. A lot of the credit for getting everyone out safely goes to several heroes mentioned in the newspapers over the next few days, among them E.F. Fudge, T.P. Keater, Russell Harrison, E.F. Segerson, and B.B Paddock. But Al Hayne got the overwhelming majority of the after-action reporting, no doubt because he alone lost his life. The *Fort Worth Gazette* dubbed him "the Hero of the Spring Palace Fire" and said, "No truer hero ever died on American soil or for the American people."[6]

Only after a glowing description of Hayne's heroics did the same newspaper get around to mentioning a "brave colored man" who "did his best to save poor Al Hayne's life." In the newspaper's telling, Hayne was "the hero" while Williams "performed a heroic act." It was an important distinction. The only other African American connected to the Spring Palace fire was an unnamed "Negro boy" on whom some sources would later blame the fire, saying his energetic dancing had ignited the fire when his shoe struck a phosphorus match, a story akin to the legend of Mrs. O'Leary's cow starting the great Chicago Fire.[7]

Six days after the fire, an anonymous person wrote a "note" to the *Gazette* pointing out there were two heroes that night: "The white hero, Al Hayne, gave his life to save others, and it was a black hero, Jesse Williams, who risked his life to drag the white man from the burning Palace." After that, Jesse might have dropped off the face of the earth. The only notice Fort Worth took of him was a series of ads he placed in the "Help Wanted" columns as a "young colored man" looking for work. At the time he was living over Bill Love's saloon on Twelfth St. Love was a leader in the black community and may have been another one of those "excellent recommendations" Jesse mentioned in his "help wanted" ad. There is no way of knowing if he found a job though it is hard to imagine why someone would not hire the fellow who risked his life trying to save Al Hayne.[8]

Fort Worth was never going to forget Al Hayne. Three years after the fire the Woman's Humane Association erected a monument in his honor in front of the T&P passenger station. The Al Hayne memorial was the first thing people saw when they emerged from the train station. And in Fort Worth Fire Department history he was transformed into a full-fledged fireman. (A full-time fire department was created the same year the memorial was put up.)

As for Jesse Williams, he was almost erased from the pages of history. In only fifteen years the *Fort Worth Telegram* could write about the "obscure hero's memorial," lamenting that people knew almost nothing about Al Hayne except his place of birth and his exploits on that fateful night. But if people knew little about Hayne, they knew even less about Jesse Williams. *Star-Telegram* newspaper columnist Amos Melton tried to keep his memory alive in 1930 when he wrote a recap of the fire, crediting Jesse with "rushing into the building to pull Hayne from the structure." And a couple of Fort Worth old-timers who had been around in 1890 still remembered Jesse when they were interviewed sixty and sixty-seven years after the fact respectively. D.E. Claypool told a reporter in 1950 that he had helped an unnamed "Negro" pull Hayne from the fire that night. And Clay Sandidge in 1957 was still sharp enough to remember "the Negro who braved the wreckage to pull Hayne out." But memories are not the same as monuments.[9]

Aside from the fact that Jesse Williams has been nearly erased from the story of the Spring Palace's fiery ending, tracking him as a person through the historical record does not turn up much else. From the 1880 Census record we know he was born in Virginia about 1864, almost certainly as a slave. As a black man who grew up under slavery and Reconstruction, he was fated to remain practically invisible for the rest of his life. We do not know where or when he died. By 1900 he is not even traceable through Census records. He could have still been living in Fort Worth and just been overlooked, or he could have been living somewhere else. He virtually drops off the face of the earth after his fifteen minutes of fame on the night of May 30, 1890, this mysterious black man who stepped from the crowd to perform a heroic deed then returned to obscurity.

Chapter 7

The Devil in Cowtown

Erik Larson's best-selling 2003 book, *The Devil in the White City*, told the story of Dr. H.H. Holmes, America's first known serial killer, who found his first victims among the throngs of visitors to the 1893 Chicago World's Fair. One of the things Larson revealed is that Holmes had a Fort Worth connection: Two of his victims were local girls, and he even came to Fort Worth long enough to build a house here.[1]

But his story starts in Chicago. The thirty-year-old Holmes came to Englewood, a Chicago suburb, in 1886 locating to Sixty-third St. where he ran a business and rented out guest rooms upstairs while he himself lived elsewhere. The slightly built, nervous little man presented himself as a physician and pharmacist, but he was first and foremost a swindler and sociopath.

He was born Herman Webster Mudgett in Gilmanton, New Jersey, in 1861. He had a normal childhood that contained no clue of his future behavior. He did not torture animals or terrorize the neighborhood children. In 1878 he married Clara Lovering and they started a family. They would remain married for the rest of his life although Holmes was also a bigamist who had at least two or three other wives stashed out in various places. He studied medicine under a local doctor, then he and Clara and their infant son moved to Ann Arbor, Michigan, so he could attend medical school at the University of Michigan. Clara supported them for a time before taking the baby and moving back home. They never lived together again. Mudgett graduated in 1884 and moved to New York state to open a practice and teach school. Two years later he was a licensed pharmacist living in Boston, using the name "Henry Howard Holmes, M.D." Passing himself off as a bachelor now, he took up with several women and lived habitually in debt. He possessed two traits that guided him the rest of his life: he felt no empathy for anyone and was a pathological liar; he never told the truth where a lie would do. He also had a certain sinister sort of charisma and was a smooth talker. It is no surprise that he got an early start as a criminal. He did not make friends; he made "marks" and future victims. Acquaintances all agreed he had "the most winning ways toward women" of any man they had ever known, and that he "never mixed up with any [women] that were not good-looking." They also described him as "mild-mannered, courteous, and affable toward men." In other words, like many sociopaths, he was not threatening in the least.[2]

In 1886 Holmes moved to Chicago with a new wife in tow and soon went to work at Holton's Drug Store on Sixty-third St. working for Dr. Elizabeth S. Holton. He subsequently arranged to buy the place, but it is doubtful if money ever changed hands, and Dr. Holton and her husband subsequently disappeared mysteriously. The building had the pharmacy on the first floor and rooms to rent on the second floor. The site would later become known as the "Holmes Murder Castle" that included a third floor added in 1892. The building had a number of odd, custom-made features later described as "secret rooms" and "hidden staircases."[3]

Holmes's principal business was not medicine but swindling. He embarked on a series of ever more complicated schemes shifting money from one fraudulent enterprise to another before ultimately leaving someone holding the bag. It was impossible to keep track of all his swindles; it's not even certain he could keep track of them. When he left Chicago, he left a string of unresolved lawsuits in the courts that could never be untangled.

It was as a cold-blooded murderer that Holmes achieved immortality. His list of victims includes nine people that he dispatched between 1891 and 1894, and another 27 that he probably did away with during his career, most of them women, earning him the title "America's Jack the Ripper." Legend attributes dozens of other victims to him that are either unprovable or have been debunked.[4]

Minnie and Nannie Williams became entangled in Holmes's web willingly or otherwise. They were sisters from Mississippi whose father was killed in a railroad accident in 1872 and whose mother died shortly thereafter. About five and three respectively when their mother died, the two orphans were split up with Minnie going to live with an uncle, Dr. J.N.B. Williams of Mansfield, Texas. It was perfectly acceptable to split up siblings if one relative could not or would not take them all (both). He died when she was about ten or eleven, leaving her some property on both sides of the Trinity. Fort Worth businessman John J. Massie served as her court-appointed guardian and unofficial advisor on her inheritance. She converted some of it to cash which she used to study elocution at Mansfield College before going to Boston to attend the Boston Conservatory. She dreamed of launching a stage career but put her dream on hold after meeting the dashing Dr. Holmes. She was immediately smitten with this smooth-talking gentleman. She came back to Texas in 1889 where she reconnected with her sister, the quiet, shy Nannie, a devout Christian with little education who had followed her sister from Mississippi. Minnie supported them both before returning to New England to resume her stage career. When that fizzled, she moved to Chicago purportedly to "become self-sufficient" by putting her considerable education to work. At the beginning of 1893 she went to work as Holmes's secretary at his Sixty-third St. office. That spring she wrote her sister that they were engaged and invited her to come live with them. She also wrote Fort Worth friends gushing about her plans to marry "Harry Gordon." By the time Nannie arrived in Chicago in June, Minnie and Holmes were living as husband and wife in "the Castle." Holmes still had a wife and daughter living in another suburb of Chicago.[5]

Whatever their marital status, Holmes used Minnie as a front in his various schemes. It is unclear whether she was a willing accomplice or not. In either case, she was soon the defendant in a number of court cases. Holmes moved the three of them into another apartment in the suburb of Wilmette to avoid being served. They lived well and he told others he was taking them on an extended tour of Europe. In July 1893 all three disappeared although not at the same time. Nannie disappeared first, then her sister and finally Holmes himself but not before moving his other Chicago wife and child into the Wilmette apartment. After Holmes's story broke in the national news, the *Chicago Tribune* led a search for the sisters that turned up Nannie's unclaimed trunk at a Wells Fargo office but no clue of what had happened to them. Wells Fargo shipped the trunk to relatives in Tarrant County whom Deputy Sheriff Bill Rea interviewed, but the fate of the girls remained an unsolved mystery. All that is known for sure is that they were never seen alive again.[6]

Holmes next turned up in Fort Worth in January 1894 intent on claiming Minnie's inheritance, which the lady herself had no more use for. But first he stopped in Denver to claim the insurance payout for Minnie's deceased brother who had recently suffered a fatal accident. While there he married yet again, this time to the much younger Georgiana Yoke whom

(a) America's first serial killer, Dr. H.H. Holmes. (b) Minnie Williams, paramour (wife?) of H.H. Holmes. Both courtesy of Chicago Historical Society.

he may have first met when she attended the World's Fair in Chicago. When Georgiana turned twenty-five later that year she would come into a sizable inheritance from her grandmother. This was most important to a man like Holmes and must have played a part in his decision to properly marry the lady before whisking her away to Fort Worth. Meanwhile, Holmes had an accomplice in Fort Worth, Benjamin Pitezel, who had been in town for some time arranging their next swindle. Holmes arrived in Fort Worth with a new wife, a new name (D.T. Pratt), and a new get-rich-quick scheme.[7]

What remained of Minnie's inheritance was a piece of property on the southwest corner of Second and Rusk (now Commerce) in Fort Worth and another in Oak Cliff (Dallas). At different times, Holmes estimated the value of the Fort Worth real estate as low as $10,000 and as high as $40,000. Pitezel had already arranged for the property to be transferred to Holmes under yet another name. Holmes parked his wife in the Arlington Inn and began construction on a building on the site, using a variety of aliases to hire contractors and buy materials on credit. The construction project was listed under Pitezel's name, but that, too was a cover. Holmes personally oversaw construction, discouraging inspectors and the curious from coming around. By all accounts the building was remarkably similar to the Chicago Castle with similar mysterious features. At 100 × 100 feet, it was twice the size of the usual town real estate, which typically had a frontage of 50 feet and a depth of 100 feet. It was also three stories but nearly twice the size of the Chicago Castle. It had its own artesian well in the back, not an unusual feature in downtown buildings of the day. It backed up to Greenwall's Opera House, which was a city landmark for years. By April 1894 it was nearly finished with a large "No Admittance" sign hanging on the door.[8]

The biggest mystery is what he intended to do with it. The best authority on Holmes believes the wily swindler never had any intention of moving into the place and taking up permanent residence in Fort Worth. Rather, it was another deal to create a real asset then mortgage it to the hilt before skipping town with the cash.[9]

He might have succeeded but for a slipup that brought the local law down on him. His mistake was buying Texas horseflesh with worthless promissory notes, then selling the animals for cash, a practice he and Pitezel did repeatedly. Texans could grudgingly appreciate a wheeler-dealer, but a horse thief was something more despicable. When Holmes tried to work his usual scam on the owner of the Exchange Stable on Rusk St., that gentleman refused to fall for it, insisting on cash for a pair of matching horses Holmes wanted. By now friends of Minnie Williams were also beginning to ask awkward questions, making things too hot for the pair of swindlers. In May 1894 Holmes and Pitezel slipped out of town one jump ahead of the law, leaving behind an empty building, some personal papers, and a lot of angry creditors. Holmes had only been in Fort Worth five months, long enough to build a "castle" and create a legend.[10]

That legend would have a particular Fort Worth twist. According to the *Dallas Morning News*, Holmes had lived with and been intimate with "at least four women" during his time in Fort Worth. The newspaper called it a "rumor" and did not give a source, did not provide the names of the paramours, and offered no explanation of how he found time to build a house, conduct multiple swindles, and keep a wife happy while engaging in all these sexual liaisons. However, Tarrant County Deputy Sheriff Bill Rea confirmed the story. He told the same newspaper,

> I know of three women Holmes was intimate with. I have never heard of more, and I don't remember seeing him with but one blonde in whose company he seemed to be fascinated. I think the report that he had four on the string is incorrect.[11]

Dallas newspapers always enjoyed dishing the dirt on Fort Worth, but there may have been some truth to this story. It certainly made better copy than an empty building. A few months later, while the fates of Minnie and Nannie Williams were being widely debated, the *Fort Worth Gazette* dismissed the empty building as "the Rusk Street Fire Trap." It was only later, as the full story of Holmes's crimes emerged that the local newspapers began calling it, "the Fort Worth Castle."[12]

Holmes, Pitezel and Georgiana landed next in St. Louis where Holmes purchased another drug store with worthless paper and equally worthless promises. He was ready to start a brand-new chapter in his life. He just needed a bankroll. Ben Pitezel brought his family to St. Louis, and while waiting to cash in on Georgiana's inheritance, the pair began planning the biggest swindle of their career. Unfortunately for their plans, it only took St. Louis authorities a month to catch on and throw them in jail. Georgiana, who was either a thoroughgoing accomplice or a gullible patsy, hired a lawyer to bail them out, using another piece of Minnie's property as collateral. They promptly skipped town, next stop Philadelphia.[13]

Holmes was eventually joined in Philadelphia by the Pitezels. The two men put their big plan into action to defraud Fidelity Mutual Insurance Company by taking out a big, fat policy on Pitezel then faking his death to collect. Unfortunately for Pitezel, the fake victim became a real victim when Holmes murdered him. Then Holmes persuaded Mrs. Pitezel to take their two children, Alice and Nellie on a cross-country trip during which he also murdered them. Eventually, the law caught up with Holmes and brought him back to Philadelphia where he stood trial for the three murders known to Philadelphia authorities.

When questioned about Minnie and Nannie Williams, Holmes expressed concern but offered no help locating them. In the gaslight era it was easy for people to drop completely out of sight, willingly or otherwise. Holmes's answers were as slippery as they were suspect. He said Minnie was "a great friend of mine," adding,

> She was an unfortunate in more ways than one. I cannot but believe she is still alive. God only knows where, as she is a fugitive from justice.[14]

When pressed he insisted Minnie had been only his secretary, but she became infatuated with him and jealous of her sister's affection for him. Minnie killed Nannie, he said; he only helped dispose of the body then buy the Fort Worth property from Minnie to give her enough money to leave the country. No one believed that story; the Philadelphia authorities were convinced he had killed both sisters, but they could not prove it, and Holmes kept changing his story: the girls were alive; the girls were dead; Minnie had killed Nannie; Minnie had taken Nannie with her to England to avoid prosecution for financial shenanigans. Like other pathological liars, Holmes could not tell the truth, and he could not keep his lies straight.[15]

Despite everything, Holmes still had friends in Fort Worth who believed in him or at least hoped the stories of Minnie and Nannie were untrue. While locked up in a Philadelphia jail, he corresponded with some of his creditors, suggesting to one that he journey to Philadelphia and escort him back to Fort Worth to face his accusers after he was found innocent in Pennsylvania, of course. Fort Worth banker J.W. Spencer did make the trip to Philadelphia in December 1894 to meet with Holmes in jail and inquire about the Williams sisters. Holmes offered his assistance if Spencer could get him out of jail. The *Fort Worth Gazette* speculated that what he really had in mind was an escape. Even in absentia, Holmes's long shadow fell over other Fort Worthers. Local lawyer William Capps, representing the heirs of the Williams sisters, went to Chicago to gather information and to Philadelphia where he also met with Holmes in his cell. (The Philadelphia authorities were quite generous in letting Holmes have as many visitors as he wanted.) Interviewed by the newspapers in both cities, Capps offered unsupported theories about everything, earning him the scorn of the national press. Among his off-the-cuff opinions was this one: "I never thought that [Minnie] was dead. The Fort Worth people think she is alive, but it seems mighty hard to locate her." It was not Capps's finest hour as a lawyer.[16]

Not until the end of July 1895 did local attention focus on Holmes's Fort Worth Castle as perhaps another crime scene, and even then, all the attention came from the other side of the Trinity. Fort Worth newspapers followed the story of his crimes but did not seem to regard the building itself as part of that story. The *Dallas Morning News* jumped all over it, sending its Fort Worth stringer inside the posted building twice to explore its dark corners and test the authenticity of the rumors making the rounds. He found a house that was "a labyrinth of small rooms and narrow passages," including a chute from the third floor to the basement, but no secret chambers upstairs or acid baths and dissecting tables in the basement. That did not keep the newspaper from concluding that the Fort Worth castle was "built for murder."[17]

Holmes's trial for the murder of Benjamin Pitezel took place in Philadelphia under tight security at the end of October 1895. District Attorney George S. Graham was the prosecutor. Among his witnesses was Fort Worth attorney Sidney Samuels who was queried about the accused's wheelings and dealings in Fort Worth. Samuels added nothing of significance to the state's case, but he proved to be an entertaining witness who was obviously not shy about testifying under oath.[18]

Holmes was found guilty on November 2, 1895, and sentenced to hang. His lawyers filed the usual appeal which was denied by the Pennsylvania supreme court. He was executed on May 7, 1896. On the scaffold he protested his innocence of all but two killings, neither of them a Williams sister. The newspapers had already dubbed him America's Jack the Ripper, a claim reaffirmed by the History Channel in 2018. The connection to England's most infamous killer derived from the coincidence of their being contemporaries and that both preyed on young women. Some writers even attempted to make the case that they were one and the same, that after Jack dropped out of sight, he came to the United States to start a new life of crime as H.H. Holmes. Preposterous, of course, but that never got in the way of good newspaper copy. Since everything had to be bigger and better in the U.S., the number of his victims was even inflated to as many as 200 by some writers. Others claimed he had not actually died on the gallows but somehow managed to cheat death and go free, making his ultimate fate as mysterious as Jack the Ripper's.[19]

Unlike Jack, Holmes had plenty of time to tell his own story. The publicity attending his trial, which included a jailhouse confession, made newspapers all over the country. Every city where he had lived had its own tale of murder and/or swindling, starting with Chicago where every unsolved murder during the World's Fair was laid at his feet. Fort Worth authorities made a halfhearted effort to extradite Holmes, but Pennsylvania had a stronger claim on him. Besides, reportedly he begged not to be sent back to Texas to stand trial for horse theft, knowing full well Texas' reputation for dealing with horse thieves in summary fashion. Joseph C. Terrell, a Fort Worth pioneer father, observed there were only two crimes "absolutely not tolerated" in Texas, horse stealing and disruption of Sunday worship.[20]

H.H. Holmes may have been dead and buried, but his ghost continued to haunt Fort Worth for years to come. Somehow, the Fort Worth Police Department acquired a mug shot of Holmes although he was never arrested during his brief stay in the city. Nonetheless, the *Morning Register* reported in 1897 that the Department's "Rogue's Gallery" possessed a mug shot of the man the newspaper called, "the most noted fiend in criminal history." The same newspaper, which leaned toward tabloid-style journalism, reported three years later that Nannie Williams' head had been found "floating in Lake Michigan." In 1905, palm-reading clairvoyant Prof. Bentley Sage claimed to have contacted Holmes in a spiritual "reading." He did not say what he learned, but obviously he felt confident that readers of the *Telegram* knew who H.H. Holmes was. In 1907 the same newspaper could still call him, "the grandest scoundrel that ever struck Texas."[21]

Meanwhile, the empty building in Fort Worth was tied up in court for years by contractors, creditors, and the heirs of the

Williams sisters. While waiting for the legal claims to be settled, it was turned into a walk-up boarding house with monthly room rates at $5 (unfurnished) or $10 (furnished). Finally, in 1900 with all the claims finally settled, the building was sold to Thomas Presnall who announced plans to convert it into a proper hotel, the Laclede, after he had "thoroughly painted, papered, finished, and furnished" it. The shabby building was famous enough that its sale was reported on both sides of the Trinity. It sold again a few years later to be reopened as the St. Elmo Hotel. It continued a steady decline until World War I when it was converted into a "detention hospital" for women infected with social diseases, not because of any real sense of compassion for the working girls but to keep the boys training at Camp Bowie healthy. The hospital closed after the war, and it was empty again for a few years until Theo Cromer opened

The two infamous Holmes Castles: (a) Chicago, *ca.* 1893. Courtesy Chicago Historical Society. (b) Fort Worth, *ca.* 1895. Courtesy Robert Smith.

his locksmith shop there in 1932. It finally fell to the wrecking ball in the 1940s (after 1943). Considering how cheaply and in what a rush it was thrown up, it is amazing the building stood for half a century.[22]

Recently, that historic corner of Second and Commerce was redeveloped as an outdoor cafe, during which the old basement space was opened up for the first time in nearly a hundred years. A mysterious vault discovered there was the subject of much discussion among local historians speculating that it might have been used for another round of murders, which ignored the fact that the Great Satan never actually occupied the building.

All we are left with today are some shadowy images in old newspapers and an old photograph and an equally shadowy connection to a man who may be the greatest serial killer of the 19th century.

Chapter 8

Death on the Tracks

The coming of public transportation to Fort Worth in the form of railroads and streetcars, both in 1876, represented a great leap forward in Fort Worth's growth from a small, frontier hamlet to a major metropolis. Yet there was also a dark side to the story: trains and streetcars posed an ever-present danger to people moving about the town; country folks were not used to looking both ways before crossing the street. Making things worse, the streetcar companies and railroads acted like they owned the streets where their tracks were located. Accidents became regular occurrences, and as deaths and injuries mounted, lawsuits multiplied. The embattled companies fought back to keep the cases out of court and away from sympathetic juries.

To the companies, lawsuits were one of the costs of doing business. They kept high-priced lawyers on permanent retainer to handle the frequent cases. Victims who survived their encounter with an iron monster found battling a powerful corporation was even harder than battling city hall. And the dangers were not limited to man vs. machine. Every aspect of the company's operations posed risks to the population. In 1891, an unidentified newspaperman fell into an uncovered ditch of the North Side streetcar company. He sued for $7,500 in actual damages but settled for far less.[1]

The Northern Texas Traction Company (NTTC), organized in 1902 to consolidate Fort Worth's streetcar lines, tried to burnish the public image of its Fort Worth-Dallas Interurban service with the slogan, "Speed with Safety." Interurbans were larger, heavier cars that used the same tracks as streetcars in the city but raced at high speeds between cities (Fort Worth to Dallas, Fort Worth to Cleburne, etc.). In 1904 the company started using a promotional campaign bragging that they had never lost a single passenger on the Fort Worth-Dallas line, which was true as far as it went. What it left out was all the animals and persons traveling by buggy or other conveyance or even walking that were mowed down in the course of operations. Four-legged victims included "Tom Powell," a beloved horse of the Fort Worth Fire Department struck and killed by the Interurban while pulling a fire wagon across the tracks in 1906.[2]

Streetcars were hailed as a great urban advance, speeding up the movement of people and tying distant suburbs to the central business district, but they also proved to be accidents just waiting to happen. The cars were of flimsy construction, and their only safety equipment was a "clanging" bell to warn anyone on the tracks ahead that they were coming. Streetcars were easily derailed if they struck anything substantial and likely to tip over. And though they shared the streets with pedestrians, horse-drawn vehicles, and automobiles, it was assumed by those who operated them that they possessed the right of way. The tracks were laid down the middle of the street on poorly prepared roadbeds, and over time the ground eroded beneath them, leaving the rails up off the ground. This meant any vehicle with a low clearance crossing the tracks was liable to get hung up in midair, wheels off the ground. Then there were the men who drove the streetcars (motormen) who were poorly paid and underwent little training. Many were former conductors (ticket-takers) who worked their way up to being motormen as a reward for long service. The companies did not improve safety by setting tight schedules that forced the cars to run at dangerous speeds. A 1910 Chicago study found that most streetcar accidents were caused by cars being operated at excessive speeds, but that did not change the practice. Finally, operating rules were vague or nonexistent. For instance, by law there was no maximum number of passengers a car could carry. The rule was as many as could squeeze on board, and people jumped on and off while the cars were moving. Motormen were known to halt between designated regular stops to let a friend hop on. Jim Crow rules added to the unsafe operating conditions because if all or even most of the seats in the car were occupied by white people, blacks had to crowd onto the rear platform, hanging on by their fingernails and unbalancing the car. This was only a problem if they tried to find a seat inside the car.[3]

Fort Worth streetcars were electrified in 1889, creating yet another danger for anyone involved in an accident: electrocution. Overhead lines providing DC current (600 volts) that ran them could bring instant death if they came down on the street. And the little electric motors on the cars that ran off the current were equally dangerous. In 1915 a collision with a motorcycle caused a streetcar to jump the tracks, but the trolley pole remained connected to the overhead wire. Without the grounding provided by the rails, every piece of metal on the car became a potentially lethal current conductor. Fortunately, a hero appeared, butcher J.R. Townsend, who ran to the scene from his nearby shop and jerked the trolley pole down.[4]

In 1890 the North Side Street Railway Company, which had converted to electricity, went back to mule-powered cars. According to the company, it could not stay in business if it had to convert to electric cars. But what was more revealing was all the reasons given by the company for its problems, which included "poor track, incompetent help, and inferior, second-hand cars." These same problems plagued electric streetcar companies in the years that followed.[5]

When accidents inevitably occurred, companies could choose from a variety of legal and public relations defenses. One defense strategy was to characterize the accident as an "act of God" or a "natural disaster." For instance, if rain limited visibility or washed out the tracks, it was not the company's fault. Almost everything else could be attributed to an act of God. Another favorite defense strategy was to blame "motorman error" or "indeterminate causes," either of which absolved them from legal liability. (At the time, the courts were willing to separate the motorman's responsibility from the company's responsibility, not an acceptable defense today.) When all else failed, the companies settled out of court. A few thousand dollars waved at a victim (or their family) was usually sufficient to get a lawsuit dropped.[6]

The poor motormen who were thrown under the streetcar by their employers became sympathetic figures compared to the heartless corporations that employed them. The NTTC motorman whose streetcar struck and killed Ryan Godwin in 1915 became so hysterical at the scene he could not make a coherent statement to police. No surprise, the company quickly distanced itself from him. Fortunately for the company and the motorman, the investigation put the blame on the victim who should not have been on the tracks. In 1895 after Joe Wilson was run down and killed by a car of the Fort Worth Street Railway Company, the company quickly pointed out that Wilson was "deaf and dumb" so it was his own fault for "allowing himself to be caught on the tracks" even though witnesses said the car was "running at a rapid rate" of speed when it struck him. The motorman was reportedly "almost prostrated" by what had happened but managed to continue his route. By bizarre coincidence, a deaf-mute friend of Wilson's had been run down and killed by the same car at almost the same spot one year previously.[7]

No surprise, the law was on the side of the companies. Legal precedent put all the onus on the person crossing the tracks to look out for their own safety. The first time the operator of a streetcar was found legally responsible for causing an accident resulting in a fatality was in New York City in 1906, and it was the conductor, not the motorman or the company that was blamed. The motorman got up from his seat to speak to a passenger, leaving the conductor to operate the car. The conductor lost control and hit a mail wagon, killing the driver. A jury found the conductor guilty of negligence, which should have had major legal implications, but it did not set much of a precedent in conservative heartland cities like Fort Worth.[8]

As the years passed and streetcar lines multiplied, so, too, did accidents between streetcars and pedestrians and streetcars and vehicular traffic. Many involved carriages or buggies whose human drivers sometimes let the horse do the driving because they had traveled the same way so often. The horses could be relied upon to look out for each other and thus avoid collisions. Electric streetcars were not so forgiving of driver error. It just took one inattentive motorman or buggy driver to cause an accident. Naturally, inquests were held afterwards which generally assigned no responsibility for the cause of death. Things got so bad the *Telegram/Star-Telegram* began reporting the annual death toll as box scores. Accidents were so common the newspaper often grouped them together two or three at a time in one story, placed on an inside page. Some stories rated front-page coverage, such as the accident that came with this gory headline in 1912: "6 Injured When Crowded Street Cars Collide. Motorman crushed, Dragged from Burning Debris."[9]

In reporting accidents, newspapers followed the tried-and-true journalistic principle: "If it bleeds, it leads." That meant gruesome details. In the 1895 accident mentioned above, Joe Wilson was run over by a streetcar on Main. As the *Gazette* told the story, his body was dragged forty yards before the motorman could stop the car. "When extricated it was mangled almost beyond the semblance of a human form. The arms and legs were crushed, the head gashed, and the abdomen and breast so torn, even that the entrails protruded and fell upon the ground." The bloody corpse was removed from the tracks and laid on the sidewalk where "hundreds" soon gathered to view the "ghastly spectacle."[10]

And the more casualties, the bigger the story. In 1907, twenty people were hurt when an overloaded NTTC car overturned going up North Main to the stockyards. After the *Star-Telegram* tallied up the 1909 casualties (four children killed, two adults injured through November), a good year by streetcar standards, a public outcry arose to put "fenders" on the front of the cars, "people-catchers," as they were also known. City commissioners responded to the outcry with an ordinance requiring the equipment, but the companies did absolutely nothing until after twelve-year-old Otto Berger was run over by a NTTC car on December 16, 1909. Only then did the NTTC agree to install the fenders "out of deference to public opinion," as the newspaper put it, although the company's manager warned that "this will not prevent accidents." He said the NTTC was doing everything possible to avoid accidents, which, he added, were "expensive and cost the company large sums of money each year." A rival streetcar company, Citizens Railway, made no such promise to install fenders.[11]

Sure enough, installing fenders did not decrease the number or the severity of accidents. The cause was usually defective equipment and/or poor track maintenance, both the result of companies scrimping on operations. What they saved in maintenance, however, they spent defending themselves against lawsuits. Most victims were not pedestrians run down by the slow-moving (seven mph) cars; rather, they were passengers killed or injured when the cars they were riding in ran off the tracks or collided with another vehicle. In January 1920, nine passengers were injured when the Arlington Heights streetcar they were riding on was hit by a Frisco train where the two sets of tracks crossed on Seventh St. The accident was the result of a series of bad decisions by employees for both companies. The streetcar driver had stopped on the tracks to let off a passenger, and the locomotive was pushing a string of sixteen cars so the engineer could not see down the tracks ahead.[12]

Victims of streetcar accidents did not shy away from taking on Goliath. All it took to win was a good lawyer and a sympathetic jury. Some victims even had legitimate cases. Big, fat paydays were rare but not unheard of. The amounts won in Fort Worth cases varied from as little as $15,000 to as much as $50,000 in actual and exemplary damages. It never hurt the plaintiff's case if the victim were a child or an important person. Little piddling cases, like Mrs. Margaret Treadwell's 1918 suit against the NTTC for $2,000 after a streetcar struck her buggy while it was crossing the tracks, were settled on the courthouse steps, usually for a fraction of what the victim had asked for originally. Notices of pending lawsuits were as routine in the newspaper as reports of streetcar accidents, and like the latter, they were sometimes grouped together in a single article, as on December 5, 1918, when U.A. Zimmerman's suit against the NTTC for $10,000 and Dada Ward's against the same company for $5,000 were reported together in the *Star-Telegram*.[13]

Not even a good lawyer and a sympathetic plaintiff were any guarantee of a big payoff. A "disastrous trolley-car accident" on Thanksgiving Day, 1907, took the life of one person and injured fifteen others. It was investigated by the authorities and the NTTC with both the company and Justice of the

Peace Thomas J. Maben concluding that it was impossible to determine why the streetcar had left the tracks and plunged down a steep embankment. Without a definitive cause, the victims had no case for negligence under the law. End of story. The plaintiffs were victimized twice: first by the company and then by the legal system.[14]

The Fort Worth Police Department seemed to have a particularly problematic relationship with streetcars. In 1918, Dallas traffic cop Max Doughty told a reporter how officers on traffic duty had to be nimble ("good dodging ability") because they were regularly "side-swiped" by passing streetcars. The risk is understandable for traffic cops, but other officers also seemed to have an unfortunate affinity for streetcars. In July 1906, Henry P. Shiel, ex-policeman, saloon owner, and alderman, was struck by a streetcar "while walking on Main St." He suffered an unspecified "permanent injury" that led him to file suit against the NTTC for $10,000 on July 19. On May 7, 1919, Officer Sterling Price "Dick" Warren of the FWPD was getting off his shift about 6:15 in the morning, heading home in the pouring rain. He ran to catch a streetcar on Front St. and did not see another streetcar going in the opposite direction. It hit him, killing him instantly. Then on August 8, 1920, a Sunday night, three officers including the night captain were involved in an accident while answering a call in the department's "emergency automobile." Apparently, upon arriving at the scene they stopped in the middle of the street and were sitting there when a streetcar came along, did not see them in time, and struck their car, knocking it onto the sidewalk. Three pedestrians were injured, but no police officers.[15]

While streetcars were involved in far more accidents than Interurbans or railroads, both of the latter were more lethal because they were so much heavier and traveled so much faster than streetcars. The Interurban sped between Fort Worth and Dallas and Cleburne at breakneck speeds that could reach sixty mph. Worse, their tracks were largely at grade level

(a) One of the new "safety cars" put in service by the Northern Texas Traction Co. in 1927. Note the warning signs plastered all over it. (b) An Interurban speeding between Fort Worth and Dallas. Both from author's collection.

with no crossing gates or signals to halt approaching traffic. On November 16, 1916, Col. Paul Waples, a wealthy businessman who lived in Arlington and commuted to his Fort Worth office, was struck and killed by a speeding Interurban when his chauffeur-driven automobile drove across the tracks just outside the gates of his estate. Waples's subsequent funeral caused city and county offices to shut down and brought out thousands of mourners.[16] On September 26, 1918, J.D. Spearman was killed when his motorcycle was struck by an Interurban car on the Cleburne line near Everman. His death did not bring the same public display of grief as Waples's, but his widow won a judgment of $50,000 against the Tarrant County Traction Company.[17]

Railroad safety issues started with the fact that trains passed through town at grade level, and even the busiest traffic intersections had nothing but a "watchman" to prevent mayhem. The days of mechanically lowered crossing guards and electrically triggered signals were far in the future. In Fort Worth the busiest intersections were where Main and Jennings Avenues crossed the T&P reservation on their way to the Near South Side. Pedestrians and vehicular traffic took their life in their hands every time they crossed the eight sets of tracks. And as settlement of the Near South Side grew and automobiles were added to the mix, the potential for accidents only became greater. The clamor for underpasses and overpasses fell on deaf corporate ears.

Railroad accident victims usually did not live to sue; that was left up to their families. The causes for such accidents were usually the same as for streetcar and interurban accidents: poorly maintained equipment, careless employees, inattentive victims. It was not always a matter of being mowed down by a speeding train. The slow-moving behemoths could be just as lethal, and human carelessness was often a contributing factor. On March 30, 1890, William Dial, "a well-known newspaper man," was struck and killed in the T&P rail yards by a switch engine about five o'clock one morning after he sat down on the tracks and apparently dozed off. That is the only way to explain how he did not hear it coming. Another victim of a rail-yard mishap was Capt. H.C. Edrington. On May 7, 1915, the seventy-three-year-old Confederate veteran and bank president died while cutting through the Texas & Pacific yards on the way home. His fine home on Pennsylvania Ave. was on the south side of the Reservation and Edrington preferred to go through the rail yards rather than use the Jennings Ave. Viaduct. He stumbled and fell into the path of a slow-moving train and was "run over by a string of freight cars." The engineer could do nothing. Edrington's body was so badly mangled he was barely recognizable by the coroner who was called to the scene. Because of his social standing, his death was front-page news.[18]

Fortunately, in the city limits trains moved more slowly and made lots of noise, but hazardous crossings and inattentive drivers still produced disasters. Grade crossings that did not merit a watchman were posted with signs that said, "Stop! Look! Listen!", which were less about safety than about avoiding legal liability. It was left up to those using the roads to keep a sharp eye out for oncoming rail traffic. In 1913, Dr. and Mrs. R.H. Gough and their five-year-old daughter were motoring along Ballinger St. paralleling the T&P tracks when Dr. Gough made a left turn across the tracks. He did not hear the clanging of the warning bell or see the approaching freight train. The engine struck the rear of the car, but none of the occupants were seriously injured. Still, the accident was newsworthy because the crossing had long been recognized as exceedingly dangerous. The street was a popular shortcut to the Near South Side, and a high board fence along the road blocked the view of the tracks. Earlier complaints had caused the railroad to put up the warning bell as a "compromise." The narrow escape of the Goughs, especially their small daughter, caused a public outcry. The city commission demanded an explanation from the T&P, which responded by posting a full-time "watchman" at the crossing. But the hard feelings against the railroad did not go away so easily. Fort Worth could not live without the railroads, and sometimes it seemed it could not live with them.[19]

The most spectacular accidents were three-way collisions involving a horse or horse-drawn vehicle, a streetcar, and a train. Since train tracks were at grade level in the city limits, they often crossed streetcar tracks, and both crossed busy streets, setting up potential disasters. Accidents involving multiple vehicles were a legal nightmare to sort out because each party blamed the others. In 1905 a Frisco freight train plowed into a NTTC streetcar near the northern city limits in the pre-dawn hours. The streetcar was crushed, a cattle car derailed, pinning the animals within. Twenty persons were severely injured. The crossing was a particularly dangerous one because two sets of railroad tracks (Frisco and Cotton Belt) crossed two sets of streetcar tracks (NTTC and Rosen Heights), and there was neither a crossing gate nor flagman at the crossing. It was one of the worst accidents in Fort Worth rail history. But it was hardly unique. In 1912 a horse on South Boaz was struck by an automobile, knocking it into the path of an approaching streetcar that crashed into the horse. Fortunately, the only fatality was the horse. Three years later, an accident on the Paddock Viaduct involved two automobiles, one trying to pass the other, and a streetcar. The newspaper reported, "Passengers thrown in all directions," with two injured so severely they were not expected to live.[20]

Most of the people injured or killed in accidents on the tracks were nonentities whose deaths were reported on an inside page and mourned by only a few family and friends. But a few victims, like Paul Waples, were leading citizens, the kind of people whose death merited front-page reporting. On April 12, 1890, Joe Rowland, a longtime city employee and candidate for street commissioner, was run over and killed by an electric streetcar at the intersection of W. Weatherford and Main streets. As the *Dallas Morning News* told it, "The poor fellow's body was badly mangled" and a coroner's inquest was investigating.[21]

On the morning of February 12, 1912, Neil P. Anderson, one of the richest cotton dealers in the state, was going into the office

Col. Paul Waples, founder of Waples-Platter Grocery Co. and an Interurban casualty. Courtesy *Fort Worth Star-Telegram* Collection, Special Collections, University of Texas at Arlington Library, Arlington, TX.

in his big, chauffeur-driven car with two companions. Their car was traveling north on the Hill St. Viaduct when it ran head-on into a southbound Summit Ave. streetcar. The car was demolished and the streetcar heavily damaged. Anderson, who was riding in the front passenger seat, was the only person seriously injured, leading the *Star-Telegram* to comment, "It was little short of miraculous" that no one was killed. Following common practice of the day, Anderson was transported home and a doctor summoned to care for him. The doctor prescribed bed rest for a few days, and by the 15th the sixty-five-year-old tycoon was reported "slightly improved." But on February 27 he passed away, the delayed result of the injuries he had sustained. It was never explained how a head-on collision could occur in broad daylight and clear weather on a straight stretch of roadway. It may have had something to do with the fact that the relatively narrow roadway was shared by streetcars and other vehicles with the streetcar tracks taking up the middle of the road.[22]

Some other Fort Worth VIPs survived their encounters with streetcars. On May 15, 1894, Will F. Lake, one of the city's most prominent cattlemen, was injured while crossing Main St. one morning in front of the Pickwick Hotel. He stepped in front of a streetcar, which sounded its bell in warning. The startled cattleman tried to jump out of the way, which took him into the path of an oncoming delivery wagon that knocked him down and ran over him, breaking his leg. The accident was not the streetcar motorman's fault, of course, but it illustrates the ever-present danger of public transportation on the streets of the growing city. In 1917, John W. Baskin, a distinguished lawyer and former county attorney, was driving east on Second, crossing Houston, when his automobile was struck by a northbound streetcar and spun around then struck by a southbound streetcar. Fortunately, Baskin was not injured, but his car was "practically demolished." An investigation attached no blame to either party.[23]

The Missouri, Kansas & Texas railroad (the KATY) had the worst record, specifically the KATY Flyer, which flew down the tracks barely slowing even after entering the city limits. In 1905 alone it claimed two prominent victims. On July 5, the northbound Flyer going an estimated 30 mph smashed into the Oldsmobile of Dr. Charles Harris at the East Second St. crossing. The car was demolished and a sixteen-year-old passenger seriously injured, but the doctor escaped without injury, which was a good thing since he went on to enjoy a distinguished career that later led to his name being attached to Harris Methodist Hospital.[24]

Almost exactly three months later the KATY Flyer took out beloved Fort Worth photographer Charles Swartz. "Charlie" as he was known to one and all had accepted a commission to photograph the Fort Worth Iron and Steel Manufacturing plant on South Hemphill for advertising purposes. On the morning of October 6, he arrived on the scene with his box camera and picked a site for the best shot, setting up on an elevated railroad embankment. While clearing the sight line in front of his camera for the shot he heard the southbound KATY Flyer approaching. He raced to save the camera and lost. The cow catcher on the locomotive caught him and the camera and sent them both flying. Neither survived the collision. A doctor summoned to the scene pronounced Swartz dead. But that was not the end of the story. An insignificant item in the *Fort Worth Telegram* just a few days earlier now seemed to foreshadow the tragedy. It was an announcement that said, "C.L. Swartz No More." Placed by Charles himself, it was not intended to be prophetic, just to advise the people of Fort Worth that he was closing his long-time studio. In hindsight, it seemed eerily prescient if one believed in such things. The victim's family received a small settlement from the KATY railroad.[25]

On April 25, 1916, the KATY was in the headlines again. A switch engine was moving a string of cars north of Fort Worth.

Where the tracks crossed the Denton Road near Hodge, the train struck the roadster of E.A. Jackson carrying Jackson and his wife. The crew afterwards claimed the train was moving "only four or five miles an hour," but it demolished the car and dragged the Jacksons' bodies ninety yards up the tracks. The couple were horribly mangled, dying shortly afterwards in the hospital. They were among Fort Worth's beautiful people, wealthy landowners and residents of Quality Hill on the city's south side. The place where the accident occurred was a blind crossing where the embankment prevented a clear view up and down two sets of tracks. It had been recognized for more than twenty years by people going back and forth to Denton as a "death trap" just waiting to happen. Fort Worth officials had long tried to get the railroad to fix the crossing, but since it lay outside the city limits, they could do nothing. This time County Judge Jesse Brown swung into action, not with the intention of suing the railroad (heaven forbid!), but to get it to finally fix the crossing. It is interesting how it took the death of two prominent citizens to move the authorities to do something. In the aftermath, the city also pressured the Texas & Pacific and the Frisco lines to do something about the Ballinger St. crossing.[26]

Track-related accidents kept a lot of Fort Worth lawyers busy, substantially padding their bank accounts, not just the corporate lawyers on retainer but the small-time lawyers who took on outgunned clients and sometimes won nice settlements. The state of Fort Worth medicine also got a boost from these cases. Some of the first use of X-ray machines came about to support plaintiff's lawsuits. Jurors no longer had to take this doctor or that doctor's testimony as final. In the long term, the city also benefited when the railroads grudgingly built overpasses, starting with the 1903 Jennings Viaduct, across their tracks to facilitate the flow of traffic and, not inconsequentially, reduce the number of accidents they had to deal with.[27]

Chapter 9

When Men Were Men and Women Were the "Fairer Sex"

This far into the 21st century we have learned to be less judgmental, more accepting of gender equality and more sensitive when it comes to physical appearance. "Diversity" and "political correctness" are in; sexism and gender bias are out. No surprise, it has not always been that way. Not so long ago, men ruled the world and judged women by their domesticity and their appearance. The most desirable kind of woman should be able to "spin, sew, cook and clean house to perfection." In the looks department, females were categorized on a descending scale as pretty, handsome, plain, homely, or ugly.[1]

Even before Fort Worth was a wind-swept military post on the Trinity River, social mores routinely characterized women as either "ladies" or otherwise. In 1838 the *Houston Telegraph & Texas Register* was outraged to learn that 3,000 Boston women had signed a petition against the annexation of Texas to the Union. The editor scornfully declared these were no "young ladies." Rather, they were "ugly, sour old maids passing themselves off for young ladies," motivated by jealousy that so many

Boston young men had gone to Texas. Partisan politics obviously had a beauty component.[2]

The early judges of feminine pulchritude in north Texas were equally blunt and critical when it came to rating the local girls. At Christmastime, 1850, the army officers at Fort Worth decided to hold a dance, and since the only lady on the post was Mrs. Arnold, the commander's wife, they reached out to the local farmers. A wagon was dispatched to pick up the farmers' daughters. When it got back, to the men's shock the girls were not just on the homely side, they were a little hazy on the essentials of a dance; they were barefooted ("shoeless"). The enterprising officers outfitted them from the supply room in army brogans, and the dance proceeded. They were so glad to have female companionship of any kind, they did not complain about the gracelessness of their dates, though one man marveled over a "six-feet-high" gal who towered over all the officers.[3]

Dallas Judge John Jay Good traveled through north Texas as a district court judge between 1854 and 1861. He wrote to his wife, "I have not seen a handsome woman or baby since leaving home. This country is not famed for either."[4]

The little settlement that grew up on the site of the old army post atop the bluff did not have many females, handsome or otherwise. Single young ladies did not move to the frontier unless they already had a mate lined up. That left the daughters of local settlers, and there were mighty few of those of marriageable age. Florence Peak, wife of early Fort Worth doctor Carroll Peak, many years later recalled there being just eight women in the little village, all of them married. Unmarried gents seeking female companionship had to get to know one of the local farmers or else go all the way to Dallas to find an unmarried young lady.[5]

In 1889, with all the furor created by early rumors of the coming of the Texas Spring Palace, the *Denver Republican* sent a reporter down on the train to investigate the rumors. His report

The only known portrait of Florence Peak, close observer of Fort Worth society. Courtesy Julia Kathryn Garrett Collection, Special Collections, University of Texas at Arlington Library, Arlington, TX.

to his editor commended the state's fauna and flora, Southern chivalry, and the industry of Fort Worth businessmen. He also added this observation: "The ladies here stand as a living and perpetual monument to the falsity of the assertion that the state cannot produce good-looking women." Without this actual on-the-scene report, we would never know today that Texas women were known for their homeliness![6]

In the years that followed, the *Fort Worth Gazette* confirmed the generally high quality of the local female population, noting in 1894 that one seldom met truly "ugly girls" on the streets of the city although "plain girls are plentiful." Not to despair; the writer noted that a plain girl could make herself attractive with the right temperament and sense of fashion. Better yet, he noted, men looking for a mate were more interested in other qualities than physical beauty: could she cook, keep a neat house, be a good mother?[7]

And what about working girls, meaning not prostitutes but those engaged in respectable labor? In 1883 the *Journal of Commerce* did some research that revealed that just 13 percent of the country's working population were "women and girls." Not surprisingly, most of those were in "domestic service." Big surprise, however: the second biggest source of livelihood for the fairer sex was "agricultural labor" where twice as many worked as in the traditional female occupations of "millinery, dress-making, and sewing." And more men than women were salesclerks and nurses, something that would eventually change. The *Journal* struggled to draw any conclusion from its findings about the "general occupational tendencies of the ladies," leaving most men to conclude that a woman's place was still in the home. Good looks and a sweet manner only boosted her chances of finding true happiness.[8]

A few years later, Fort Worth men found themselves being encouraged to read a new book by a French author titled, *Tween You and I; Some Little Problems of Life*, because it included useful things to know about women. Who better to advise the male sex on relations with women than a Frenchman? One of the author's main points was denouncing the tendency among girls to flirt. "A serious woman, a sensible woman … who has the consciousness of her womanly value, does not flirt," he stated flatly, not if she wanted to attract a "sensible" man.[9]

Another one of those wise male authors asked, "Can a girl be brainy and a beauty, too?" This may have been one of the first attempts in print to address the age-old myth about "dumb blondes." His answer: "The heavy, ugly girls are not half as intelligent as the bright and pretty girls." He dismissed the identification of beauty with stupidity as "a relic of Puritanism," which is another bad thing to blame on the Puritans besides blue laws and witch burnings. In the end, he associated beauty with intellect and homeliness with vanity, thereby turning conventional wisdom on its head.[10]

These sort of op ed pieces were much in vogue in the early 20th century when men ruled not just at the ballot box and in the courtroom, but in all areas of American society. Women, too were part of what modern feminists call the "patriarchal culture." Beatrice Fairfax in a 1909 edition of the *Star-Telegram* offered "words of cheer for the girl who is plain." Whatever comfort her female readers took in her advice column, men still read "plain" as "homely" or downright ugly. By the way, Mrs. Fairfax's advice for the "plain girl" was to be "sunny tempered," "fun-natured," and have a "good, sweet heart."[11]

By 1916 the prototypical feminist had come around to embracing homeliness as a badge of honor. A group of girls attending the Denton College of Industrial Arts (forerunner of Texas State College for Women and Texas Woman's University), an institution that in its literature bragged of turning out "first-class wives," banded together to form an "Ugly Girls' Club" (UGC). The UGC was dedicated to "cultivating *in both men and women* [emphasis added] an appreciation for the finer qualities of humanity" that would naturally produce better marriages. "There never yet lived a girl who believed down in her heart that she was so ugly that she couldn't convince some man to the contrary," said a spokesman.[12]

To put all this in perspective, one must remember that until well into the 20th century, newspapers had all-male staffs, from the managing editor right down to the lowliest cub reporter. There was no one in the building to call them on their shameless chauvinism. No Fort Worth newspaper had a female on the staff until Kitty Barry was hired by the *Star-Telegram* in 1912.

Chapter 10

Fort Worth: Candy-Making Capital of the Southwest

Once upon a bon-bon, Fort Worth was arguably the candy-making capital of the Southwest, perhaps America, although Hershey, Pennsylvania got all the publicity. That was because Fort Worth was home to two of the six largest candy-making companies, Pangburn's and King Candy Co. (The other four were Hershey, Russell Stover, M&M Mars, and Whitman's.). King Candy was established in 1905; Pangburn's came ten years later, and for the next half-century Fort Worth was the only city that could make such a claim.[1]

Fort Worth as a candy-making center goes back to the earliest days of the city. In 1878 Frenchman John F.P. Capera opened Capera Candy Manufacturing at 106–110 Throckmorton, enjoying great success in the years that followed. By 1890 Capera & Bro. was "the largest concern of the kind [candy-making] in the state." In 1889 he joined with other leading manufacturers of the city to form the Manufacturers' Association of Fort Worth. They even placed an exhibition at the Spring Palace. In 1890 he added crackers to his product line and changed the name to Fort Worth Candy & Cracker Co.

He employed fifty, mostly female, workers, and had three salesmen on the road covering Texas, New Mexico, and Indian Territory. His production went through 5,000 pounds of cane sugar a day to produce 10,000 pounds of rock candy. His chief competition came from J.S. Clark who opened the Queen City Candy Works in 1888 (1600 Houston). Clark turned out 4,000 pounds a week of "plain and fancy stick candies." Capera's remarkable success story has been overshadowed by the success of King Candy Company and Pangburn's in the 20th century.[2]

That gave little ol' Fort Worth two thriving candy manufacturers that we know about. The candy business ranked right behind owning a saloon as a sure-fire money-maker, and just as easy to get into. Candy, like liquor, was cheap and everyone liked it, and unlike liquor there were no social prohibitions against indulging a taste for it. After retiring, August R. Mignon, one of Fort Worth's leading photographers of the 19th century, became part-owner of Fort Worth Candy & Cracker.

The candy-making business could also be a launching pad to bigger things. Fort Worth cattle baron Sam Davidson got his start ramrodding a "confectionary store" in Granbury, Texas. The man who would later run in the same circles as Samuel Burk Burnett and W.T. Waggoner was not born to be a cowpuncher. He was a Jewish immigrant from eastern Europe who came west for his health and settled in the little town of Granbury. His first entrepreneurial venture was a little candy store he opened just off the public square. His fortunes rose rapidly from there. He moved to Fort Worth in 1892 and subsequently became vice president of King Candy Co. His interest in the cattle business came only after he had conquered the candy business.[3]

There was just one problem with the candy business in the Southwest: the warm climate made it impossible to market chocolate bon-bons and creams for most of the year—or at least that was the conventional wisdom that held the industry back.

It took John P. King to disprove that notion with a little help from the invention of industrial refrigeration. In 1905 King started a "small-scale" candy-manufacturing business in a second-floor rented space of a wood-frame building at 918 E. Ninth. At first, he only produced the usual stick candies, but soon he began turning out chocolates. He was the only local candy-maker doing so. He filled his work force with boys until necessity forced him to begin hiring young women. The boys by temperament and upbringing did not take to candy-making. Young women were an untapped labor source. He advertised for "bright" and "experienced girls" and put them to work dipping chocolates, which required dainty skills. Within a year he had twenty girls working in his "Chocolate Dept.," and business was booming. The following year he hired another ten girls to pack and ship the chocolates to his growing list of mail-order customers. In August 1906 he rolled out a Christmas line of "fancy candies" that he boasted were "equal to any of the larger candy manufacturers in the east." He backed his boast with a product of delicious high quality.[4]

King was not just the Willy Wonka of Fort Worth; he was much more. He was an excellent businessman who steadily grew his business. In January 1909 he filed the paperwork to incorporate King Candy Co., along with partners R.H. McNatt and Sam Davidson. There was no doubt who the senior partner was or whose vision the corporation was built on. In 1910 he constructed a "modern, four-story building" next door to the original site, and two years later expanded into a third building, going from 10,000 square feet and fifteen employees to 80,000 square feet and 275 employees. In 1913 he expanded into peanut sales because of the huge popularity of peanut candies. By 1915, he was producing 30,000 pounds of candy daily. In 1921 he purchased the old Southern Cold Storage Plant next door to his candy-making plant, and re-chartered it as King Ice Co., capitalized at $300,000. There was a natural synergy between the two businesses that he brilliantly exploited. His candy factory had a "sample room" that sold a good selection of what was made on site, but the location and the factory ambience did not draw a lot of customers, so in 1922 he opened the King Candy Store and Tea Room at 810 Main. The Victoria Building, as it was called, was strategically located for his purposes right across the street from the Hotel Texas. It offered the usual candies, but also had a soda fountain that sold his own ice creams and ices, and a menu that offered an assortment of French pastries and other "dainty foods." King never had any trouble raising money for this latest venture, any more than he did his earlier expansions. He seemed to have the Midas touch. His monthly payroll was $25,000, and that was before he hired forty more employees for the tea room.[5]

Like any good tycoon he turned it into a family business, bringing in sons Porter and R.H. as secretary and treasurer respectively of the company. Later they took over the business, but like many second-generation family businesses, things were not the same.

The heart of the business was still candy-making, chocolates to be more specific, which explains the company slogan, "King's for Southern Queens." (There was nothing of the sexual connotation that would have today.) The Ninth St. factory was an efficiently laid-out operation with offices and walk-in sales on the first floor; chocolates and creams on the second floor; stick, peanut, and crystal candy production on the third floor. Boxing and shipping were in the basement.[6]

What the candy plant did not have for years was a restroom for the female employees or a dining room. The former lack was an obvious problem for a business that employed more women than men, but the latter was also a problem because the building was a healthy walk from the business district, and employees were only allowed a half-hour lunch break. Eventually both problems were addressed. John King was neither more nor less callous than most of his contemporaries when it came to taking care of his employees. In 1913 he acknowledged the lack of bathroom facilities for the girls and admitted, "We are going to be forced to provide [a restroom] … Working women should have such a place." Perhaps he had learned the hard lesson earlier that Texas girls were not a bunch of docile wage-slaves. In 1906 when he refused to address their complaints about working conditions, twenty girls walked off the job, the whole Chocolate Department They were not part of a union but acted strictly on their own. But since experienced chocolate-dippers were not easy to find and milk chocolate is a perishable item, they were able to negotiate some improvements in the workplace, although those improvements at that time did not include a restroom or dining room. Those would not come for another decade. King was also not averse to putting his pretty "girl candy-makers" front and center "entertaining" factory visitors; nothing untoward, but a pretty smile could also help sell the product. King was not alone in identifying his chocolate candies with pretty girls. There was a natural connection between the two.[7]

Pangburn's story starts in 1902 with Hugh T. Pangburn who operated a drug store at 501 Houston. He opened a second store on West Seventh selling ice cream and ices, then in 1915 he turned the upstairs over the ice cream shop into a "candy factory" using the most "modern candy making equipment." He began selling his own candy ("Ragtime Chocolates") to customers of the ice cream shop. He had learned an important lesson from John King: successful chocolate manufacturing required a refrigeration plant, and he had that on site. His goal was to manufacture "the highest grade of candies at the lowest prices," breaking the stranglehold of the big out-of-state manufacturers over the candy business in Texas. He was the owner and "general manager."[8]

He threw down the gauntlet to John King, advertising that his candy was "Fort Worth's newest and best," and it was not just candy; it was "pure candy," whatever that meant. His special creation was "Ragtime Chocolates" that he described as chocolate "rough-dipped" in a coating of chopped nuts. Eventually, "Texas Millionaires" replaced "Ragtime Chocolates" as the company's signature candy. Millionaires were a perfect combination of pecans, caramel, milk chocolate, and "just a touch of honey." Come Valentine's Day every year, gift boxes of the candy flew off the shelves and straight into the hands of wives and sweethearts.[9]

Pangburn's had a synergy with another Fort Worth mainstay, the Ellis Pecan Company on North Main. Ellis produced the pecans that went into Texas Millionaires. Both companies thrived from the popularity of the candy. Ellis Pecan Company, therefore, was another element in making Fort Worth the candy capital of the Southwest.

Hugh Pangburn and John King were both first-rate businessmen and patriots who found ways to combine the two. When Camp Bowie came to Fort Worth in 1917, Pangburn loaded tubs of his ice cream onto streetcars and sent them out to the doughboys as a gift from the company. In World War II, John King provided free chocolate bars for Red Cross packages to G.I.s.

The 1920s were a boom time for Pangburn's operations. When Americans were not dancing and drinking hooch in the Roaring Twenties, they were eating candy and ice cream like there was no tomorrow. By 1922 the business had expanded beyond the original drug store to include an "ice cream and candy factory," a "chocolate shop" (609 Houston), and a cafeteria (1007 Houston). The cafeteria concept was a new type of American dining, family "eating out." Hugh Pangburn jumped on the bandwagon early. Pangburn's Cafeteria advertised "home-cooked food at reasonable prices" with breakfast, lunch, and dinner service from 6:00 AM to 8:00 PM Tuesday through Saturday. They also added a little class to the experience

Pangburn's Cafeteria, Fort Worth. The candy-maker branches out into dining. Author's collections.

by having an orchestra entertain diners nightly between six and eight o'clock.[10]

In time the candy business far outstripped the cafeteria and drug store business. He focused on the holiday business that flourished between Thanksgiving and Mother's Day every year, putting his product in beautiful decorative boxes that were part of the magic of the gift. Many of the boxes bore the striking silhouette of the Pangburn Candy Cowgirl, which was the face of Constance Campbell, an Arlington Heights High School graduate who became the company's face in 1942. The president of the company in 1942 said Pangburn's had built its packaging and advertising around "the natural beauty of the Texas outdoor girl, admired by the world and its artists." Production had to ramp up to meet national demand, and they moved into a modern, new plant at 2000 White Settlement Road in 1947.[11]

John King and Hugh Pangburn revolutionized the candy business in the Southwest. Before they came along, any Texan with a discriminating sweet tooth for soft candy had to rely on goodies shipped in from the east. King and Pangburn changed the dynamic of the business, making Fort Worth a candy manufacturing *and* distribution center for more than hard candies. Their sales reached far beyond the boundaries of Texas. They also introduced assembly-line techniques to candy-making, which allowed them to mass-produce their popular candies. The assembly-line girls were valued by how many pieces of candy they could "dip" on an eight-hour shift. Less well known, they changed the labor market in Fort Worth. Candy-making employed mostly women, and they put more women to work than any other employer except the phone company. Candy-making, like teaching and working a switchboard, was a respectable occupation that seemed peculiarly suited to women.

King Candy Co. and Pangburn's were the pride and joy of Fort Worth, but they did not have a complete monopoly on candy-making even in their heyday. Their chief competition came from Greek immigrants Nick Gavril (originally Gavrelos) and John Sideris who started Tripoli's Confectionary Company in 1911 on the corner of Main and Eleventh in the same building with a Renfro's Drug Store. They started with just hard candies which they sold in the Greek community on the North Side but soon expanded into "high-grade home-made" chocolates, ice creams, and ices. They also offered Christmas boxes "packed in our own shop" and delivered to the buyer or mailed. Business was so good by 1919 they had to advertise for additional "chocolate dippers." The candy business was ration-proof in wartime, too. In 1942 they were one of only three firms in Fort Worth that paid bonuses to their employees, 25 percent of weekly salary. Not even King's and Pangburn's did that.[12]

By the 1970s, as the giant manufacturers took over the business, as social conventions changed (fewer people giving gift boxes of candy), and as Americans became more conscious of healthy eating, Fort Worth candy manufacturing came to the end of the line. Hugh Pangburn died in 1928, John King in 1948. After Pangburn died, the company he founded went through several changes in ownership, none of whom had the founder's touch. In 1999 the Fort Worth plant closed, and Russell Stover Candies acquired the name. They continued to produce

Two views of King Candy Co.: (a) Artist's representation for PR purposes; and (b) The reality, *ca.* 1907. Both from author's collection.

Texas Millionaires in Corsicana. John King left his company in the hands of his son, but business slacked off for a lot of reasons. The final straw came in 1978 when the FDA ordered a recall of 11,000 cases of King's candy due to "bacterial contamination." The company closed shortly thereafter. What was it about the two founders that made them so successful? John King once explained the philosophy that made him and Hugh Pangburn successful: "We aimed for quality from the start—to turn out as good a candy in Texas as could be made anywhere. We did it at the start, and we have continued doing it … that's the secret of our success."[13]

Chapter 11

It's About Horsepower, Not Horse Flesh

The Automobile Age arrived in Fort Worth in the summer of 1902 when bicycle-shop owner H.R. Cromer proudly steered his two-cylinder, sixteen-horsepower Rambler down Main St. at the terrifying speed of eight mph. Horses snorted and reared, people gawked or jumped out of the way, and Cromer plowed on heedless of the alarm he was causing. Within two years there were fifteen automobiles in Fort Worth, and the owners held the first auto rally, parading down Houston and up Main to the Courthouse. A.B. Wharton, adventurous son-in-law of cattle baron W.T. Waggoner, opened the first automobile dealership and repair shop in 1904, selling Wintons and Franklins, but only on special order because there was no sales floor. He had no showroom. The first generation of automobile owners was a wealthy, privileged bunch who could afford to purchase and keep up one of the new toys. They formed an Auto Club in 1904 and took the entire city council for a spin one Tuesday afternoon. The following year photographer Charles Swartz lined them all up with their vehicles for a group picture in front of the Texas & Pacific passenger station.

Fort Worth automobile owners line up in front of the T&P passenger station for Charles Swartz's camera. Author's collection.

He was the first but not the last professional photographer to find automobiles fascinating.[1]

The list of those early automobile owners (called "autoists") reads like a Who's Who of Fort Worth elite. Speeding around town in their little open-air flivvers was the very definition of "conspicuous consumption." Their exclusive ranks included Drs. J.D. Mitchell and I.C. Chase; cattlemen A.F. Crowley and J.P. Daggett; Police Chief James Maddox; architect Marshall Sanguinet; L.P. Robertson, owner of Robertson's Funeral Home; and Guy Waggoner, son of another cattleman, W.T. Waggoner. One newspaper described them as the proud owners of "the finest vehicles to be found in the state." They also seemed to think they owned the roads, driving with the sort of reckless abandon that produced the city's first automobile accidents. The first recorded accident occurred in October 1904 when

Albert B. Wharton, doing 20 mph on a busy main thoroughfare, barreled into a Western Union delivery boy on his bicycle. The boy's family sued Wharton for $1,000 but settled out of court a year later. In 1906 Dr. Chase collided with a horse and buggy at the corner of Main and Ninth. He was transported home suffering from "a very painful head injury." Fortunately, no one else was injured. He was treated by his fellow physicians and lived to drive again.[2]

The first area speeder to find himself in legal hot water was an unnamed driver stopped in Dallas by a local policeman in 1900. The police court let him go because at the time there was no law on the books making speeding a crime. Fort Worth city fathers first set a speed limit of ten mph inside the city limits, following Dallas's lead, but after a series of accidents and near-accidents, they revisited the question of "the proper speed for autos" at a January 25, 1907, council meeting. They did not reach a decision then but a few months later, responding to citizens' complaints, they lowered the speed to seven mph. That brought complaints from car owners that the legal speed limit was ridiculously low. The little runabouts on the roads at the time overheated at such low speeds. Most of the privileged young men chose to simply ignore the legal speed limit and go on their merry way. Two speeders who were cited, Marshall Sanguinet and Guy Waggoner, were only caught because a sharp-eyed policeman recognized them as they sped past. At this date the police still had no way of catching speeders. A man on foot cannot hope to catch a man in an automobile, even if the automobile is going only 10 mph. In another couple of years, responding to the complaints of the growing number of automobile owners, the council raised the speed limit to 12 mph, still not high enough for those who enjoyed the wind in their hair and scenery flashing by.[3]

Since only the wealthy owned cars, there was definite class prejudice involved in the enforcement of the traffic laws.

Marshal Sanguinet (L) and Guy Waggoner (R). Known to their peers as "Makers of Fort Worth." Known to Fort Worth police as speed demons. Courtesy Dalton Hoffman.

On July 4, 1904, Sanguinet was speeding along through City Park (now Trinity Park) going about 20 mph when he struck and killed A.B. Wharton's dog, ironic considering Wharton's own history of reckless driving. Sanguinet did not slow down, but he was recognized and reported to police by Wharton. An officer thoughtfully came to Sanguinet's office to deliver the summons. The city's police court, which handled all traffic violations, administered nothing more than a slap on the wrist to violators, assessing fines of one dollar plus minimal court costs (typically five dollars). For some of the privileged few, the court was even more understanding. In 1909 Col. H. E. Crowley and three ladies were racing through the night trying to beat a rainstorm that would have ruined the ladies' ostrich-plume hats. Crowley was ticketed by a policeman, but the police court judge dismissed the charge because of the extenuating circumstances.[4]

The Fort Worth Police Department had to hustle to catch up with the times. In 1909 city commissioners (taking over from the city council under the 1907 revised charter) created a "traffic squad" to direct traffic on downtown streets. To make them stand out, only the tallest officers were picked, and they wore white gloves while on duty. This did not address the problem of speeding, however. The first stab at addressing that problem was when the Police Department posted mounted officers in "speed traps," raising the specter of a horse in hot pursuit of an automobile through town. In 1909 the department finally addressed the strategic imbalance by purchasing two Indian motorcycles. Henry Lewis, a former trick rider in the circus, was the FWPD's first motorcycle cop. He made the first traffic stop for speeding a few months later when he pulled over Pete Vernon for going a remarkable twenty-seven mph in the city where the speed limit was twelve mph. Lewis and his fellow motorcycle cop Bill Little were kept busy thereafter.[5]

It was only a matter of time before some of the town's prominent young ladies got behind the wheel and showed that having a heavy foot was not just boys being boys. In August 1911 Police Court Judge B.D. Shropshire announced, "If women violate the law they will be punished just as the men are for the same offense." The first test of that pronouncement came the following month when Martha Shelton, daughter of wealthy cattleman John M. Shelton, was stopped while speeding down Lipscomb. Motorcycle Officer J.W. Edwards caught her after a short pursuit. It was not her first speeding citation, but it was the first one she pleaded "guilty" to and paid the fine. The city had recently raised the fine to $5, so she (or daddy) had to pay $12.95 total. Because of her gender and family name she was not required to appear in court.[6]

Fort Worthers had to get used to seeing the privileged zip around town in their ever-more-powerful vehicles. Fort Worth police were not so accepting. Motorcycle officer Bill Little chased a young stud with his lady friends who were speeding through town. When the joyriders would not stop, Little pulled his pistol and opened fire over their heads. The driver pulled over, and Little took him in, leaving the young ladies sitting in the car.[7]

Amon Carter, always a fan of the latest technological advance, purchased an automobile for himself, then had his newspaper put out a special, twenty-eight-page automobile edition on March 16, 1910. And the city extended Cowtown hospitality to long-distance road racers coming through the area, including one race that started in Fort Worth before going to Beaumont, and another that went from Denver to Mexico City.[8]

The city council wrote traffic laws to put some controls on the dangerous new vehicles, trying to walk the thin line between individual freedom and public safety. The "automobile ordinance" of 1909 set a maximum speed limit of seventeen mph "anywhere in town" in accordance with state law. In earlier years, the Fort Worth speed limit had been set at 8 then 12 mph. The ordinance also made it unlawful to drive "in a careless or reckless manner at any speed." It further required every machine to be registered with the city and given a number which was to be displayed on the rear of the car in "white figures not less than six inches high"—the first license plates! The ordinance required every vehicle to have brakes, horn or gong, and "lamps" front and back. "Sounding the gong or horn so as to willfully scare horses" was prohibited. Fines for violation of any of these provisions ranged from $1 to $200. Alas, traffic problems only got worse. The city posted the speed limit on the main streets so no one could claim ignorance of the law and put up first STOP signs then traffic signals at major intersections. As drivers began heading for the open roads, county authorities got involved. In 1919 Tarrant County commissioners authorized "traffic officers" as part of the Sheriff's Department. That same year, Police Chief Oscar Montgomery called "handling traffic" the "chief problem" of his department. Catching horse thieves was yesterday's problem. This was a new, 20th-century Fort Worth, more concerned with horsepower than horse flesh.[9]

Chapter 12

Market Day

In Fort Worth's early years market day was one of the most important days on the calendar. It was when local farmers and stockmen brought their products to town to sell. Market day was once a month, held on the public square. One of the few surviving photos of 1870s Fort Worth shows a typical market day with the square filled with wagons and rough-dressed people. Fort Worth was more than the county seat of Tarrant County; it was the distribution center for a vast hinterland to the south and west. There was no such thing as urban sprawl. Beyond the city limits was open country dotted by farms and ranches and populated by "countrymen" meaning rural residents, not fellow Americans as we think of the term today.

By the early 1890s market day no longer took over the public square on Saturdays. Retail business owners objected, and it interfered with normal courthouse business. Furthermore, a massive new courthouse was in the works that would occupy most of the old public square. It was not completed until 1895, but market days on the public square were a thing of the past even as bonds were being issued and plans drawn up. There was

(a) Market day in Fort Worth on the public square, *ca.* 1870s. Author's collection. (b) Public markets have been a part of Fort Worth life ever since, including this one on Henderson built in 1930. Courtesy Scott and Linda Jo Barker.

also talk of fencing off the square during construction, a prospect the *Fort Worth Gazette* warned would be "a serious inconvenience" for the farmers and stockmen who had sold there historically. No one wanted to eject honest, working folks who depended on that area to market their goods, and of course, city residents also bought their fresh vegetables and meat from the local farmers who came to town. Fort Worth for all its metropolitan airs was still a little country town in many ways.[1]

In 1892 the *Fort Worth Gazette* championed the need for a "commodious public market" where the working man could buy his meat and vegetables cheap. The farmers' market was a cheaper alternative to the town's retail grocers and butchers. The question was where to put it. When city fathers began making plans in 1891 to build a new city hall, one of the suggestions of the "building committee" was to put a public market on the ground floor of the building, police court and public offices on the next floor, and council chambers on the third floor. The revenue from the market would help pay for construction in addition to the public service provided by the market itself. It would also make it easier for the city to "regulate and control the sale of meats, articles of produce, etc."[2]

When saner heads on the city council prevailed and the new city hall in 1893 did not include a farmers' market on the first floor, Fort Worthers had to look elsewhere. Attention turned to nearby empty property in the Jennings Addition. The city's business district virtually stopped at about Eighth or Ninth streets east and west of Main. The only substantial buildings south of that until the Railroad Reservation were St. Patrick's, the 1893 city hall, and the 1896 federal building. Some "public-spirited" property owners offered two sites: a couple of empty blocks between city hall and the federal building or a single block bounded by Tenth and Eleventh, Houston to Throckmorton. It just depended on how much land the market needed. In either case "countrymen" could bring their wagons in without having to drive through the center of town, and city residents could easily make their way there, too. All that was needed to get things going was a few hitching posts and a watering trough. (Curiously, no mention was made of providing toilet facilities. Presumably, either people would use the facilities at city hall and the federal building, or they would step behind a wagon to take care of business.) The *Fort Worth Gazette* was in favor of getting it up and running as soon as possible, dangling the possibility that a large covered market ("market house") might be built on the site someday.[3]

The discussion grew remarkably heated, showing that Fort Worth was still invested in its rural way of life despite the growing skyline, electric wires, streetcar tracks, and other signs of urbanization. No one could open a public market without a permit from the city council, and those gentlemen were under pressure from several sides. They debated where to place the market, whether to push for an open market or a market house, and how to regulate it. One group of businessmen strongly opposed both Jennings sites. They were not opposed to a farmers' market, but they had their businesses on the north end of town and thought they would suffer financially if the public market located on the south end of town. They dangled a proposal to put up a market house on four empty lots on the north side of the courthouse square. One writer to the *Gazette* grumbled that until the market opened, the city's residents would continue to pay exorbitant prices for their meat and vegetables.[4]

The two-block Jennings site won out. A covered structure went up, and the council licensed it. In the discussion leading up to the decision other reasons emerged for relocating the public market to the south end of town away from the city center: getting the peddlers and "wood sellers" off the public square. The former in particular were a nuisance, taking over the sidewalks and pestering passersby. Police could now move them well away from the business district or shut them down entirely if they refused to move. In the next few years, the market on Jennings "near Thirteenth" prospered. Instead of market day once a month, it was open six days a week (Sundays excepted). It proved as big a hit as the old market on the bluff had been. A reporter for the *Fort Worth Morning Register* visited it and commented on the "cosmopolitan crowd" he saw there. Vendors offered everything from melons and pumpkins to stove wood and patent medicine. Everything was for sale, including livestock, farm equipment, and furniture. The owner did not even have to do the selling; there were auctioneers for that. It was a touch of the county fair every day (except Sunday) just a couple of blocks from city hall.[5]

The operation was so successful it stirred more jealousy among uptown merchants who coveted all the customers who took their business to the public market. A group of them banded together and purchased an empty piece of property between Belknap and Bluff just east of the Courthouse to revive the old open-air market. Their site proved so successful they drove the Jennings market out of business. The growth of the city south into the Jennings Addition also played a part in killing it. As property in that part of town became more valuable, a farmers' market/flea market was a poor use of real estate. The last thing to go was the shed, torn down after all the vendors had cleared out in 1906. The land was cleared for redevelopment, and that is where the first Majestic Theater (1308 Jennings) went up eventually. In the meantime, the vendors did not go far, just back uptown.[6]

The city council recognized the civic value of a public market, enough to underwrite the $35,000 bond drive it would take to build it in 1906. While Fort Worth could rightly claim to be a regional metropolis (population more than 50,000) by this date, the area's farmers and stockmen still sold direct to the public. And it was no longer just countrymen who wanted a public market; business interests saw a chance to make a killing. A group of retail merchants, calling themselves the Market House Company, believed they could do very well by putting up a public market and charging vendors to rent space instead of letting them use the empty land. They acquired clear title to the piece of land on the corner of Houston and

Belknap across the street from the county jail (two lots) then offered to let the city have one lot in return for the city erecting a covered structure on it and letting them use it for free. The deal also required the city to purchase the second lot for an open-air market. Farmers had been coming into town "to sell and exchange their products" as far back as anyone could remember, using those lots without paying a cent in rent. As the city grew up around the site, the land increased in value by roughly a thousand dollars a year, and still the farmers did not pay taxes or even have to buy a license. On any given day except Sunday from a dozen to fifty wagons were parked there. The farmers were practicing the oldest trade in the world, feeding the city, marketing their produce straight to the public. This cozy arrangement was interrupted in 1906 when the Market House Co. bought the land. If they got their way, free enterprise would no longer be free. The city council voted to accept the deal. It did not hurt that one of the Market House investors, Ben L. Waggoman, was also a councilman, guaranteeing at least one vote for the deal.[7]

Those corner lots were historic because they were the last bit of undeveloped land where once the 1849 fort had stood. A little grove of trees that had been there when the first soldiers arrived still stood on the west side of the property. One vocal element in town favored making it a memorial park. Others saw only its potential commercial value. That corner would be the object of a bitter fight for years to come, pitting preservationists against county commissioners against real estate developers who could agree on nothing.[8]

When the Market House investors and the city did nothing with their little piece of real estate, the county stepped back in and purchased it for $20,000 in 1912. For the first time ever, the county had "clear and unrestricted title" to all the land from the public square to the river. Neither city nor county elected officials were willing to give up entirely on having a farmers' market downtown, an indication that Fort Worth was not as urbanized as people liked to think. In 1912 city officials proposed a joint project to put up the long-promised covered market on the bluff plus a much-needed public auditorium on the same site. However, county commissioners were no longer interested in farmers' markets in any form. They had another idea in mind for the site: a new county jail. Tax Collector Robert M. Davis was in favor of relocating the jail and urged them to turn the old site into "a resting place for farmers when they come to town," *i.e.*, a farmers' market. Not wishing to alienate any group of voters, commissioners promised the empty lot on the corner of Houston and Belknap would continue to be used for "a market square and nothing else."[9]

The truth was, by 1917 the decision to move the jail across the street was final. The county owned the property and needed a new jail, and that jail had to be close to the Courthouse for convenience and security reasons. No amount of arguing for using the property as either a farmers' market or heritage park was going to change the decision. Nearby businessmen on Belknap argued that putting a jail there would substantially harm commercial property values, but their resistance was nothing compared to the Federation of Women's Clubs who descended on commissioners' court like angry hornets. They argued that "the only historical spot" left on the bluff should not be turned into a lockup. Mrs. J.J. Jarvis, their spokesperson, threatened, "If they start it, I for one will be in favor of tearing it down, and I wielded a hatchet before Carrie Nation did!" Commissioners finally bought off the ladies by promising to turn the old jail site over to them once it was cleared for a public park. That finally happened in 1921. Lost in all the back-and-forth between commissioners and the preservationists was the fact that regardless of which one won, the farmers were the big losers. There was no longer room for them in the heart of Fort Worth.[10]

The new county jail at 200 W. Belknap took the better part of two years to go up. In 1918 the county moved into what was grandly named the Tarrant County Criminal Courts Building. It still stands there today, atop land where once soldiers drilled and farmers spread their wares.

The appeal of a public market did not die so easily, however. Decades after suburban sprawl had stretched to the horizon in every direction and long after the last farmer's wagon was seen on a downtown street, the old idea was revived. In 1930 developer John Harden opened a new Public Market in a magnificent building in Art Deco and Spanish Colonial Revival styles at 1400 Henderson. It closed in 1944 and passed through several hands in the next seventy-plus years before landing on Historic Fort Worth's list of "most endangered properties" in 2008. It still stands empty today waiting for the right owner, a monument to Fort Worth's rural roots. Meanwhile, there's still a place for a "public market" even in the 21st century. The name evokes images of the freshest produce, friendly prices, and knowledgeable sellers even if the building does look like just another supermarket.[11]

Chapter 13

Jewel Heist at Thistle Hill

Thistle Hill, the last of the great cattle-baron mansions of Fort Worth (1509 Pennsylvania Ave.), was built by W.T. "Tom" Waggoner for his daughter Electra and her husband Albert Buckman Wharton. It was a wedding gift that came with strings attached: papa wanted to keep his little girl close. The couple were married June 10, 1902, and while they were honeymooning, Tom purchased a piece of land on the heights just south of town and started construction. Albert and Electra moved into their new home in 1904. She was already the toast of Fort Worth for her beauty and charm, and hubby was the scion of Philadelphia blue bloods who fit easily into Fort Worth society. He opened the city's first car dealership in 1903, which allowed him to make a little money while indulging his love of cars. He spent more time tooling around in his own Winton than he did selling them. He and pal Roy Kamp took an adventurous, cross-country trip from Denver to Fort Worth that same year in one of the temperamental machines. Back in Fort Worth there was not much of a market for what were essentially expensive toys, but that did not bother the baby-faced playboy. Albert and

Albert and Electra Wharton go for a spin in their Winton (with friends), 1903. From severely damaged original. Courtesy Shirley Ross and Scott Barker.

Electra were Fort Worth aristocracy. In a later generation, they would have been counted among the "beautiful people."[1]

Electra slipped easily into the mantle of "First Lady of Thistle Hill," hosting lavish parties while managing a sizable staff that included a gardener, a groom, a nursemaid for their son (born in 1903), and her own personal maid, Mabel Palmer. Mabel, who like Albert came from Philadelphia, was not just hired help; she was more like a personal friend to Electra. The mistress of Thistle Hill may have been rich and privileged, but she liked to treat her personal servants like members of the family, even including them in vacation photos. Nor did she recognize conventional social boundaries with other working-class women. She gave little gifts to shop girls, manicurists, and others who waited on her regularly. Whenever one of her pet girls was worn down by her work,

Electra invited her to the house to rest and have some refreshment. More than one working-class lass could boast she had been in Thistle Hill and had tea with the mistress![2]

Thistle Hill, as it turned out, was not a happy home for the Whartons. In 1905, Electra gave birth there to their second child, a girl who died almost immediately. Afterwards Electra did not stop socializing entirely, but she became more reclusive. She was at home when tragedy of a different sort struck on December 19, 1906, a Wednesday. The couple had been out the night before at a holiday party for which Electra wore a gorgeous gown and her finest jewelry. When they got home instead of returning the jewels to the safe, she stuck them in a leather box and stashed them in a dresser drawer. Albert tossed in his own diamond-and-emerald ring, shirt studs, pocket watch, and cigarette case. That Wednesday afternoon Electra told Mabel to fetch the valuables so she could put them away in the safe. A few minutes later the maid came back and said they were not in the drawer. Electra was not alarmed, thinking Albert had put away his own things and taken her jewels to have them cleaned when he left that morning. She phoned the office, but he was not there. When he returned her call a couple of hours later, he told her he had not taken the jewels. Now panic set in. He rushed home, and they searched the house, aided by Mabel and the other servants. It was only at that point, late Wednesday afternoon, that he called the police. Since this was the Whartons, the police came running promptly, led by Chief James Maddox, a twenty-year veteran of the force. The Chief and his detectives declared it an inside job, "the work of professionals." Support for their theory? The jewels were upstairs in a dresser drawer, nothing else had been taken, the mistress and servants had been there all day, and the isolated location of the house made it unlikely that some petty thief had found his way there from town then slipped in and out without being seen. Also, their experience was that jewel thieves typically tried to pawn their loot as soon as possible, and nothing had showed up in the local pawn shops.[3]

The police interrogated all four servants who were working that day but left still scratching their heads. The story was headline news in both Fort Worth and Dallas newspapers. By Thursday afternoon, the Fort Worth paper was saying the police were "hopelessly at sea." They did not have a "single clew" and no likely suspect(s). The stolen jewels included several rings, one of which they valued at $1,000, plus stick pins and brooches. They were vague about the total value of their loss; at different times the value was reported as $3,000, $6,000, and $7,250, even different values in the same edition of the newspaper! Nor apparently were the jewels insured. Regardless of whether they were valued at the high end or the low end, the thief or thieves had gotten away with quite a steal. Albert offered a $500 reward for the recovery of the jewels *and* the arrest and conviction of the thieves.[4]

Stung by the criticism, the police on Friday arrested two people, Mabel Palmer the maid and Sam Dunn, the black butler. Interrogation revealed that Mabel had worked as a domestic under several different names and had a criminal record in Philadelphia. They let the butler go and continued to interrogate Mabel through Sunday. A search of her house turned up some other items belonging to the Whartons but no jewels. For those items she was charged with "theft over $50." At a dead end, the police planned to transfer her to county lockup to be prosecuted for the provable crime. Meanwhile, Mabel, who was no neophyte in the criminal justice system, hired a defense attorney and vowed not to answer any further questions.[5]

Eventually, day after day of "sweating" the prisoner (AKA, the third degree) broke her down, and she gave what passed for a confession in the presence of Chief Maddox, a city detective, Albert Wharton, and Tom Waggoner. The presence of the latter pair is an indication of the high importance attached to the case. Mabel also implicated a "male accomplice" who now had possession of the jewels and was in Philadelphia. Fort Worth authorities contacted the Philadelphia police and set an examining hearing for Tuesday morning, January 1. It was indeed going to be a "Happy New Year" for Fort Worth police.[6]

Mabel was charged as "Miss Rosa Devoe, alias Rosa Doran, alias Mabel Palmer." She was charged in Justice of the Peace Hugh Bratton's court with "theft over $50" and bail was set at $10,000. Then she was returned to her cell in the county jail to await the action of the grand jury. The authorities and of course the Whartons wanted her remanded without bail, but the weakness of the evidence against her and the relative insignificance of the charge against her made that impossible.[7]

The Philadelphia police sent a rap sheet and photograph ("a perfect likeness") for Mabel whom they knew as "Rose Palmer." (Unfortunately, Mabel's picture, so thoughtfully provided by Philadelphia police, never made it into the local newspapers.) The only charges Philadelphia had against her were for larceny (twice), both of which had been settled out of court. Philadelphia's Rose was no saint, but neither was she a jewel thief. However, she was the only suspect the Fort Worth authorities had, so they continued to search for an accomplice. Even the Fort Worth newspaper referred to him as her "supposed accomplice." It was the prominence of the robbery victims that drove the investigation. Someone had to pay.[8]

A month later, a new player entered the picture, Mabel's husband. The well-dressed stranger walked into Sheriff Tom Wood's office and introduced himself as the husband, just arrived from St. Louis. He explained that they had been separated for some time, which was why he was just hearing about her plight and asked to see her. Sheriff Wood allowed him to speak with her in her cell then directed him to her lawyer's office. Up to now, Mabel had not mentioned anything about being married or having a husband in St. Louis, and as the *Fort Worth Telegram* observed, "This adds interest to the history of the prisoner."[9]

Mabel (Rose) sat in jail for more than two months while her case languished. Detectives could not identify an accomplice, though they were convinced she had one, and the Wharton jewels were still missing. The case against the accused was as weak as dishwater. A good defense lawyer would have little trouble getting her off or at least getting a sentence so light as to be meaningless. Neither prospect particularly pleased the Wharton or Waggoner families.

Finally, in April 1907 the state moved on the case, but not in the direction everyone expected. Instead of seeking a criminal indictment, the county attorney charged Mabel with "lunacy" in county court, where such cases played out. The evidence bar was not as high for a lunacy conviction; all it took was the testimony of a competent doctor or two and a couple of witnesses who would attest to her acting strangely. And the jury, of course, would be all-male. Mabel's jailers obligingly testified that she went for "long periods without food" and sometimes "tore her clothing off." Clearly, she was not all there. The prosecutor also entered into evidence statements she had made under questioning that could be "construed as confessions." Mabel may or may not have been certifiably nuts, and her so-called confession may or may not have been coerced, but the prosecution was desperate for a conviction to appease Fort Worth society, and Mabel was all they had.[10]

One week after being convicted of being "of unsound mind," Mabel was shipped off to Terrell State Hospital, a remarkably fast transfer to get rid of a major embarrassment. Usually, it took anywhere from months up to two or more years for a bed to become available at Terrell. The authorities, it seemed, were very anxious to send Mabel away – anywhere as long as she was out of Fort Worth. However, the bogus insanity conviction proved to be a less than satisfactory resolution to the problem. Five months after being shipped off to Terrell, Mabel was pronounced "cured" by doctors there. They awaited only word from Fort Worth authorities before releasing her. The county attorney's office announced they had no intention of prosecuting her further, releasing this statement: "Mabel Palmer is no longer wanted by the state on the diamond robbery or any other charge. She is at liberty to go where she pleases when released." The *Star-Telegram* added gratuitously, "The belief is prevalent in official circles that the woman is innocent of the diamond robbery."[11]

Mabel was returned to Fort Worth under guard and locked up again in county jail, but with no criminal charges against her, the authorities could not hold her. Four days later her attorney filed a writ of habeas corpus in Sixty-seventh District Court. Judge W. T. "Tom" Simmons held a perfunctory hearing at which Mabel testified. The state opposed her release, but not even the prosecutor's tough cross-examination could shake her story; she doggedly asserted her innocence just as she had previously. With no new evidence in the case, Judge Simmons had no option but to release her. She promptly disappeared, never to be seen in Fort Worth again. Fort Worth police had good reason to remember her name, however. A few years later, another "Mabel Palmer" set up shop in town as a madam, operating a house in the Acre. The dismissal of all charges against the original Mabel Palmer was a good and a bad thing. On the one hand it took the case out of the headlines. On the other hand, it was a reminder that Fort Worth authorities were no closer to solving the Thistle Hill jewel heist than they had been ten months earlier. Upon her release from custody, the *Star-Telegram* helpfully reviewed the history of the case for its readers.[12]

Still, the case would not die. A few days after Mabel was released, the *Telegram* reported the appearance of a ghostly manifestation when the Fort Worth Police Department (FWPD) took its annual group photograph on the steps of city hall. A wraithlike ring appeared over the face of Detective J.D. Allgood.

Some called it a manifestation of "spirit photography," the name given to unexplained things that showed up in photographs supposedly revealing the world of people who had "crossed over." In the case of Detective Allgood, true believers claimed they could make out the details of a jewel setting in the ring over his face, constituting a spectral message from … *who exactly?* It was not clear who was reaching out from beyond the grave, but the newspaper cruelly taunted the police by asking if the "Wharton diamonds" would ever be recovered. The answer was no.[13]

The Wharton robbery would go down in history as a cold case and eventually be forgotten, to the relief of the FWPD. It is a textbook example of how *not* to conduct a criminal investigation. Chief James Maddox's theory that it was an inside job may have been right on the mark but focused on the wrong suspect. He never seems to have considered that one or both the Whartons might have been involved. No one ever accused either Albert or Electra, but supporting the possibility of their involvement is the fact that the year before the robbery Albert had been $2,124.50 in arears on his property taxes, and whatever his net worth might have been, at the time he was far from being a millionaire. He filed an appeal arguing that he was not a resident of Fort Worth when some of the property had been assessed, and furthermore that some of it was "non-assessable" (*i.e.*, not taxable). He lost his appeal and had to pay all the back taxes, which left him in something of a financial bind. What is certainly true is that Electra's jewels fenced on the black market would have gone a long way toward restoring his finances. Both Albert and Electra were used to living lavishly, and a reduction in lifestyle would not have come easily. (Electra could have moved back home with daddy, but that would have been equally humiliating.) By this time, Albert was vice-president of the Waggoner Bank and Trust, a considerably more stable and financially lucrative position than selling automobiles.[14]

The Fort Worth police got a chance to redeem themselves in late 1914 after a similar jewel robbery at the home of Mr. and Mrs. C.H. Bencini. Some $14,000 worth of diamonds disappeared about the same time as a mysterious fire. Lena Bencini kept the jewels concealed in a closet when she was not wearing them. As they had after the Wharton robbery, police first suspected a long-time black servant of the crime although Mrs. Bencini refused to believe it. More than a year later, detectives police traced the diamonds to several black men and charged them with arson and robbery. They also recovered some of the diamonds, unlike the Wharton case. Detectives made it a point of characterizing the accused as "remarkably clever negroes." The Fort Worth Police Department's record in jewel robberies became an issue in the 1915 race for police

(a) Albert B. Wharton, first master of Thistle Hill. Courtesy Historic Fort Worth, Inc. (b) An older Electra Waggoner Wharton, grand dame on both sides of the Trinity. Courtesy Thomas Kellam and the Tarrant County College Heritage Room.

commissioner. Candidate Mordecai Hurdleston accused the incumbent, Robert M. Davis, of failure to close such cases and won the election in April 1915.[15]

Due to the tragedies associated with their dream home and probably their own growing estrangement from each other, Albert and Electra decided to sell Thistle Hill in February 1911. Their split-up was hastened if not provoked by a stroke he suffered in September 1909 while in Colorado on business. He was rushed home in a special train where he began his recovery at Thistle Hill from "paralysis." The stroke may or may not have also affected his mind. Such things were not aired in the newspapers, but a year later one of the servant girls at Thistle Hill sued him for "physical and mental abuse." Twenty-four-year-old Margaret Butler had been with the family for less than a month when, she claimed, Albert beat her so severely she could not work and had to get medical treatment. She sued for $10,000 in actual damages and $10,000 in exemplary damages. The case must have been a terrible embarrassment for Electra who would have been called to testify had it gone to trial. It was settled out of court.[16]

The Whartons' one-time storybook life had turned into a nightmare. They sold the mansion to Winfield Scott, a cattleman pal of W. T. "Tom" Waggoner's, for $90,000 and separated. Albert moved into the Westbrook Hotel, and Electra eventually settled in Dallas. The marriage officially ended in divorce court on January 12, 1921, with Electra getting a fat financial settlement and custody of the two children, Albert, Jr. (eleven) and Tom (seventeen).[17]

She began a new life as a "colorful, wealthy divorcee," the toast of Dallas society now instead of Fort Worth society. She was never short on expensive jewelry, only now her emeralds, diamonds, and pearls were locked away in a vault when she was not wearing them. Meanwhile, Albert's own luck with jewelry did not improve with the separation. In January 1911, the Westbrook Hotel barber came to his apartment to give him a shave. When the man left, he took a pearl-and-diamond stick pin with him worth $350. Police caught the thief, wearing the stick pin in his tie before he left work that same day.[18]

Thus ended the mystery of the Great Thistle Hill Heist. Mr. and Mrs. Wharton were no more, Mabel Palmer, or whoever she was, was gone, the jewelry was never recovered, and Thistle Hill had a new owner. It all adds up to an unsolved mystery and a cold case for the Fort Worth police.

Chapter 14

When Is a Miranda Warning not a Miranda Warning?

Fort Worth prides itself on being "Cowtown" and "The City Where the West Begins." (Eat your heart out Dodge City and Tombstone!) Newspaper publisher Amon Carter emblazoned "Where the West Begins" as a slogan on the masthead of the *Fort Worth Star-Telegram* starting in 1923, and the city embraced it.[1] The "cowboy culture" extended to our police. Many officers continued to wear six-shooters even after automatics came into vogue, and the Police Department maintained a horse-mounted division until 1927. The cowboy culture was an attitude as much as anything, and it did not end with the frontier era, but remained alive and well deep into the 20th century. Fort Worth cops preferred to "buffalo" obstreperous arrests with the butt end of their pistols rather than use standard-issue billy clubs. And in 1904, Night Captain Joe Witcher was still making his rounds on his faithful horse Old Baldy, whom he tied up to a convenient telephone pole behind city hall when he was not on the street. For all these reasons, it is a surprise to find the issue of defendants' rights coming up in

Cowtown criminal cases long before there was a Miranda Rule (made famous by the 1966 Supreme Court decision).

On three known occasions in the early 20th century, murder suspects were "Mirandized," or at least officers informed them of their constitutional rights. It was not a requirement, and it did not always happen. To understand how someone could be Mirandized before Miranda was adopted, it is necessary to understand the concept of defendants' rights at the time. What was called a "spontaneous confession," as opposed to one obtained through interrogation, was admissible in court. If a killer blurted out, "I did it," that utterance was admissible as evidence against him. This is the principle of *res gestae* (Lat. for "the thing done"), meaning a statement can be admitted if "it constitutes part of the criminal act." *Res gestae* does not apply if enough time passes between the arrest and the confession that it can no longer be considered "spontaneous." Another part of the principle is that any confessions must be "freely and voluntarily given," meaning it cannot be beaten out of a suspect by means of the old-fashioned "third degree." At least that was what the law said. In actuality, Fort Worth police considered the third degree to be standard practice, especially with recalcitrant black and Mexican prisoners. Former police chief James Maddox defended it at a convention of the International Chiefs Association in 1910. And local newspapers praised the department on more than one occasion for effective police work.[2]

The Fort Worth Police Department was representative of law enforcement in general. Men learned how to be policemen on the job. There were no training academies or instruction manuals. How Fort Worth officers and prosecutors wrestled with the issue of defendants' rights is part of the story of the passing of the Wild West. The frontier may have closed in 1890 according to historian Frederick Jackson Turner, but the men charged with upholding the law were still products of the frontier era.[3]

Three Fort Worth cases in particular demonstrate how Fort Worth officers and courts were more responsive than most when it came to recognizing defendants' rights. In 1902, Jeff Vann was a Fort Worth cabbie making his living picking up fares at the Texas & Pacific passenger station on the south end of Main. Vann was supposed to park his horse-drawn rig behind the "dead line" across the driveway in front of the station entrance, waiting his turn like all the other cabbies to pull around and pick up passengers exiting the station. Officer Andy Grimes was on duty at the station on May 12 to see that, among other things, the cabbies did not block traffic or get out of line. Vann refused to wait in line and parked his cab right in front of the entrance. Officer Grimes strolled over and looked up at him sitting on his high seat and ordered him to move. Vann had been ticketed for the same violation before, and he also had a history with Grimes, so he began to curse the officer. "You are nothing but a God-damned old jobber, and if you want anything out of me you can get it!" he ranted.

Grimes took out his "bond book" and filled out a bond, which worked like a ticket today. He tried to stuff it in the cabbie's hand, but Vann angrily jerked his hand away and reached under the seat box for the .45 revolver he kept there. He opened fire at the officer at point-blank range. Grimes ducked toward the back of the cab, and Vann jumped down on the opposite side. By now, Grimes had pulled his .38 revolver and begun firing back. Bystanders and nearby cabbies dived for the ground as an old-fashioned Western shootout followed with both men using the cab for cover, firing over the top and through the windows at each other. They worked their way to the rear of the cab where they came face-to-face. Both fired simultaneously, but only Vann's shot found its target, striking Grimes in the abdomen. The officer died on the spot. In all, eight or nine shots had been exchanged, exploding the Western myth that all men were armed *and knew how to use a gun.*

Eight or nine shots fired, and only one shot hit home is not a very impressive record.[4]

Officers John Fulford and Joe Witcher came running from the train station, disarmed Vann and placed him under arrest. Before being taken away, Vann blurted out to them, "I did it." Later, after he was indicted for murder, Vann's fellow cabbies took up a defense fund and hired William P. McLean, one of the top lawyers of one of the top firms in Fort Worth, to defend him. Vann also changed his story to better fit an "innocent" plea. At trial, the jury still found him guilty and sentenced him to hang. Then the appeals started. One of the major points was that Vann's confession was not admissible since he "had not been warned first" by the officers that anything he said could be used against him. The Texas Court of Criminal Appeals agreed and overturned the conviction, but not on that point alone. They also cited other missteps in the prosecution's case. Even if Miranda had existed, Jeff Vann's confession would have been admissible as a "spontaneous utterance," so the defense's objection was more a matter of a tactical ploy than the heart of their appeal. But the fact that they cited it shows that it was a constitutional matter for the court to consider. Jeff Vann went back to court for two more trials before he was finally acquitted in 1904, on technical grounds naturally. The best lawyer always wins![5]

The second case came a few years later, in 1908, involving Ike Knight. In 1908, he was living in North Fort Worth, an incorporated city of its own, just across the Trinity River from Fort Worth, with his common-law wife Florence and her daughter Nellie by a previous husband. Nellie never took kindly to mama's new man, and that was before she married the "strikingly handsome" Ed Larmon, and the couple moved into the house with Ike and Flo. With mama's blessing they took the master bedroom while Flo moved into the second bedroom, putting Ike in the "shed room" on the back of the house. Ike took an instant dislike to Ed, which had nothing to do with fatherly feelings for Nellie.

Things deteriorated to the point where Flo ordered Ike to move out. On Saturday morning, April 11, Ike went to work as usual but left work to go to the County Attorney's office. He intended to file a complaint about being thrown out of his own house. When the clerk told him the County Attorney could not do anything until after a court had decided the matter, he stormed out. A little later he showed up at the back door of his house with a double-barreled shotgun and forced his way in. Ed and Nellie were home, and while Nellie ran to call the police, Ike chased Ed from room to room. He finally caught up with him, and Nellie heard two shotgun blasts then a pause then a third blast. She ran outside thinking she was next and went down the street screaming. As a mob gathered in the yard, Ike stalked down Lake Street with the mob trailing at a safe distance. When North Fort Worth Officers Dick Howell and Oscar Montgomery arrived and tried to stop him, he gunned them both down. Eventually, the mob brought Ike to bay inside the Panther City Creamery where he surrendered to sheriff's deputies.[6]

Officers Howell and Montgomery survived, and Knight was charged with murder and "assault to murder." On Monday morning, April 13, County Attorney R.E.L. Roy paid a visit to Ike, who had not yet seen a lawyer, in his jail cell, and told him ominously, "It will be better for you if you make a statement." Ike meekly confessed to everything with a court recorder present to take it all down. Ike signed his statement, which was witnessed by an assistant county attorney and a deputy sheriff. With a signed confession, Roy figured he was home free. He asked the grand jury for and got an indictment for first-degree murder. By the time Ike got to trial on April 29 he had a court-appointed lawyer who argued Ike's confession had not been "freely and voluntarily given." Rather, it had been "induced" from a man without legal counsel, fearing for his life and unacquainted with the legal system. On the witness stand Ike swore that no one ever told him his confession might be used against him, which was a statement by an incredibly naïve man, or one who had been well-coached by this new lawyer. The jury found him guilty anyway and sentenced him to hang. Among the twenty-seven "bills of exception" filed by the defense, the clincher was the challenge to the admissibility of the jailhouse confession. The appeals court agreed and overturned the conviction, citing a "chain of mistakes" starting with the defendant's confession. They ruled it too late to be "spontaneous" besides being without benefit of counsel. It was the first time in Fort Worth history that a defendant got his conviction overturned (at least in part) on the assertion that he had not been duly advised of his rights. This was an application of the Miranda principle even before there was such a thing. The farmers and stockmen who tended to fill Fort Worth juries at this time were not typically moved by appeals to defendants' rights. It was not customary to find a man innocent because his rights had been violated; either he did the crime, or he did not. Ike Knight went through four more trials in the next five years before the prosecution finally settled for a conviction for manslaughter with a sentence of five years in trial #6. Two years later, Texas Governor James Ferguson bestowed on Ike one of his annual Christmas paroles.[7]

The third case of a Miranda-style warning was in 1920, involving Jeff Couch and Tom Vickery. Fort Worth Officer Couch was the victim and Tom Vickery was the man accused of murdering him. Couch came from an extended family of lawmen. He grew up around the station house but did not put on a badge until he was twenty-six. Soft-spoken and non-violent, Officer Couch was a far cry from old-fashioned lawmen like Timothy Isaiah "Longhair Jim" Courtright who ruled the town with fists and six-guns in the 1870s. Couch joined the FWPD in April 1920.

Tom Vickery was a typical bad guy, abusive, a heavy drinker, belligerent, and habitually armed. In 1920 he was working as a driver for the Dollar Dodge car-rental company.

On December 20, he returned to the garage with an inebriated Fort Worth city councilman, Robert Dawson, in the backseat. Vickery had also been drinking, perhaps the same bootleg hooch as his passenger. At the garage they got into an argument over the fare, and Vickery punctuated his demand for payment with a couple of shots fired into the air. Jeff Couch, who was still a rookie cop patrolling Hell's Half-acre, was nearby and came running when he heard the shots. Instead of arresting anyone, Couch tried to settle things amicably, but when he made the rookie mistake of turning his back, Vickery disappeared. Couch turned his attention to getting Councilman Dawson to a hotel where he could sleep it off. He was just getting ready to put Dawson back in the car and take the driver's seat when Vickery reappeared, this time waving a pair of six-guns. Vickery forced them back into the garage along with the owner, lined them up against a wall, and opened fire, St. Valentine's Day Massacre-style but with six-guns instead of tommy guns. The other two got away untouched, but Couch took seven slugs. He went down without ever pulling his weapon. Someone across the street called the police who showed up in a hurry. An all-points-bulletin went out on Vickery, and Police Chief R.R. Porter instructed his men to shoot to kill. Less than an hour later, Vickery, accompanied by his lawyer, strolled into the sheriff's office and surrendered himself.[8]

Later that same day, Tarrant County District Attorney Jesse Brown came to the jail to interview the accused. He had barely started his questioning when Vickery blurted out, "I shot him, I know I shot him." Vickery kept on talking, implicating Dawson and accusing Couch of trying to "job" him. Brown let him talk, no doubt thanking his lucky stars for such a cooperative perpetrator. Unfortunately, no court reporter was present to write Vickery's confession down, and Vickery had not yet seen a lawyer. No problem. Back in his office, Brown wrote down the "detailed statement" from memory, considering it admissible evidence under the principle of *res gestae* because he was not really interrogating the prisoner when he made his confession. In his eyes, it was a "spontaneous confession … freely and voluntarily given."

However, no one ever saw the tell-tale confession; its admissibility was never challenged in court because it was never entered into evidence. That is because Tom Vickery never got to trial. On the night of December 22, while the Tarrant County jail's two duty officers were mysteriously busy, Vickery was dragged out of his cell by unidentified vigilantes, thrown into the back of a car, and driven out to Samuels Ave. where he was lynched from a large hackberry tree. Those responsible were never brought to justice though several names were

Fort Worth's infamous "Death Tree," on Samuels Ave. where two men were lynched, 1920 and '21. From newspaper clipping. Author's collection.

knowingly bandied about on the street. The grand jury indicted no one for breaking Tom Vickery out of jail and stringing him up. The decent people of Fort Worth, it was said, were tired of delayed justice and criminals getting off on technicalities. Most people felt that Tom Vickery got what he deserved. The Texas Criminal Court of Appeals never had to rule on the admissibility of the confession or on DA Jesse Brown's unorthodox method of securing it.[9]

There is a myth of Western law enforcement that justice in the old days was more direct, less obsessed by legal technicalities, and therefore more efficient. These three cases show what happened when old-fashioned notions of justice collided with law-book niceties. The appeals court usually sorted things out if a case got that far. Critics have said the Texas Criminal Court of Appeals liked to overturn cases just to show that they were smarter than local judges and juries. Whether that is true or not, the good citizens of Fort Worth were not much on appeals and legal technicalities. They did not know anything about *res gestae*, but they knew when a man was guilty and what punishment was called for.

Chapter 15

President Roosevelt Plants a Tree

One of the most historic moments in the history of Fort Worth was the visit of President Theodore Roosevelt in 1905. Any moment can be called "historic" later, but Fort Worthers of the time recognized the visit as a singular moment. Everyone who had a camera grabbed it and turned out to see the president. They cherished those photographs afterwards, which is why there are more surviving pictures of that event than any other in early Fort Worth history.

At the time, Fort Worth as an incorporated city was barely thirty years old (1873*ff*), and no other visitor had stirred as much interest. This was the first president or even former president to come to visit. In 1889, the city had invited President Benjamin Harrison to come to town for the opening of the Texas Spring Palace, but he had not surprisingly declined. What possible political gain was there for the President of the United States to journey to the north Texas plains, especially if that president were Republican?

This was not Roosevelt's first visit to Texas. He had been here twice before, the first time in April 1892 to do some hunting on W. T. "Tom" Waggoner's ranch. He was back four years later to train the "Rough Riders" in San Antonio for the Spanish-American War. Now he was back in 1905, and it was still not about politics. This was another hunting trip. Modern-day presidents escape from the cares of their office by hitting the golf links. Roosevelt found escape in hunting. Two friends, Burk Burnett and Tom Waggoner, both Fort Worthers, invited him to go wolf hunting in the Indian Territory, do a little male bonding, and delay the end of white grazing leases on Indian reservations. Quanah Parker made the local arrangements, another reason Texas ranchers loved him.[1]

The trip was also timed to coincide with a reunion of his Rough Rider regiment in San Antonio. He had not seen the boys since 1898, and this was a chance to get two birds with one stone. The president planned to be away from Washington for nearly two months on vacation. While not politically motivated, the train trip was definitely a whistle-stop tour through Texas. The first stop was in Denison on April 5 then it was on to Sherman that same day where 30,000 people were waiting, and Dallas where an even bigger crowd welcomed him. He also stopped briefly to say a few remarks from the back platform in Hillsboro, Waco, Temple, Austin, San Marcos and New Braunfels before arriving in San Antonio on April 7. It was truly a punishing schedule, but the kind Roosevelt loved. In San Antonio he did not relax either, celebrating with his old comrades that evening. At midnight he was on the train headed back north.[2]

He arrived in Fort Worth at 9:45 on Saturday morning, April 8, after snatching a few hours' sleep on the way. The city had pulled out all the stops to welcome the first president to ever visit Fort Worth. The *Fort Worth Telegram* had covered every step of the president's journey since he left Washington and the planning for the big reception when he reached Fort Worth. (By contrast, the Dallas newspapers barely covered the president's trip.) City fathers were determined that Fort Worth's welcome would outdo all other stops on the presidential route. Although the state's politics were strongly Democratic, Fort Worth was not so partisan against all things Republican. Fort Worth was home to the first Republican political club organized in the state, 250 strong in 1905, which also happened to be named the Central Roosevelt Club in the president's honor. In addition, the city's labor unions had been asked to turn out in force for the presidential parade through town. The Cattle Raisers' Association considered Roosevelt one of their own (he had been a rancher in the Dakota Territory years before), and they put up a huge banner over Main St. bearing a picture of the president and the words, "The Cattle Raisers' Association of Texas Extends a Welcome to the President, the Cattlemen's Friend." Roosevelt would have to pass under it on the way uptown.[3]

The welcome at the Texas & Pacific station was tumultuous. It was estimated that more than 20,000 had turned out. They filled the platform and spilled over onto the tracks: men in suits and ties, women in dresses and hats, children sitting on their fathers' shoulders, and more than a few dressed in military uniform. A reception committee of Fort Worth notables officially welcomed him to Fort Worth and escorted him to a platform erected in front of the station. The crowd filled the street, stood on the monument in the Al Hayne triangle, hung out the windows and sat on the roof of the T&P freight depot, and stretched up and down Front St. (now Lancaster) hoping to get a glimpse of him even if they could not hear him. They waved both American and Confederate flags, which did not bother Roosevelt. He was fond of saying his parents were from both sides of the Mason-Dixon line, and he himself stood for a reunited nation. The reception committee had decorated for the president's visit, hanging red-white-and-blue bunting on both the passenger station and freight

(a) President Theodore Roosevelt plants a tree at the Carnegie Library, April 8, 1905 (3-D stereoscopic view). Courtesy Tarrant County Archives. (b) The city honored Roosevelt with a parade through downtown. Author's collection.

depot. Among the professionals busy taking pictures were Fort Worth photographer Charles Swartz and presidential photographer H.A. Stohmeyer.[4]

Roosevelt was introduced by Mayor T.J. Powell and in his booming voice thanked the crowd for their effusive welcome. Then heedful of the time, the president boarded a waiting carriage joined by his secretary William Loeb, Mayor Powell, and Sam Davidson representing the Cattlemen's Association and Board of Trade. The open surrey was the finest in Fort Worth, pulled by a team of "perfectly matched [white] trotters," its wheels decorated with flowers and the sides bearing the presidential seal and the letters "T.R." in script. An American flag hung over the rear of the carriage almost dragging on the ground. Originally, the parade route had been laid out going up Main St. to the Courthouse then west on Weatherford to Houston then south on Houston to Ninth with a detour by city hall and the federal building before returning via Eleventh to Houston and proceeding on Houston back to the train station. But as it turned out, Saturday was also Arbor Day and the president was a big nature man, so the route was changed to incorporate a stop at the Carnegie Library for a tree-planting ceremony before returning to the train station where he was supposed to give a prepared speech. Time was of the essence because the schedule called for Roosevelt to be in Fort Worth only a little more than an hour. The revised route took him up Jennings past the Federal Building and city hall to Ninth and a quick stop to plant the tree then over to Houston, up Houston to the Courthouse then back to the station by way of Main. A special parade stand had been erected on the Peter Smith triangle (where Jennings and Throckmorton merged) for top city officials and their families. The city's white schoolchildren were gathered at the Courthouse to greet the president as he passed while another group of 600 "negro school children" awaited him in front of city hall waving American flags and singing the "Star-Spangled Banner." This was important because Roosevelt was behind the "Black and Tan Alliance" aimed at turning out voters of both for the Republican party. He was so moved he ordered the carriage to stop so he could wave his hat and them and accept a bouquet of carnations from one little girl.[5]

The parade consisted of a marching band, mounted members of the Sheriff's Department, several state military companies from all over north Texas including the Fort Worth Fencibles, numbering as many as 500, veterans of the Mexican War, Civil War, and Spanish-American War, being all those who could still squeeze into their uniforms and march. All participants were asked to line up on Front St. no later than 8:30 that morning. The crowd that lined the parade route was estimated to be 30,000, many of them having been at the train station before hurrying uptown to find a place along the route. Though it was Saturday, the windows of every office were filled with people waving flags and cheering. Not all were residents of Fort Worth. A delegation of 336 came in from Weatherford for the occasion. They sat in open windows and stood on awnings and rooftops in addition to filling the sidewalks. Shutterbugs found elevated perches to snap pictures. Several surviving pictures were taken from atop the Flatiron Building (Ninth and Houston across from the library). Immensely pleased by the turnout, Roosevelt stood up during the entire parade, doffing his top hat to the crowd on both sides of the carriage.[6]

The tree-planting was all for show. The east lawn of the library was the spot selected, beating out Hyde Park across the street and the front lawn of city hall. The hole had already been dug, and a little elm sapling was waiting in a root bag. No one expected the president to actually do any work. He bent to his task without even taking off his hat or frock coat, throwing a few shovelfuls of dirt into the hole while dignitaries held the tree in place. The well-dressed wealthy and common folk in working clothes all crowded together. Librarians stood primly at the windows looking on. Because of the press of time, he did not make a speech. That would come at another time and place on another Arbor Day a couple of years later when he said, "A people without children would face a hopeless future; a country without trees is almost as hopeless."[7]

The president was back at the station in time to deliver his address standing at a flag-draped podium speaking without notes. Aides told reporters it was "the best speech of his trip." (They probably said that at every stop.) He was back on the train ready to leave at 11:00 AM. As he stood on the rear platform, the crowd pressed in close. One old soldier in a gray uniform climbed up on the car to shake the president's hand. In all, he had been in town only seventy-five minutes but in that time he had made two speeches and planted a tree. It was arguably the most memorable seventy-five minutes in Fort Worth history. So many people had never before filled the town at one time, not when the railroad arrived in 1876 and not during the Texas Spring Palace run in 1889 and 1890.[8]

The visit also affected Roosevelt enough for him to write home about it, in letters to his two oldest sons, Theodore, Jr. and Kermit. Though admittedly more enthusiastic about the subsequent wolf hunt, he still spoke of his warm reception in Fort Worth.[9]

The presidential train left Fort Worth on the Fort Worth & Denver tracks headed for Vernon in the Texas panhandle. There the hunting party would disembark and cross the Red River to hunt wolves with Roosevelt pals W. T. "Tom" Waggoner and Burk Burnett. Roosevelt left most of his presidential party in Fort Worth, including his personal secretary William Loeb and fourteen others, to cool their heels until he returned. As the *Fort Worth Telegram* pointed out, a telegraph line from Kingola, Oklahoma Territory to Fort Worth was the president's only connection with the outside world or even his own government.[10]

Roosevelt's Fort Worth visit was a huge success; the tree, not so much. The *Fort Worth Telegram* quipped that it hoped the tree would "grow into a big stick," a pun on Roosevelt's famous "big-stick" foreign policy for dealing with his Latin American neighbors. And William Loeb said, while awaiting the president's return, if it died, he would come back personally and plant another. At first the sapling did seem to flourish. The *Telegram* optimistically reported on April 23 that it had put out leaves and buds. The library's janitor, charged with caring for it, offered his prediction that it would grow to "large proportions." When the city council announced plans a month later to cut an alleyway through the rear of the library property, they promised the tree would be uninjured, and the library's directors voted $30 to put a wrought-iron fence around it. All the precautions and promises proved meaningless, however. By fall the president's elm was dead. Informed of its demise at a White House reception, Roosevelt said, "I'm very sorry to learn of this," adding that he would have to investigate the matter. Sure enough, he sent a replacement, this one a Chinese cherry tree, which also died, much to the city's embarrassment. The story of the little elm tree that couldn't had turned into an epic saga of man vs. nature.[11]

The legend of the president's tree proved more enduring than the tree itself. After the Carnegie Library was torn down in 1938 to make way for a new public library, someone started the story that the now-full-grown elm had been successfully transplanted to the grounds of the Will Rogers Memorial Auditorium (WRMA). That story was finally debunked many years later when the city forester said he could not identify any tree on the WRMA grounds as old as the Roosevelt tree would have been had it lived. The moral of the story brings to mind a variation on the famous line from *The Man Who Shot Liberty Valance*: When the tree dies, plant the rumor.[12]

In 1911 Theodore Roosevelt made a return visit to Fort Worth as ex-president. As before, the invitation came from "some old and valued [cattlemen] friends." He called it a "howdy" visit and was only in town for one day, which started with an invitation-only breakfast at the Westbrook Hotel. Then he visited the Fat Stock Show and commented to reporters on "the astonishing growth of your city" since his last visit.[13]

Fort Worth had a deep affection for Roosevelt. A different type of monument to the 26th president was proposed after his death in 1919, a stone memorial to be erected at some unspecified site. Some locals helped get things going with a typical Fort Worth subscription drive, but nothing ever came of it. Among those who donated were members of Fort Worth's "Colored" baseball team.[14]

Chapter 16

The Protestant Sanitarium and the Beginnings of the South Side Medical District

Today the Southside Medical District consists of four major hospitals plus private clinics and rehab facilities too numerous to count, adding up to a multi-billion-dollar operation. It helps drive the local economy while serving Fort Worth's ever-growing population. We have not always been this blessed with first-class medical facilities.

In 1901, Fort Worth's hospital needs were handled by St. Joseph's Catholic Hospital, All Saints Episcopal Hospital, and the training hospital of Fort Worth Medical School (part of Fort Worth University). St. Joseph's, operated by the Sisters of Charity of the Incarnate Word, was the oldest and the biggest. It opened in 1885 on the far south end of Main, burned to the ground, and was rebuilt in brick in 1889. It took both paying patients and charity cases regardless of race. All Saints opened in 1900 as a project of Trinity Episcopal Church to provide "medical care for the poor." Fort Worth Medical School was established in 1891 as part of Fort Worth University by a group of physicians, including Elias J. Beall, Bacon Saunders, and William A. Duringer. Some of the city's leading businessmen also invested, seeing it as both a good cause and a boost to the city's growth. These included Julian T. Feild and Edgar D. Capps. In 1894 the school moved into its own building at Seventh and Rusk. The medical school maintained a 50-bed clinic that mostly treated charity patients as part of its student training program.[1]

The going rate for paying patients was $1 to $3 a day which got you a bed, "ordinary nursing," and all necessary medicines. An ambulance trip or "special care" nursing was extra. At this time medicine was not the big money-maker like it would become. Doctors saw a lot fewer patients because most people recovered at home under the care of family with the family physician making house calls as needed. The places where some people went to recover were generally known as infirmaries, clinics, or sanitariums. Even charity cases were overwhelmingly white because the population was overwhelmingly white but

Interior of St. Joseph's Infirmary, *ca.* 1910. Courtesy Scott and Linda Jo Barker.

also because black people did not voluntarily go to the hospital. Their medical needs were served by a handful of black doctors at home or the doctor's clinic.[2]

Of course, there is nothing wrong with doctors wanting to make money, and the privileged get sick, too. The idea of premium medical care was no different than the idea of premium hotels or premium restaurants; it was for an exclusive clientele. That was the reality behind the opening of the Protestant Sanitarium in 1901. It was strictly a private, for-profit operation to serve the medical needs of a well-heeled clientele who expected to be waited on hand and foot. It was called a "sanitarium" to distinguish it from a general hospital (infirmary). In those days, "sanitarium" was not simply a euphemism for a mental institution; it was the snobbish name for a private hospital that provided personalized care and private rooms with doctors and nurses on site 24/7. And the "Protestant" part distinguished it from St. Joseph's and added a certain all-American cachet.

The place was built on the southwest corner of Main and Railroad Ave. (modern-day Vickery) for $25,000 by investors that included Drs. Amos C. Walker and Edgar D. Capps, Winfield Scott, Sam Levy, and John B. Slaughter. They were all distinguished and all of them WASPS except for Levy (Jewish). More importantly, they were to a man motivated by more than simple altruism. Fort Worth's privileged had no interest in being treated in a charity ward or surrounded by "others" that might include immigrants. The sanitarium was laid out so it did not resemble an institution like St. Joseph's. It occupied two spacious buildings on a large lot with a sweeping view of downtown. The larger building had a 224-foot frontage with deep porches all around, divided into a "surgical wing" and a "convalescent wing." At this time, convalescing in a hospital was still a novel concept, but the Protestant Sanitarium's lucky patients would receive what amounted to spa treatment only without having to travel to places like Mineral Wells, Texas, or Hot Springs,

Arkansas. The admission building was a separate structure to keep the business and treatment ends of the operation separate. The grounds were attractively landscaped with shade trees, shrubbery, walking paths, and fountains.[3]

Since this was a money-making operation, it had to advertise; it could not just wait for people to walk in the front door. The advertising promised "the highest scientific practice of modern medicine, surgery, and gynaecology [*sic*]," the last-named being one of the most modern fields of medicine, addressing a need formerly filled by midwives and general practitioners. Other advertising boasted, "In all lines of practice this institution has at call the services of the best specialists," and went on to say it had "the confidence of the profession to a marked degree throughout the entire Southwest." Though the doctors made regular rounds, day-to-day operations were in the hands of "a competent matron" assisted by "a corps of trained nurses."[4]

The doctors were also among the principal investors and included some of the city's most respected practitioners, starting with Dr. Walker, a professionally trained surgeon who had come to Fort Worth after more than a quarter-century practicing medicine in Texas. His partner, Dr. Capps, was a "specialist in mental and nervous disorders," which put the Protestant Sanitarium in competition with the Arlington Heights Sanitarium on the far west side of town. Among the non-medical investors were cattle barons Winfield Scott and John Slaughter and businessman Sam Levy. Such men were always on the lookout for a good investment whether it was real estate or a new business enterprise. Together these men and their friends put up $50,000 to capitalize the Protestant Sanitarium. The first organizational meeting on May 25, 1901, was attended by seventeen men all of whom immediately became officers or board members.[5]

The Sanitarium's well-heeled patients were invited to involve themselves personally in their treatment and making

20 FORT WORTH CITY DIRECTORY.

Dr. AMOS C. WALKER, President. Dr. EDGAR DOAK CAPPS, Secretary.

THE PROTESTANT SANITARIUM OF FORT WORTH, TEXAS.

THE PROTESTANT SANITARIUM, HAVING BEEN COMPLETED AT A COST OF $25,000, IS FULLY PREPARED TO RECEIVE ANY NUMBER OF PATIENTS FROM FORT WORTH AND THE SURROUNDING COUNTRY. IT IS LOCATED ON THE SOUTHWEST CORNER OF MAIN AND RAILROAD AVENUE. AND THE BEAUTIFUL GROUNDS MAKE IT A MOST ATTRACTIVE SPOT.

THE PROTESTANT SANITARIUM
FORT WORTH, TEXAS.

The Frontage of the structure is 224 Feet and the Width is Forty-two Feet. There are 160 Feet of Porches. The Structure is Modern in Design. The operating Room in the South Wing of the Main Building is Said to be One of the Most Complete in the Country. The South Wing is the Surgical Wing and the North the Convalescent. Each Wing is Ninety-one Feet in Length. The Administration Building is Forty-two Feet in Length.

DAILY VISITS ARE MADE TO THE SANITARIUM BY THE SURGEONS IN CHARGE AND IN URGENT CASES ONE OF THE ABOVE MEMBERS WILL REMAIN DURING THE NIGHT.

A COMPETENT MATRON AND A CORPS OF TRAINED NURSES ARE IN CHARGE.

SPECIAL TIME AND ATTENTION WILL BE DEVOTED TO THE HIGHEST

Scientific Practice of Modern Medicine, Surgery and Gynæcology.

Dr. AMOS C. WALKER, Surgeon in Charge.
Dr. EDGAR DOAK CAPPS, Diseases of the Eye, Ear, Nose and Throat.
Dr. H. L. WARWICK, X-Ray and Radio Therapy.

THE SANITARIUM IS AN INCORPORATED INSTITUTION. THE FOLLOWING ARE THE DIRECTORS:

DR. A. C. WALKER. DR. E. D. CAPPS. WINFIELD SCOTT.
NOAH HARDING. J. E. BOMAR. WILLARD BURTON.

The Extensive Buildings and Character of the Institution Enable Us to Provide Several Rooms for Maternity Cases, Which are Cared for After the Strictest Technique of Modern Obstetrics.

PROFESSIONAL FRIENDS Who May Have Cases Requiring Treatment Such as Our Institution Specially Offers, and Who May Confide Them to Us, Will be Kept Advised as to Progress of Same, and in the Event Surgical Operation be deemed Necessary, Will be Invited to be Present with their Counsel and Assistance.

ADDRESS ALL COMMUNICATIONS TO

DR. A. C. WALKER, MANAGER.

The Protestant Sanitarium. Medical care for the privileged, as advertised in the *Fort Worth City Directory*, 1905. Author's collection.

medical decisions (with their "counsel" and family) which was more of a traditional business model than a medical model. The organizers were quite right about the need for such a facility in Fort Worth. Business proved quite profitable in the early years. Then came May 1903, and the Sanitarium's good name made the pages of the newspaper in tabloid-style reporting. One of its patients was Oran Hoskins who lived with his mother at 901 E. Belknap. Oran was not a member of the elite clientele that usually checked into the sanitarium, but he wound up there anyway after he claimed to have been struck by a Frisco Railroad train, leaving him in an insensible condition. Oran's mother filed a lawsuit against the railroad and got her son admitted to the Sanitarium for observation. After three weeks as a (paying) patient, Oran was scheduled for exploratory brain surgery by Dr. Walker. One has to wonder if the good doctor really intended to operate or was playing out his own game. Almost literally at the door to the operating room, Oran experienced a miraculous recovery and protested he did not need surgery. He subsequently confessed the swindle to the police who charged both Oran and his mother. They went to jail and Dr. Walker assured reporters he had suspected the fraud ("shamming") all along. The alternative explanation, that the high-falutin' physicians of the Sanitarium had been completely hoodwinked by a poseur, was not a good image for the Sanitarium or its doctors.[6]

The Protestant Sanitarium was in the newspaper again but for an entirely different reason in April 1909 as a result of the disastrous South Side Fire that destroyed twenty square blocks of businesses, churches, and private residences, causing losses equivalent to $44 million today. It was the most destructive fire in Fort Worth history, and it did not spare the Protestant Sanitarium. The disaster cost Dr. Walker $53,000 personally on top of the estimated $25,000 in damage to the buildings and equipment.[7]

The Protestant Sanitarium never rebuilt. Expected profits long-term were not sufficient to make up for the huge financial cost of the fire. This did not mean the city's elite had nowhere to go for the best medical treatment. It was replaced by other hospitals, both public and private that comprise our medical district today. The original southside medical district, after almost going up in flames, rose from the ashes like a phoenix. Drs. Walker, Capps, and the rest of the owner-physicians, continued to practice in Fort Worth for many years to come before retiring. Dr. Walker is buried in Oakwood Cemetery. And all the other non-physician investors found other places to invest their money and earn a good return on their investment.

Chapter 17

Fort Worth an Aggie Outpost?

Fort Worth has loved its Horned Frogs since 1911, and there are also plenty of Bevo supporters in Cowtown. But Aggies had little visible presence until 2013 when Texas A&M Law School was launched in Fort Worth by purchasing Texas Wesleyan's School of Law, thus allowing it to hit the ground running. Within four years it was ranked among the top 100 law schools in the country, proving if nothing else that Aggies do not do anything halfway. With an enrollment of nearly 500, that means a lot of future Aggie alumni will have a personal tie to Fort Worth. However, the law school was not the first Aggie outpost in Cowtown; that came a hundred years earlier.[1]

A large pool of graduates is what usually leads to the creation of an alumni organization, which then provides a vehicle for future fund-raising and recruitment in the community besides being an excuse for grads to socialize. Yet Fort Worth's Aggie alumni organization basically owed its existence to one family, the Edringtons. It all began with papa, Capt. H.C. Edrington, who came to Bryan, Texas, after the Civil War. He became "fiscal agent" of A&M College from its founding in 1876 until he moved to Fort Worth in 1892 where he founded Traders' National Bank. His son, William R. "Will" Edrington, was also a graduate of A&M (1890) and followed dad into the banking business and the lifetime fellowship of the A&M family. In 1911 Will Edrington enrolled his son H.C., Jr. in the school giving the family three generations of Aggies. Will Edrington took his family and drove down to Bryan every year for commencement and graduation exercises. He bled maroon and white. In 1912, he became fiscal agent for the college.[2]

The Edrington family really stepped up to the plate by literally saving the school from closure in 1912. Successive fires in November 1911 and May 1912 that destroyed the main building and the mess hall represented financial losses of $35,000 and $75,000 respectively to the struggling school. Trustees estimated rebuilding would cost at least $200,000, and this was long before A&M and the University of Texas began splitting the wealth from state-owned oil and gas lands, so there was no money to rebuild. The school's future was in jeopardy. Then the Edringtons, H.C., Sr. and Will, offered to float a $300,000 loan to allow the school to continue operating until the legislature (hopefully) appropriated the money. This was old hat for Capt. Edrington who had, while fiscal agent for the school in the 1880s, kept the school afloat during hard times. The Edrington family was as devoted to A&M as they were to making money.[3]

This was not today's A&M. The school was more military academy than liberal arts college, the student body was all male, and they were known as "the Farmers," not "the Aggies," a name which they wore proudly. Not a surprise since A&M stood for *agricultural* and mechanical. Since Texas was still largely a rural state despite large cities like Houston, Dallas, and Fort Worth, there was no shame being known as a "Farmer" in either sense of the word.[4]

It is no surprise that Will Edrington took the lead in organizing an alumni chapter in Fort Worth in 1914. Along with Traders'

National Bank it was part of the legacy he was preparing for his son. (His three daughters had no hope of going to A&M even if they wanted to because it was an all-male school.) Local alumni had their first big event that fall. The timing was not coincidental. Fort Worthers were devoted sports fans, and that meant football in the fall. On Saturday, October 16, A&M played TCU at College Station, winning handily. The following Saturday the Aggies were scheduled to play the Haskell Indians in Fort Worth. The Indians of the Haskell Institute (Lawrence, Kansas) were a powerhouse football team that drew large crowds wherever they played. TCU had played them in Lawrence in 1912, and now the Indians were paying a visit to Fort Worth, but not to play the lowly TCU team who were so overmatched by the Indians, a year later the "Christians" barely squeaked out a win in a game against the North Fort Worth High School team. TCU hoped to parlay Cowtown hospitality into a return game against the Indians in Fort Worth in 1915 when the Horned Frogs expected to be more competitive. In the meantime, Haskell was coming to town to play A&M. There was a catch, however. Fort Worth had to pay the Indians $1,000 up front and guarantee a certain gate to get them to sign the deal. Even without the hometown team playing, Fort Worth leaders expected this game to put Fort Worth on the map as a big-time college football town, on a par with Dallas, which hosted the annual Texas-Oklahoma game during the State Fair every year. Fully 10,000 fans were expected to show up for the game, including the entire student body of A&M, 1,000 cadets in uniform plus the sixty-piece marching band. Fans were encouraged to "show your colors!" Everyone from A&M it seemed showed up except the football team, which lost to the "Haskell eleven." The Indians could not be enticed back to Fort Worth to play the Christians (now renamed the "Horned Frogs," perhaps because the "Christian" mascot name was too meek and mild) until 1921. Fort Worth newspapers billed that 1921 game as "the feature contest of the gridiron season." TCU lost again.[5]

William R. Edrington, Founding Father of the Texas A&M alumni chapter of Fort Worth. Courtesy Quentin McGown.

Local Aggies had more on their mind than just football in the fall of 1914. The drive to organize a Fort Worth alumni chapter began with a fancy banquet in the Westbrook Hotel on October 13, 1914, put on by thirty grads who, like Edrington, bled Aggie maroon and white. At the time the Westbrook was the city's finest hostelry, stretching the full length of Fourth St. between Main and Houston (now the west side of Sundance Plaza). It was boys' night out, and the newspaper makes no mention of the boys bringing along their wives. The Farmer spirit was running especially high looking forward to the upcoming game against the Haskell Indians. But since this was still Cowtown, one of the toasts that evening was to the A&M team of student livestock judges at that year's State Fair.[6]

The guest of honor that night was C.O. Moser, a 1904 A&M graduate who went on to become a state leader in "agricultural activities" and was president of the Dallas Farmers' alumni chapter. Another honored guest was Louis J. Wortham, president and editor of the *Fort Worth Star-Telegram*, who in a burst of hyperbole, perhaps forgetting where he was, praised A&M College as "*the* most important educational institution in the state." At the very least it was obvious the hometown newspaper fully supported the alumni-club drive. The evening also drew Farmer faithful from other alumni "clubs" across the state, including Mount Taylor, Farmersville, Rockdale, and Waco.[7]

Will Edrington was master of ceremonies that night. In his remarks he admitted that "Fort Worth didn't know much about A&M" before 1911–12, observing that regrettably the cadet corps "had never marched down Main St." and that the nearest alumni club was in Dallas. The twin blazes that threatened to close the school were a chance for Fort Worth grads to step up and show their support for their alma mater.

After news of the May 1912 blaze spread, A&M alumni from all over the state had rallied to raise the money for rebuilding. Eventually more than $1,000,000 was pledged in the form of loans offered in the expectation of sooner or later being repaid by the legislature. Fort Worth alumni raised more money than any other single city, including the $300,000 pledged by the Edringtons. And carrying the ball across the goal line, it was Louis Wortham, at the time state representative from Fort Worth. who got the legislature to repay all those loans, making him virtually an honorary "Farmer."[8]

Will Edrington, ever the advocate for his alma mater, called for whoever the next governor was (with an election coming up in November 1914) to "make provision for the adequate maintenance of A&M." He suggested the state could start with the streets and sidewalks on the campus which had never been paved. A&M students, he said, "are given no more comfort than hogs." Put him on the board, he promised, and there would be plenty of changes at College Station. Before adjourning that night, the members of the new Fort Worth A&M Club agreed to hold their next meeting at the Continental National Bank building.[9]

The ulterior purpose of the October 1914 banquet did not come out until a couple of months later. Will Edrington said that in order to guarantee that A&M played TCU in Fort Worth next season ("Farmers vs. Christians!") it was essential that local alumni work together to make the case to the A&M "athletic council," who were then putting together the 1915 football schedule. It was not just the game itself that mattered; but the hope of bringing the "entire corps of cadets" to town with all their friends and relatives. The financial benefits for Fort Worth, not to mention the publicity, would be huge. The potential return was enough to persuade the TCU athletic director to ask the local Farmers' alumni club to join him in extending an invitation not just to the A&M football team but to "the entire cadet corps to come be the guests of TCU." The alumni club accepted the invitation, and a joint strategy was mapped out to line up the biggest football game in TCU history up to that date. It did not help their case that the highly touted A&M-Haskell Indians game had not lived up to all its hype. There was some thought on the Farmers' side that perhaps Fort Worth needed to be "educated up to football" before a local game could be a financial success. TCU officials and the A&M alumni club hoped to change that opinion while also making Fort Worth more football-friendly.[10]

Another outgrowth of that October 1914 meeting was the creation of a Fort Worth student club at A&M. H.C. Edrington, Jr., a chip off the old block, was one of its founders. By 1920 the club numbered fifty-five members from Fort Worth "and its environs," making it one of the largest and most active student organizations on campus. Some of Fort Worth's finest families would send their sons to A&M. And the members of the club would sing the praises of their hometown with its "aggressive spirit" and A&M with its "phenomenal record in athletics." The bond formed on that October Tuesday night in the Westbrook Hotel is still going strong today, more than a hundred years later.[11]

Chapter 18

Murder at the Metropolitan

The Metropolitan was Fort Worth's first luxury hotel. Built in 1898 by cattleman-turned-hotelier Winfield Scott, it took up the entire east side of the block of Main between Eighth and Ninth, placing it strategically on the well-traveled route between the T&P passenger station and uptown. A streetcar came by every ten minutes. The Metropolitan set a new standard for Fort Worth hotels. It was three stories tall, of red brick, and designed so every room had an outside window. Winfield Scott insisted everything be first class so there was a lot marble and mahogany. Every room had central steam heat instead of the usual coal-burning stoves, and every floor had a bath with hot *and* cold running water. There was a fine restaurant with a French chef and tuxedoed waiters, the largest banquet hall/ballroom in Texas, a gentlemen's bar and tobacco stand, and a separate lobby area for ladies. It was also the first Fort Worth hotel to operate on the "European plan" which meant meals were priced separately from the room. (On the American plan, guests ate together family style at a given hour.) Another classy touch was having diners entertained by a full orchestra on Friday and Saturday nights. The hotel even had its own wine cellar and artesian well, guaranteeing that no guest would ever have to go thirsty for either pure water or fine libations. All these amenities came at a mere 50¢ to $1 a day, the room rate at the time it opened.

The Metropolitan grew until it covered the entire block from Main to Rusk (Commerce) eventually. The first expansion took place in 1905, increasing the number of rooms to 200. In 1908 two more floors were added, bringing the number of rooms up to 425. With each remodeling additional amenities were added, such as a telephone in every room and speaking tubes connecting the rooms to the front desk.

Fort Worth's own Waldorf Astoria has been written about by Fort Worth authors Mack Williams, Bill Fairley, and Simone Ramos. But none of them delved into the darker side of the hotel's history: the homicides, police raids, and related criminal activities that went on there. More murders and attempted murders took place at the Metropolitan than all the rest of Fort Worth's hotels put together. Maybe, in Hollywood movie tradition, it was built on an ancient Indian burial ground, or something else about the place brought out the worst in men.[1]

The Metropolitan's problems with the criminal element began in 1903. About 7:30 on the evening of January 10, Carrie Turner and Cora McNeill, two black women, were on their way home, passing by the hotel on Ninth St. when Walker Hargroves and a friend, both white, in town from Bowie, Texas, went by them the opposite direction. Both men had been drinking heavily and were in a "jovial" mood. They said something to the women who ignored them and hurried on down the block. Then the women heard the crack of a pistol behind them, and a bullet ricocheted off the pavement in front of them. When they cried out in surprise a crowd began gathering. Hargroves retreated into the hotel bar where Detective Sebe Maddox found him a little later and arrested him for discharging a firearm in the city

(a) Metropolitan Hotel, Fort Worth's finest. (b) The Metropolitan's elegant lobby, site of several homicides. Both courtesy of Dalton Hoffman.

limits. Neither woman filed charges; they were just glad to get safely home. Hargroves was released on bail when he sobered up and went home to Bowie.[2]

As the classiest tourist hotel in the city, the Metropolitan also offered other services on the Q.T., namely high-stakes gambling and party girls. In 1904 an Ellis County farmer came into Fort Worth looking for his thirteen-year-old daughter who had run away from home to the big city. With the help of FW detective Al Ray he found her working at the Metropolitan as a chambermaid. Her first reaction when confronted by Ray was to insist that she was not the runaway girl, then after she was identified by her family it took considerable persuasion to get her to return home. How a 13-year-old girl got hired by the hotel was never explained although some "chambermaids" did more than clean rooms. She would not have been the first country girl to run away to the big city only to wind up working in the world's oldest profession.[3]

The most sensational case connected to the Metropolitan Hotel was the murder case of Capt. Al Boyce, Sr. He was the father of Al Boyce, Jr. and longtime family friends with the Sneed family. John Beal Sneed married Lena Snyder of Georgetown in 1898, and in 1902 they moved to Amarillo, bringing all the Sneeds and Boyces together in the same community. Since both families were rich and engaged in the cattle business, they ran in the same circles. About 1911 Al Boyce, Jr. took up with Lena Sneed. In October she confessed her affair to her husband, declaring that she intended to run away with her lover to South America. Beal Sneed did what any self-respecting husband would do: He had his wife declared insane and put her in a private institution, Fort Worth's Arlington Heights Sanitarium. But Lena sent a letter to Al begging him to come get her. He did on November 8, and they fled to Canada. Sneed filed abduction charges against Al, Jr. and hired private detectives to find the runaway couple, which they did, living in Winnipeg, Canada. He went there and brought her home. He returned her to the sanitarium and announced his intentions to pursue extradition proceedings against Sneed to bring him back to Fort Worth for justice.

Enter Papa Boyce. He came to Fort Worth and hired a lawyer, a former U.S. district attorney, who got the charges against Junior dismissed. This was early January 1912. While in Fort Worth, Capt. Boyce took a room at the city's finest hotel, which is where Beal Sneed found him on the night of January 13. He and friends were sitting chatting in the lobby when Beal Sneed walked in and confronted him. Sneed considered the elder Boyce complicit in his son's wife-stealing. Words were exchanged then the cuckolded husband pulled a pistol and pumped five slugs into Papa. He turned himself in and was indicted for murder by a grand jury. His defense was the "unwritten law," and it was good enough to get a mistrial on February 29 and an acquittal at his retrial the following December. In the meantime, two related developments occurred: Lena hired an attorney and got herself released from the sanitarium, and Beal Sneed found and killed Al Boyce, Jr. in Amarillo.[4]

There was more mayhem at the Metropolitan less than a year later. In October 1913 C.W. Hudson, an employee of the Texas & Pacific, caught Alex Friend, proprietor of the cigar stand, in the hotel lobby and clubbed him over the head with "a loaded cane." Arrested and charged with assault to murder, Hudson explained that he mistook Friend for the railroad's general manager. At the time Hudson was in dispute with the railroad for his medical bills from a severe accident suffered several months before. Friend was carried home in "serious condition," but the doctor said his injury would not prove fatal.[5]

In March 1919, another romantic triangle came to a boil in the Metropolitan's lobby. Warren Wagner, an oil man, accused fellow oil man Floyd Holmes of trying to steal his wife. For months Wagner had issued threats against Holmes, saying Fort Worth "is not big enough for the both of us." He also stopped Mrs. Holmes on the street, telephoned her, and wrote her a letter, all urging Mrs. Holmes to leave her unfaithful husband. Wagner had a violent reputation and was known to go about armed, so Floyd Holmes made it a point to avoid him. Unfortunately, they were both in town at the same time and staying in the Metropolitan. Came the day in the lobby of the Metropolitan, Wagner said, "Holmes is the cause of my troubles, and I'm going to kill him!" Then he stalked out of the hotel and up the street. That's when he ran into Holmes who saw him coming, retrieved a pistol from his car, and opened fire on the unsuspecting Wagner. He put two bullets into Wagner's back, killing him on the spot. At the time Wagner was unarmed. (It would have been a clear case of murder except numerous witnesses had heard the victim repeatedly threaten to kill Holmes. In Texas that was justifiable homicide.)[6]

On December 9, 1922, James M. Reynolds ambushed Claude Bell as Bell was crossing Main St. between Eighth and Ninth, shooting him twice in the back. Fatally wounded, the victim staggered into the Metropolitan's lobby and collapsed. He was rushed to the hospital where he died fifteen minutes later. Reynolds said he did it "in defense of his home and self-defense" because Bell had been carrying on with his wife (the "unwritten law"). As it turned out, the twenty-one-year-old victim was unarmed. Otherwise, a jury subsequently accepted Reynolds' explanation and acquitted him of murder. For the record, Bell and Mrs. Reynolds had their love trysts at another hotel than the Metropolitan, a much cheaper hotel.[7]

The last bit of violence on record at the Metropolitan occurred in March 1932 when Whitmore Stonewall ("Stoney") Phillips shot Elmer L. Churchill right in the hotel's lobby. Phillips was a thirty-two-year-old, "one-armed police character" with a long rap sheet. Churchill was a forty-six-year-old oilfield drilling contractor. Both men had designs on the same woman, Sallie Moore, a stenographer at the hotel. Phillips had been seeing Sallie before he left town on some business. When he got word that Sallie was seeing someone else, he raced back to town and on March 14 caught up with her new beau chatting with the clerk at the check-in desk. He demanded to talk to the other man, and when Churchill ignored him, he pulled a pistol and started blazing away. He emptied the pistol then retreated into the nearby men's room, reloaded and came out firing again. In all he fired five or six shots, two of which found their target. Meanwhile, the desk clerk had dived down behind the massive marble counter at the first shot, probably saving his life. Others in the lobby not in the line of fire stood where they were, stunned. Witnesses included the hotel's eight-year-old newsboy.[8]

Churchill died in the hospital the next day. Phillips was charged with murder, convicted and sent away for ninety-nine years. (He died in the penitentiary in 1936.) Sallie Moore left town and was never seen in Fort Worth again. It was another sordid chapter in the Metropolitan's history.[9]

What might be called "the Metropolitan Curse" extended beyond the doors of the hotel. Just working at the hotel could turn out badly. In 1905 thirty-two-year-old James M. "Grude" Britton, a former Texas Ranger, took over the bar at the Metropolitan. It should have been a quiet retirement plan, but Britton was a hard case with a belligerent streak. He had a lady friend who ran a bawdy house out of the Amarillo Flats on Jennings, just down the street from city hall. On January 10, 1910, Capt. Tom Blanton led a police raid on the place. Britton expected that simple professional courtesy would protect a fellow lawman from official harassment. He was wrong. He blamed Blanton personally for the raid and was prepared to have it out if he could have found the police captain. When he did not, he went home but he returned the next night to city hall to file a formal complaint. As he was unarmed, it would seem he had given up any idea of calling Blanton out. Blanton was waiting for him on the steps of city hall and put three bullets in him, the last one while Britton was on his knees. The Metropolitan Hotel had to find a new bartender.[10]

The reputation of the once-high-class Metropolitan suffered a long and sad decline. It did not help that in the 1920s major vice activities took root in its rooms and suites. It became a haven for bootleggers and shady gamblers who raked in enough money to buy a lot of protection. Things ran smoothly until the fall of 1922 when Fort Worth police in cooperation with the feds raided the place. Police Commissioner (PC) John Alderman ordered his men to lay off the Metropolitan, an order which infuriated Chief Harry Hamilton. The PC fired him for "insubordination," and Hamilton took his beef to the press. The city council held a series of hearings and wound up supporting their fellow commissioner against the ex-chief. Alderman was a one-term city commissioner, and the poor old Metropolitan took another hit to its reputation.[11]

By 1938 the Metropolitan was a sad shadow of its early magnificence. The Hotel Texas and the Blackstone had replaced it as the city's premier hotels. It was frumpy and half-empty most of the time. Visitors coming in on the train now bypassed it to get to the nicer hotels. It needed massive remodeling and repair to restore it to anything like its former glory. That did not scare away the Milner chain who bought the place, made some cosmetic improvements, and carried on as the Milner Hotel for a few more years. Finally, in 1959 the hotel shut its doors and was bulldozed to make way for the Tarrant County Convention Center. The block was a surface parking lot until it was transformed into General Worth park, the home of the JFK statue after 2012. With the JFK statue it continued its spooky connection to murder.

Chapter 19

Don't Divorce 'Em, Lock 'Em Up

In unenlightened times the law considered women to be wards of the men in their lives, a principle well-established by statute and precedent. In Texas, for instance, when a couple married, her property became his to do with as he saw fit. Likewise, women could not sit on juries, there were no women judges or prosecutors, and no woman was admitted to the Tarrant County bar until 1932.[1]

After the turn of the 19th/20th centuries, divorce was becoming a worrisome social issue; the family was under attack, Christian values were in decline, the civil court dockets were clogged with divorce suits. Men were especially worried. In some states laws were under consideration that would protect a wife if her husband defamed her character. A more radical change in the statutes would prohibit the partner bringing the divorce suit from ever remarrying! The discussion was not just happening in the decadent cities back east either. In 1900 Assistant Tarrant County Attorney Jefferson McLean proposed federalizing divorce so that the law would be the same all over the country. This sort of radical solution to the problem from a member of the establishment must have petrified husbands everywhere. If the wife was to get an equal shake in divorce proceedings or, worse, federal civil rights protections, it would mean the end of civilization as men had known it since the beginning of time.[2]

Fortunately for husbands, there was an alternate solution available, and it was entirely legal. When a wife became troublesome or a burden, he could get rid of her without the messy, potentially expensive ordeal of a divorce. He simply had to have the county court declare her insane and commit her to an asylum. Sanity hearings were "tried" before a judge and jury who heard the evidence just like in a criminal case and handed down their verdict. The difference was the accused did not have to be present or even represented in sanity proceedings. In 1904 the Texas Sheriffs' Association recommended that such hearings be heard before the county physician and county attorney, not a jury. The recommendation never went anywhere. If a husband had pull, he did not even have to go through the charade of a formal hearing; upon application, the judge signed the commitment papers, and the wife was whisked away. The concerned husband did have the option of having her committed to a state institution, such as Terrell State Hospital, as a ward of the state or to a private residential institution. Private insane asylums were euphemistically called "sanitariums," and they could appear quite inviting from the outside. Fort Worth had one such place, the Arlington Heights Sanitarium (AHS), on the wind-swept prairie five miles west of town.[3]

The AHS opened in 1906 operated by Drs. Wilmer and Bruce Allison and John S. Turner, who described their place as "a quiet retreat … strictly ethical." They specialized in "nervous conditions, selected cases of mental disease, and drug and alcohol addiction." But that was only half the story. They catered to a very exclusive clientele who wanted *discreet* medical treatment for their loved ones. It had rooms for forty patients, male and

Arlington Heights Sanitarium, a nice place to visit perhaps but … Courtesy J.W. Dunlop Photograph Collection, Special Collections, University of Texas at Arlington Library, Arlington, TX.

female. If you could afford it, it was a huge improvement over Terrell State Hospital.[4]

The cases locked up in private institutions had the best care money could buy, but they were still victims of a judicial system that treated women and children as wards of the paterfamilias who had no rights whatsoever. Three cases in Fort Worth history illustrate how the system worked, and how ugly things could get: the commitments of Mary Couts Burnett, Lena Sneed, and Irene George made newspaper headlines because the ladies in question refused to be locked away and forgotten.

Mary Couts Burnett was the second wife of Samuel Burk Burnett, wealthy cattleman and patriarch of one of the most powerful families in Texas. She came from a Parker County family and was the widow of Claude Barradell. Burk Burnett married her in 1892 after divorcing Ruth Loyd Burnett, the daughter of his banking partner, Martin B. Loyd. In most cases that would have been the end of the partnership, but not in that case.

During their happy years together Mary and Burk had a son, Burk, Jr., and she became a prominent socialite in Fort Worth. But by 1911 the marriage was on the rocks. She was not happy when Burk moved his daughter-in-law and granddaughter into their Fort Worth home. She was even less pleased by the way he doted on them. Perhaps fearing an expensive divorce, he filed court papers accusing Mary of suffering from "hallucinations" and being "hopelessly insane." Reportedly, she had accused him of trying to kill her. His pals testified against her as did Dr. H.L. Warwick. The six-man jury agreed that she was of "unsound mind" and on May 24, 1911, ordered her committed. The final insult was that the court appointed Burk her legal guardian, which gave him complete control over both her person and property. After a brief confinement at Terrell, he had her moved to a private home in Weatherford where she could receive compassionate care while still being kept out of the way. There she remained for the next eleven years, not even permitted to come home to attend the funeral of Burk, Jr. in 1916.[5]

On June 27, 1922, Burnett died. He left a very detailed will that completely excluded Mary, leaving almost everything to his granddaughter, Anne. That same day Mary left Weatherford and returned to Fort Worth where she engaged her longtime physician Charles Harris, one of Fort Worth's most respected doctors and a self-described expert on mental illness, to help get her insanity conviction overturned. They brought in William J. Slay, one of Fort Worth's most successful trial lawyers, who filed suit in county court. After Judge Hugh Small found her of "sound mind," she challenged the will and succeeded in breaking it, entitling her to the "widow's half" of the largest estate ever probated in Tarrant County up to that time. She won again and walked away with about $3 million. For his time and trouble, Harris made a nice fee of $25,000, and Slay was also well-paid by the now-wealthy widow. Mary did not have long to enjoy her wealth, dying on December 16, 1924, at the age of sixty-eight.

(a) Samuel Burk Burnett, a force of nature in Fort Worth, *ca*. 1918.
(b) Young Mary Couts Burnett, *ca*. 1898. Both from author's collection.

She left most of her fortune to TCU in trust. In death, she was virtually written out of Burnett family history for all time.[6]

The case of Lena Sneed was even messier because it involved murder and played out in the local newspapers. Like Burk Burnett, John Beal Sneed was a privileged man, the wheeler-dealer scion of a wealthy cattle family who was used to getting what he wanted, in this case Lena Snyder, a high-spirited, headstrong young woman. They married in 1900 when he was twenty-two and she was twenty. A decade later she took up with Al Boyce, Jr., informing Beal that she was in love and asking him for a divorce. Instead, he got a doctor to sign commitment papers in the fall of 1900 and without even the formality of a hearing got a court to declare her "morally insane." In keeping with her husband's wishes, she was committed to a private facility, Arlington Heights Sanitarium, for an indeterminate stay. Beal had not counted on the power of love, however, and less than a month later Al broke her out and they fled to Canada. Sneed charged him with "abduction," and hired a private detective to find the lovebirds. They were located in Winnipeg, and Sneed convinced his wayward wife to come home. Boyce stayed in Canada to fight extradition, and Lena went back to the sanitarium, only under closer watch this time. A lawyer hired by the Boyce family got a habeas corpus hearing before Judge W.T. Simmons in Sixty-seventh District Court. In the absence of formal commitment papers or any evidence that she was insane except her husband's word, the judge ordered her released.[7]

An outraged Beal Sneed could not get his hands on Al Jr., so he went after the father, Al, Sr., ambushing him in the Metropolitan Hotel on January 13, 1912, shooting him to death. He was tried for murder in Seventeenth District Court, invoking the "unwritten law" that he had only been defending the sanctity of his home. Lena's sanity and moral character were raked over the coals by the defense. The all-male jury sided with Beal and freed him. Beal and Lena reconciled, and that should have been the end of it. But it was not.[8]

Nine months later, on September 14, 1912, Sneed finally caught up with Al, Jr. in Amarillo and gunned him down on the street. Another all-male jury in Vernon again found him innocent of committing murder because of Texas' "unwritten law."[9]

The third case is that of Irene George whose husband, W.R. George, put her in the Arlington Heights Sanitarium on January 30, 1911, following what everyone called "a nervous breakdown." Like Lena Sneed she was railroaded into the sanitarium where she was deprived of her clothing and held incommunicado. A sanity hearing was held March 22, 1912,

A love triangle! John Beal Sneed (top). John Beal Sneed with children, Lena and Al Boyce, Jr. (bottom). Newspaper clipping, author's collection.

at which she was not allowed to appear. The charge was "moral insanity," which was a specious medical diagnosis saying she was morally unfit to live in decent society. The doctors at Arlington Heights did not keep Irene long before shipping her off to the Terrell state hospital, presumably either because she was a difficult patient or because her family could not foot the bill for her confinement. The Terrell doctors found her sane and released her to her family. Unlike the cases of Mary Couts

Burnett and Lena Sneed, her husband supported her stand. They sued the Sanitarium and the doctors who ran the place for "false imprisonment." In the subsequent trial in county court, the case turned on whether a jury of twelve men considered her sane or not.[10]

In the end the judicial system had it both ways: Irene George's jury found her sane, allowing her lawsuit against the doctors to go forward in district court, but at the trial the judge found the defendants innocent of the charge of false imprisonment. Everybody it seemed won; Irene was declared sane, and the authority of the medical establishment was upheld.[11]

At least the ladies in question were spared the embarrassment of having their pictures splashed all over the newspapers. This was particularly surprising in the case of two such well-known women as Mary Couts Burnett and Lena Sneed. In the case of Burnett, neither she nor her cold-hearted husband were desirous of seeing their mugs in the newspaper when he was trying to get her committed. In the case of Lena Sneed, though her husband's legal troubles stretched out over nearly two years, putting the spotlight on their marriage all that time, her picture appeared in the newspaper only twice, both times the same unrevealing file photo. Perhaps the *Star-Telegram* took to heart the old adage that says a lady's name (picture?) should only appear in the newspaper three times: when she's born, when she gets married, and when she dies.[12]

Legally. nothing really changed as a result of these cases. None was the landmark kind that makes new law. Male doctors still believed that women who acted "queer" were of unsound mind and having medical credentials meant they did not have to support their accusations with any real evidence. Usually the accused was not even present in the court when her fate was being decided, nor represented by legal counsel in the proceedings. Irene George's doctor testified that he "did not think her mind was right" and ordered her confinement because "the seclusion would be beneficial" for her. That sort of testimony was business as usual in the courts of the day. None of these three women had a prayer once they were accused by reputable (male) persons of being insane. Only *after* they were locked up did the real fight begin to win their freedom, and without a lawyer in their corner and a habeas corpus hearing, they had little chance of triumphing over their (male) accusers.

Chapter 20

That's No Lady, That's My Lawyer!

Fort Worth has seldom led the way when it comes to advancing women's rights. The men who ran the city took a very patriarchal view of women in the justice system. The only women who ever stood before the bar in a courtroom were either defendants or witnesses. So rare were women around the courthouse that a "restroom" was not put in for them until 1917, in the basement naturally. In this case Tarrant County was ahead of the legislature, which ordered ladies' "restrooms" in courthouses two years later. The Tarrant County Courthouse's ladies' restroom was installed at the urging of the Daughters of the Confederacy, an auxiliary group to the Confederate Veterans organization. The ladies pressured their husbands who got it done. That was how things worked in those days. That first restroom was not even a fully equipped bathroom; there was no toilet. For that a lady still had to leave the courthouse. This was literally a room for resting, presumably while her husband took care of business at the courthouse. It did have sofas and ice water and perhaps even a matron to keep it tidy.[1]

Obviously, if women were such an inconvenience in the courthouse, they were not expected to spend a lot of time there. That would include jury duty. By law, women were excluded from juries in Texas until 1954. That prohibition had been unsuccessfully challenged after women got the right to vote in 1920 (19th Amendment to the Constitution). Amon Carter's *Star-Telegram* had not favored the Amendment. In 1920 the newspaper editorialized that a female juror might have to ask a judge to stop the court's proceedings while she called her husband to have him pick up the kids from school, get groceries, and cook their dinner. Among the practical concerns about having female jurors was the question where would they sleep during capital cases when juries were typically sequestered? As it was, the 1918 Criminal Courts building and the 1895 Courthouse both had single "dormitories" for sequestered juries to sleep in overnight. When both buildings were built, no one imagined women would ever be serving on a jury. If the law were changed, both facilities would have to find someplace for any female jurors to sleep or else put them up in a hotel.[2]

The District Attorney's office was split over the question of having women on juries. Assistant D.A. Will Parker was not in favor because a female juror might be inclined to let a "good-looking" male defendant off. He generally believed they would be guided by their hearts, not their heads. On the other side of the argument was Assistant D.A. W.H. Tolbert who took a philosophical view that "women jurors can't be worse than the men" but added that he would try to limit them to cases involving child and woman victims. Other Fort Worth officials were bemused at best, skeptical at least.[3]

It was all just speculation until September 1920 when defense lawyer John Baskin objected to the exclusion of a woman from the grand jury on the basis that the exclusion denied his female client the right to a "jury of her peers." He lost his objection, and women had to wait until 1954 to sit in judgment on Texas defendants.[4]

Women appearing as counsel in the courtroom were another matter entirely. When they were qualified members of the bar it was hard to keep them from representing clients in court since a defendant was entitled to counsel of his choice. Here Fort Worth was one of the first cities in Texas to allow female defense counsel in court although with one important, unstated qualification initially: they only appeared in civil cases.

Mrs. Olive S. England of Houston was on the way to becoming the first woman to practice law in Texas when she applied for her license in 1902. Unfortunately, her hopes were dashed when District Judge W.H. Wilson, Fifty-fifth District Court, rejected her application on the grounds that a woman could not legally practice law in the state of Texas because the statute governing the granting of licenses stated that the applicant "must be a man of good reputation."[5]

Mrs. England was no tyro begging for a chance to prove herself. She was already a member of the Oregon state bar and among her paperwork filed in Texas was a certificate from the Oregon Supreme Court attesting to her status.[6]

Most women lawyers got their start in the same way: They were either the daughter of or married to a practicing male lawyer. They learned the trade the old-fashioned way, by helping dad or hubbie around the office. In the old days, learning the trade by "reading law" under a working lawyer was the way many men gained admittance to the bar. Going to law school made a fairly late entrance in the 19th century. The requirements for practicing law in Texas were eventually changed to say that "the person" applying for a license had only to be of "good reputation and honorable deportment," twenty-one years old, an American citizen, a resident of the state for at least six months, and with a knowledge of legal rules and court proceedings. Gender and race were not determining factors, and the knowledge of rules and proceedings could be acquired by either apprenticing under an established lawyer or attending a certified law school, which meant the University of Texas initially.

In June 1914, Fort Worth's Rose Zeloski became one of the first women to graduate from the University of Texas law school. That accomplishment got her a license to practice law in Texas. This was forty-five years after Arabella Babb Mansfield of Iowa became the first woman in the United States to pass a state bar exam, but still four years before women were allowed to vote in Texas (*cf.* the 19th Amendment). Still, she found the Texas judicial system to be inhospitable to female lawyers. She was a natural-born crusader, so she took up the woman's suffrage cause and moved to Philadelphia to work for the movement to get women the right to vote in the Keystone state. She also began working with reform-school girls, which gave her a lifetime cause. When the women's right-to-vote campaign was shot down at the polls in Pennsylvania she moved back in with her parents in Fort Worth before taking a job at the new Gainesville "state industrial school for girls." Eventually her career path brought her back to the law. She moved to New York City where she became the first woman on the legal staff of American Telephone and Telegraph.[7]

Once the door was open, other women followed the pioneers. The first woman lawyer to try a case in a Fort Worth court was Mrs. Hortense Ward of Houston. She appeared in Judge James Swayne's Seventeenth District Court as counsel for the two children of James W. Lawson in a dispute over an insurance settlement of his ex-wife's estate. Mrs. Ward argued successfully that the money in question rightly belonged to her clients, not the ex-husband. The newspapers at the time made a big deal out of the fact that Mrs. Ward was "best known" for pushing the "married women's bill" through the Texas legislature. She was fortunate that the case was heard in Judge

Miss Rose Zelosky, 1914, when she graduated from University of Texas law school. Courtesy *The Cactus Yearbook*, 1914, Dolph Briscoe Center for American History, The University of Texas at Austin.

Swayne's court. He was a long-time advocate of minority rights going back to his days as a defense lawyer.[8]

In 1917, Texas Christian University, which had just moved back to Fort Worth from Waco in 1911, enrolled its first female law student, Geneva Bradley, daughter of a judge. According to reports, her male classmates were "pleased to have a lady student" in their midst. The student newspaper opined that she would keep them on their toes out of fear of being shown up. Apparently, they need not have worried. There is no record that Bradley graduated before the school closed the law department in 1920.[9]

By 1930 there were seventy-five women lawyers in Texas (versus 6,571 men). Almost all of the women were in civil practice as opposed to criminal practice or corporate law because the courtroom was still considered too tough for ladies, especially in brutal murder and rape cases. Some were reduced to working as stenographers or law clerks in a male law office.[10]

Years later, Hollywood character actress Florence Bates would claim to have been "the first woman lawyer in Texas" before she took off for Hollywood. As she told it, the Texas-born woman decided to become a lawyer when she was twenty-six. She eschewed the law-school route and instead studied on her own "eighteen hours a day for eight months" before taking and passing the bar exam. She then opened an office in her hometown of San Antonio where she practiced for four years until a court tried to force her to betray the confidence of a client. She "resigned" and went to work for her lawyer dad. She subsequently married a Texas oil man, and they moved to California where she launched her acting career in 1938. She was fifty years old. She enjoyed a successful Hollywood career as a character actress but never forgot her Texas roots. Whenever she did come home, she was always greeted as a hometown celebrity. Apparently, no one ever checked out her story of her beginnings in the legal profession.[11]

Chapter 21

America's Dance King Becomes a Fort Worth Flyboy

Before World War I, Vernon and Irene Castle were the toast of the stage on both sides of the Atlantic. They were the original "beautiful people," the first "power couple" before there was a Brad and Angelina. As a dance team they popularized the foxtrot and the tango. With their athleticism and elegance, they made dancing respectable for the masses. As music publisher Edward B. Marks said about the music scene after 1910, "The public demanded tunes to dance to." And the music that got everyone on the dance floor was called "ragtime." Social dancing was born![1]

Vernon Castle, his stage name (he was born Vernon Castle Blythe), was a proper Englishman educated at Birmingham University, who started his career as an engineer. But the tall, rail-thin Castle discovered his real talent lay in tripping the light fantastic. While visiting the United States in 1906 he also found he enjoyed being on stage. He launched a career in Broadway musicals, specializing in comedy pratfalls. He met Irene Foote in the summer of 1910 while vacationing at New Rochelle, New York. She was six years younger than Vernon and already

Vernon and Irene Castle, sweethearts of the dance floor. Author's collection.

stage-struck when they met. She was not impressed with the less-than-handsome Englishman until she learned of his show-business pedigree. They also shared a love of dancing, Irene having studied ballroom dancing with a respected teacher. He introduced her around Broadway, and she picked up some bit work as a chorus girl.

Somewhere along the way the love bug bit, and they were married in May 1911. Irene, who longed for more recognition than she was getting as a chorus girl, had the idea of putting together a dance act. Though they had undeniable talent and charisma, dance teams were a hard sell. Most were hoochy-kootchie girls who were not showing off their dance moves on the stage. The Castles had to go to Paris to find success. They returned to the U.S. in 1912 and began playing small clubs in New York where they re-created their Paris cabaret act. Their star really took off after they improvised a brand-new dance, the "Castle Walk," that quickly caught on with the society set. They got bookings on Broadway where they introduced a series of new, refined dances that were variations on the waltz and foxtrot. They became America's dance teachers as they toured the nation playing to packed houses. They were also America's darlings, the beautiful couple who demonstrated their love in wholesome fashion on stage nightly. They were rich and famous, and the future was bright. Vernon cultivated a playboy image, within polite boundaries, of course, that included buying an airplane and learning to fly. Irene became a fashion horse, setting new styles.[2]

Then came the war. Vernon, twenty-eight years old and an experienced pilot, heard his country's call. In 1916 he sailed to England and enlisted in the Royal Flying Corps (RFC). He demonstrated genuine talent at the stick of the crates the RFC flew, and they soon shipped him off to the Western Front where he distinguished himself flying 150 combat missions. Equally remarkable he survived that many without a scratch. Capt. Castle seemed to have a charmed life. Then he was recalled from France and sent to America to train a new generation of pilots. While Vernon had been off fighting in Europe, Irene pursued her own dreams, making a splash in silent films and developing a solo dance act that was a hit. Apparently, America's darling couple could live as happily apart as together.

The British made a deal with the U.S. Government to train their pilots in the United States, which made sense in terms of training conditions, financial arrangements, and the diplomatic designs of the Brits. In October 1917 Vernon and the No. 84 Canadian Training Squadron moved their training from Camp Mohawk, Ontario, to the balmier climate of Fort Worth, Texas. They took up residence at Carruthers Field (one of three fields known collectively as Camp Taliaferro), carved out of the prairie at Benbrook, southwest of Fort Worth. It was a spartan, desolate home for the irrepressible playboy though he did not let the isolated field prevent him from socializing. To get around he purchased a Franklin roadster in Dallas that got him around town, allowing him to hobnob with Fort Worth society during his time off.[3]

The locals were a bit put off by the reserved Canadian boys, but they were charmed by the dashing Capt. Castle and his pet monkey. They were already familiar with Vernon and Irene by reputation if not in person from hearing their music and learning their dance steps on the exclusive rooftop garden at the Westbrook Hotel. Ironically, the same dances Fort Worth socialites were doing on hotel dance floors uptown—the turkey trot, the grizzly bear, and the bunny hop—were another matter when black Fort Worthers did them in the Acre. Uptown they were more politely known as the "one-step," the "long Boston," and the "fox trot" respectively to pass public censorship. Performed in black dance halls by dark-skinned patrons twisting and gyrating was sufficient to get such places closed up tight "by order of the police." Meanwhile, white patrons uptown danced the night away trying to be Vernon and Irene.[4]

Vernon gushed to a reporter that he really liked Texans whom he called "Westerners." Aside from a disdain for rules and regulations, he was an excellent teacher. On his own, he was a daredevil who took too many risks in the underpowered Curtiss JN4 "Jennies," which had a top speed of 75 mph. With America in the war after April 1917, he also trained American boys. When not racing around the countryside in his Stutz, he "borrowed" aircraft without authorization to go barnstorming, dropping in on pilot

(a) Vernon Castle shows off his Dallas-purchased Franklin. (b) Castle beside his airplane at Benbrook Field. Both from author's collection.

training camps in Dallas. His superiors took a dim view of wasting fuel and putting government property at risk, but he did not care. In the winter of 1917–18, his shenanigans were reportedly on the verge of getting him court martialed out of the RFC.[5]

Though the newspapers played up Vernon and Irene's separation as a mutual wartime sacrifice, the truth was something else according to recent biographer Eve Golden. Both had taken up lovers, and they quietly filed for divorce intending to announce it after the war. During his stay in Fort Worth, there were rumors that Vernon was involved with a local girl, Inez Childers. None of this mattered after February 15, 1918.[6]

That was Vernon's last day on this earth. Word had come down that he was being recalled to Canada to command a new RFC flying school. While waiting for orders to come through he continued to train his current crop of students. On that Friday morning he went up with American cadet R.O. Peters. Usually, the instructor took the back seat, known as the "safe seat" because the Curtiss Jenny was front-heavy and tended to go nose-first into the ground when it cracked up. But Capt. Castle preferred to sit up front for reasons of his own, perhaps to show his students how much confidence he had in them. Whatever the reason, Peters took the back seat and in another violation of regulations Castle did not bother to fasten his seat belt. The training flight went well until they were coming in for the landing. Peters carelessly brought them down directly over another plane piloted by an RFC cadet that was just taking to the air. Neither pilot saw the other until it was too late. Vernon, whose view of the ground was blocked by the nose of his plane, at the last minute tried to grab the controls and veer away into a half loop, a maneuver he had performed many times before, but the Jenny stalled and plunged forty or fifty feet nose-first into the ground. Vernon's body slammed into the instrument panel, breaking his neck and causing severe head injuries, either of which was sufficient to kill him. He was dead when they pulled him out of the wreckage. The pilots in the other plane and even Cadet Peters escaped with their lives. A board of inquiry that same day cleared the instructor of any blame, ensuring he would be remembered as a hero who "gave his own life to save another." Vernon Castle was the thirty-first casualty at the three flying fields around Fort Worth of 101 casualties during the entire thirteen months the fields operated.[7]

Fort Worth gave Vernon Castle a first-class sendoff. His body lay in state in a closed casket at Robertson's Funeral Parlor (Tenth and Throckmorton) on the morning of February 16. The unusual closed casket for the popular aviator suggests that the body had been horribly mangled in the accident. The casket was draped in the Union Jack and surrounded by piles of flowers. After the public viewing the funeral service was preached by the Rev. Henry Eckel, pastor of St. Andrew's Episcopal Church. Vernon Castle had never been a faithful church-going man, but the Episcopal was the American cousin of the Church of England, which every Englishman belonged to by birth. Then the body was taken in a grand military cortege to the T&P station for transportation to New York City where Irene waited. An honor guard of Fort Worth mounted police led the procession followed by the Camp Bowie marching band and an honor guard of 250 American and British aviators, then the flag-draped casket on a gun carriage pulled by six horses. They proceeded from Robertson's Funeral Parlor up Throckmorton to the courthouse then back down Main St. to the station. Thousands of mourners lined the route to pay their final respects to the soldier who had been as much American as English. When the body arrived in New York City he was laid to rest in the Bronx's Woodlawn Cemetery surrounded by similarly famous statesmen and celebrities. Prominent Fort Worthers immediately started a fund-raising drive to build a monument to the fallen hero. It was never built, but the city did rename a stretch of Circle Park Blvd. from Grand Ave. to Circle Park "Vernon Castle Blvd." in his honor.[8]

Irene Castle made it to Fort Worth for the first time in November 1922. She had remarried in the meantime and was on tour with a one-woman show, "Dances and Fashions."

Vernon Castle's funeral cortege through Fort Worth, Feb. 16, 1918. Author's collection.

The troupe stopped over in Fort Worth toward the end of the tour. With some time on her hands Irene went sight-seeing, looking for Vernon's memorial in Greenwood Cemetery and for Vernon Castle Blvd. She laid a wreath at the memorial but was disappointed when she found Vernon's namesake street. Instead of a nice, tree-lined boulevard with stately houses on both sides she found a working-class street that she dismissed as "rough and unlovely … unworthy of the illustrious name that has been given to it." She never came back to Fort Worth, and the city never invited her to return. Fort Worth had opened its heart to Vernon Castle, and that was enough.[9]

Chapter 22

Amon Carter Is Rejected by the Masons

This story comes from the dark secrets of Masonic lore. Fort Worth Masons go clear back to 1854 when the first Freemason lodge, No. 148 in Texas, was founded, which also happened to be the very first fraternal organization. Thereafter, the Ancient Free and Accepted Order of Masons held bragging rights as the most distinguished and secretive of all fraternal organizations. Lodge 148 counted such notables as Ephraim Daggett, John Peter Smith, Julian Feild, brothers Addison and Randolph Clark, B.B. Paddock, and W.P. Burts. Membership was both a privilege and a valuable network with other, like-minded gentlemen of distinction. All the best people were Masons. And it did not hurt that lodge brothers patronized each other's businesses and invested in each other's enterprises. According to the reminiscences of Capt. Joseph C. Terrell, the Masons built the first substantial building in town, a two-story brick structure that did double duty as the only public meeting hall and the first school. Lodge 148 also brought the body of Maj. Ripley Arnold home from Fort Graham in 1855 for interment in the soil of the community he had founded.[1]

Amon G. Carter was born in Grafton, Texas, in 1879. He left school at eleven to go to work. His first job was as a dishwasher in Bowie for $1.50 a week. His life had a steady trajectory upward from there. He was a natural-born salesman and was drawn to the advertising field. In 1905 he moved to Fort Worth and opened an advertising agency. When the *Fort Worth Star* began publishing in 1906, he was hired as advertising manager. As the paper grew by absorbing the *Evening Telegram* and the *Morning Record*, he moved up the ladder to business manager then vice president before becoming general manager and part owner of the *Star-Telegram.* Thereafter he became the face of the newspaper and the No. 1 booster of Fort Worth.[2]

Carter was a big-time joiner; it was part of his social networking that kept him connected to everything that went on in "his city." He was a full-fledged member of several fraternal organizations and a charter member of the Ad Men's Club and Rotary International of Fort Worth. He did not regularly attend meetings, but he knew everyone. And Carter was not content to be just a member; he had to hold high office, or the group was not worth belonging to. Thus, he became president of the Chamber of Commerce, Exalted Ruler of the Elks, secretary of the Ad Men's Club, and president of the University Club. He was also a lifelong Democrat, which similarly paid dividends.[3]

His penchant for joining an organization and then not attending meetings got him in trouble with the leadership of Fort Worth's Rotary International chapter. One of the items on the agenda at the August 18, 1922, meeting of the board was a letter from Carter about his string of absences. He explained they were the result of his being so often out of town on business. The letter was more a courtesy notification than a plea for forgiveness. The board let him off the hook, merely requesting he notify the secretary when he was going to miss meetings in the future. A month later, at the next directors' meeting, the minutes noted that Carter had missed four meetings "without a valid excuse," and the members voted to drop him from the organization. Three days later after the secretary had met with him, the directors "reconsidered" and voted him back in. That was how it worked in Amon's world.[4]

The only important fraternal organization Carter did not belong to was the Masons. It was only natural that "Mr. Fort Worth" should want to join the city's most prestigious fraternal order. He certainly had all the necessary credentials: sterling reputation, social prominence, and devotion to public service. In addition to publishing the *Star-Telegram*, he created the Amon Carter Foundation, was a director of the Southwest Exposition and Fat Stock Show, and president of the Fort Worth Club. He was a living legend, largely of his own creation.

So, what possible objection could there be to him joining the Ancient Free and Accepted Order of Masons? He applied to Lodge 148 with the necessary endorsements, and it seemed only the formality of a vote remained to be done. As was traditional, several lodge members came to see him. Part of the traditional interview was to ask the applicant why he wanted to become a Mason. There is almost no "wrong" answer to this question, whether the reason was a family connection, social ties, a do-gooder spirit, or what have you. It was a perfectly natural question, anticipated by everyone who ever wanted to become a Mason. So, imagine the surprise when Carter responded with blunt frankness: He did not really want to be a Mason, he explained; he just wanted to become a Shriner so he could bring more conventions to Fort Worth. The Shriners were the Ancient Arabic Order of the Nobles of the Mystic Shrine, restricted to Masons of the highest degree. Being a Shriner would help bring Masonic-related events to Fort Worth. It was an honest answer from a man who was not used to being denied anything he really wanted.

The committee went back to the Masonic temple and reported on their interview. Then it was time to vote. Historically, lodge

Amon Carter, master of all he surveyed, being honored by the Fort Worth Advertising Club, February 26, 1936. Courtesy *Fort Worth Star-Telegram* Collection, Special Collections, University of Texas at Arlington Library, Arlington, TX.

members voted with black balls and white balls. At that time, it only took one black ball to torpedo an application, but the normal vetting process typically prevented that embarrassment. Not this time. Somebody, nobody knows who, cast a black ball, and Amon Carter's membership was rejected. Wouldn't you

(a) Until 1932, Fort Worth Masons met downtown in this unpretentious building at Second and Main. (b) The inner sanctum where Lodge No. 148 held their meetings. Both from author's collection.

have hated to be the man who had to go back and tell Mr. Carter he had been turned down? There is no date to this story, so it is impossible to say when it occurred. Most of his other memberships date from before World War I. By the 1920s he was bigger than any fraternal organization. They would have come to him begging him to join, just so they could have his name on the rolls. His ever-expanding list of organizations that he belonged to included the board of Texas Tech University (1923–27), the American Petroleum Institute, and the Fort Worth Club.[5]

Amon Carter died on June 23, 1955, leaving behind a legacy of having succeeded in virtually everything he ever set his mind to excepting one glaring failure. The story of his rejection by the Masons entered the lore of Lodge No. 148 to be whispered to future Masons in the strictest secrecy. Since all Masonic voting is secret no one would ever be able to confirm the story, not even through the records of the Grand Lodge in Waco. Amon's embarrassment was buried with him, safe from public exposure—except for the usual "loose lips" that have a way of sinking ships and revealing secrets sooner or later.

Chapter 23

Redemption for a Tired, Mistreated Building?

For years, if you happened to drive out North Main from downtown, you passed a crumbling building on the right side that had long stood empty. If you asked around, old-timers either called it the old Klan Hall or the Ellis Pecan Company. There was nothing on the building that said one way or the other. Now, as the wrecking ball draws closer and closer to that old building, it may be helpful to know its history—before it is history.

That present building whose address is 1012 N. Main was erected in 1925 as a Klan meeting hall, replacing one on the same site. Since then it has gone through multiple owners, but it is the original owner that stirs the passion. This was the second of two klaverns (Klan meeting halls) built on the site. The first was built in 1920 so that the Klan could stop holding its meetings in the basement of the courthouse. This was the second or revived Klan. The first Klan, founded in Tennessee by embittered Confederate veterans after the Civil War, directed its vitriol at freed slaves and the Yankees who protected them. It was shut down in the early 1870s by federal law and federal troops. The Klan name and organization were revived in 1915 in Georgia by a new generation of Southerners. This time its targets were not freedmen and Yankee carpetbaggers but immigrants, non-Protestants, and the unpatriotic. Their stated creed was "God, Home, and Country." As the self-styled defenders of Anglo-Saxon purity, the Klan was still at heart a white supremacist organization, just with a longer enemies list.[1]

The Fort Worth outpost of the Klan was launched the following year by officers in the police department. They had no trouble signing up their fellow officers and a lot of other people besides. Klan marches, Klan parades, and Klan auxiliaries followed. There was no shame in being a Klan member. Respected lawyer W.A. Hanger and respected Judge Julian C. Hyer were Klan leaders and counted it an advantage politically. The Klan's candidates swept county elections in 1922.[2]

Someone in the organization suggested raising money to build a memorial to the "historic Klan." After some debate, they decided instead to build their own meeting hall. It took several years and an aggressive fund-raising drive to transform the dream into brick and stone. To facilitate fund-raising and protect themselves legally they formed the American Building Corporation which sold stock to raise the necessary $90,000 for the building and a piece of property on North Main. They laid the cornerstone in a big ceremony on Sunday, May 18, 1924. An impressive, four-story building quickly went up on the site (1006 North Main). From the start it was intended to be more than just a meeting place for their weekly Friday night gatherings. It had a stage and an auditorium reportedly seating 4,000 that could be rented out for "public gatherings and concerts." Klavern No. 101 needed a grand building since Fort Worth was the headquarters of the organization in Texas and probably its largest chapter. The furnishings included a "fireproof vault" for record-keeping. Though it would be a multi-purpose building, there could be no mistake about whose building it was.

The Klan's name was in stone over the front entrance and an electric "fiery cross" sat atop a telephone pole at the southwest corner of the property.[3]

The building went up in remarkably short time, just a month from the laying of the cornerstone. On July 28, Hiram Wesley Evans, the Imperial Wizard of the Knights of the Ku Klux Klan, helped dedicate the new building when he addressed a standing-room-only crowd that turned out to see and hear the organization's national leader. The next biggest star to play Klan hall was famed magician and escape artist Harry Houdini who was a fading attraction when he spoke and gave a "demonstration" there on October 18.[4]

The Klan was not able to enjoy its new digs for long. In the early morning hours of Thursday, November 6, 1924, the building burned to the ground in less than two hours despite the best efforts of the Fort Worth Fire Department. Arson was never proven although it was strongly suspected, and a police investigation was launched. The total loss was estimated

1924 Ku Klux Klan Hall on North Main. Klan headquarters in Texas. Author's collection (from a postcard).

at $70,000–$90,000. The Klan had a close connection to First Baptist Church's flamboyant pastor, J. Frank Norris, as evidenced by the fact that the Klan's official organ and the church newspaper bore the same name, *The Searchlight*. That connection proved a life-saver as the Klan contemplated what to do about a scheduled Friday-night minstrel show preceded by a parade through downtown and featuring "star performances" by popular local baseball players, Clarence "Big Boy" Kraft and Ziggy Sears. (Kraft went on to become a Tarrant County judge.) The show was sold out. As disaster loomed, Norris rode to the rescue. From Houston he telegrammed, "Let the klan have the auditorium over all engagements." That command posed another problem because it threw the church's own Euterpean Club, which had planned to use the auditorium for a performance that same night, out on their ear. They immediately filed suit in district court for breach of contract, and on Friday Norris backed down. The Euterpean show would go on as planned. But after that, Norris honored his promise to let the Klan use his church's facilities as long as necessary.[5]

The building had been only partially covered by insurance, putting the burden of rebuilding on the membership. There was never any question that they would rebuild. By the time of their Christmas program in 1924 they were announcing that architectural plans had been drawn up, and they were soliciting money to begin construction. One fund-raising measure was to sell small tokens at fifteen dollars each. On the front was an embossed figure of a Klansman in full regalia. On the back as a reminder of why the token was issued it said "Ft. Worth Klan Hall. Bombed Nov. 6, 1924." (The tokens are collectors' items today.) Earl Glasgow, a Klan member, was the architect of record. The new klavern with an address of 1012 N. Main was slightly smaller than its predecessor. It was only three stories, and the auditorium seated no more than 2,000 people. Otherwise, the two buildings looked very similar. The first official function was on June 5, 1925, the installation of new officers for the coming year. In the intervening months Klavern No. 101 had held their weekly meetings in a rented space at Fourth and Commerce. Apparently, J. Frank Norris's generous offer to use his church only covered special events.[6]

The new hall, like its predecessor, was more than just Klan central Fort Worth; it was a multi-purpose community center that could be rented out for religious revivals, celebrity appearances, and music concerts. Prominent on the schedule in the next year were a black-face minstrel show put on by the Fort Worth Police Benevolent Association as a fund-raiser, and an "Old Time Gospel Revival" by evangelist Bessie May Randall.[7]

Still, the place was a money-loser, and as the Klan's power and influence declined, they decided to sell it. In 1927 Marvin and Obie Leonard of Leonard's Dept. Store bought it to use as a "retail and grocery" warehouse. Apparently, that was another losing proposition because in 1929, they sold it to a group that sponsored dance marathons, a growing craze nationally that offered prizes to couples that could stay on their feet for days. The promoters cleared out most of the seats to make room for a dance floor and threw open the doors at 50¢ a head, promising "laughs galore." They also changed the name to the less exceptionable North Main St. Auditorium, which was as much about the image of the place as it was about the new owners.[8]

In 1934, as the building continued to decline, it was turned over to professional wrestling for the next six years with the cards made up mostly of local unknowns able to pack the house with friends and relatives. The building's rapid decline was slowed in 1937 when the *Star-Telegram* began sponsoring Golden Gloves matches there, showcasing the best of young, homegrown boxing talent. It was a venue for local folks in hard times to enjoy a night out without spending a lot of money. The crowds were raucous and mostly male.[9]

In 1946 with its glory years far behind it and no longer attractive as an entertainment venue, the building sold again, to Lonnie V. Ellis, owner of Ellis Pecan Company. Ellis, one of the largest commercial pecan operations in the state, employed mostly North Side Latinos, more than half of them females, to crack, shell and package their product. Employing some fifty workers during the season (November to March), Ellis was one of the largest employers of Latinos in Fort Worth. It brought shelling out of homes and backyard sheds, turning it into industrial labor. The jobs were low-paying, manual labor that made a lot of money for the owners, not so much for the work force. There was a degree of irony in the fact that a building once dedicated to white supremacy was now the workplace for so many Latinos. Ellis Pecan Company remained a family business for the next half-century, until 1991 when it was sold to a Missouri corporation that continued to operate it under the same name as before. It moved in 2000 to a more upscale neighborhood near Ridgmar Mall. The 1012 North Main building has been empty and for sale ever since.[10]

Over the years its past was occasionally recalled. In 1962 Rudolph Ganz, the legendary concert pianist and orchestra conductor, was in Fort Worth as a juror for the Van Cliburn International piano competition. The Fort Worth League of Composers made him an honorary member, and old-timers reminisced about his fifty-one-year musical connection to Fort Worth, which included a 1924 appearance conducting the renowned St. Louis Symphony Orchestra when it performed at the Klan Hall. The packed house that night was a well-dressed assemblage of Fort Worth society with not a single white hood and robe to be seen.[11]

In 2019 a determined movement calling itself the 1012 Leadership Coalition began a determined push to save the old building. By that date it was known vaguely as Klan Hall or the Ellis Pecan building depending on how far back one's

North Main Auditorium as it looks today, exterior and interior. No sign of either pecans or Klansmen. Author's collection.

memory went. The drive coincided with a visionary project to re-channel the Trinity River, creating an 800-acre island that would include the land the building sits on. Suddenly what had been a relatively worthless piece of property became highly valuable real estate for retail space or maybe condos. The fight was on: historic preservation vs. economic development. And that is without factoring in all the emotional baggage the building carries. Its very existence is an affront to many in the black community who consider it "a monument to violence." There are others in that same community who argue for saving it, not for the sake of something esoteric like historic preservation but to turn it into "a living monument to liberation, to love, and to freedom." There is talk of naming the restored building for Fred Rouse, a black man and the last lynching victim in Fort Worth in 1921. For a small band of preservationists, the building represents a unique historic artifact. Architecturally it is nothing special, but it is the only purpose-built Ku Klux Klan headquarters still standing today. As such, it deserves to be saved from demolition for the same reason we have saved slave quarters and listed them on the National Register of Historic Places—not to celebrate the people who built them but to preserve a piece of history that has much to teach us. If a picture is worth a thousand words, how much more is a historic building worth?[12]

The argument for saving is appealing on more than one level. For those who see only the bottom line, the building could become a major anchor on the North Main corridor between the Courthouse and the Stockyards. As a combination performing arts center and history museum telling the story of race relations in Fort Worth, it would be a must-see stop for the curious-minded. An old, empty shell of a building that was once a monument to hate would have been redeemed, and everyone loves a good redemption story. On the other hand, if you pass by 1012 N. Main years from now and see nothing but a strip shopping center or condominiums, you will know the developers won.

Chapter 24

Harry Houdini Makes an Appearance in Fort Worth—Twice!

Harry Houdini (1874–1926) was the biggest showman of his time. The escape artist/illusionist born Erich Weiss created his own legend by putting on spectacular demonstrations of an uncanny ability to escape from the seemingly inescapable: handcuffs, padlocked chains, straitjackets, bank vaults, and prison cells. He did not just perform; he dared others to expose his "magic" or put him in a place he could not escape from, and in countless appearances dared others to discover his secrets. He took the ancient art of necromancy to new levels inventing his own props, like the "Chinese Water Torture." He entertained audiences on both sides of the Atlantic, and at a time when the average American was making $500 a year, he pulled down $3,500 a week by putting his life as well as his reputation on the line every time he stepped on the stage. It was said that there was not a day in his performing life that a newspaper column had not been written about him somewhere.[1]

But by 1916 he had been performing for fifteen years, and he was on the downhill side of his career playing the vaudeville circuit. His act had become stale with big-city audiences and outclassed by the new magic of moving pictures, so he was reduced to touring smaller towns in the heartland where the locals had heard of him but had not seen him perform. He came to Fort Worth in January 1916, a mid-sized city of 105,000, and his first visit to Texas.

The Majestic Theater on Commerce booked him for a week filling out the bill with a full program of comedy and musical acts. But make no mistake about it; manager Oscar Gould was counting on the man known as "The Elusive American" to fill the house every night. The name Harry Houdini was still magic. However, the Great Houdini came with a lot of baggage. Any venue he played had to be able to hold the sets he brought along. The climax of his act in 1916 was a dramatic escape from the "Chinese Water Torture Cell," a tank holding thousands of gallons of water with a hoist to lower him into it and pull him out again after he had done his thing. (Other parts of his act in the past had featured an elephant.) To add to the element of daring, he offered $1,000 cash to anyone in the audience who could prove he had access to an air supply while freeing himself from shackles and a straitjacket dangling upside down underwater. The Majestic anticipated a packed house every night of the show plus a matinee on Monday.[2]

Public challenges were a big part of Houdini's show. His biggest attention-getter was the challenge he issued to the police in every town he played that they could not confine him in any way, shape, or form that he could not escape from in under five minutes. For some reason police in every town took up the challenge, and Fort Worth police were no different. Never one to settle for a simple trick when it could be made more spectacular, he sweetened the offer. Not only could the police truss him up in any combination of handcuffs, shackles, and straitjacket, but they could suspend him in the air over the street while he tried to escape. In this way the shrewd showman was adding another layer of risk to his performance while inviting all of Fort Worth to turn out to see him fail (?!), thus taking street performing to new heights literally and figuratively.

The site selected for the big show was the *Star-Telegram* building at Throckmorton and Eighth. The newspaper was more than willing to go along with anything that might sell more newspapers and give them a leg up on the competition. They promoted it in the days before the event like a prize fight between two heavyweight contenders: "The skill of the Fort Worth police department matched against the skill of a man who has escaped from everything in the world!" If that did not draw a crowd to Eighth and Throckmorton, nothing would. Every time Houdini's name was mentioned, so was the *Star-Telegram* building. On Thursday afternoon, January 13, a crowd estimated at 4,000 gathered to see Houdini's challenge play out. This was the biggest thing since President Theodore Roosevelt came to town in 1905. The crowd was so large it spilled over on nearby streets, relying on those in front to relay what was happening to those in the back. What those in front saw was Police Chief Cullen Bailey and Detective Tom Blanton put Houdini in a straitjacket, put handcuffs on his wrists, and tied a rope around his ankles. A team of burly policemen hoisted him upside down to roof level, three stories above the ground, then they started the clock.[3]

Houdini's 1916 visit to Fort Worth was ballyhooed with this publicity stunt at the *Star-Telegram* building, Eighth and Throckmorton. Author's collection.

Of course, "The Great Houdini" escaped from his restraints and did so in less than five minutes. Lowered to the ground by the sheepish policemen, he smiled and bowed, soaking in the adulation of the crowd. Then he invited them to come see him at the Majestic during his last two shows. He had also received another challenge, relayed by the ever-obliging *Star-Telegram*, from the packing department of Washer Brothers clothiers. Three "expert" packers challenged Mr. Houdini to try to escape from "a packing case of heavy lumber in which we believe we can so nail and rope you that you will be unable to make your escape." Of course, the master showman accepted the challenge, insisting only on the condition that the box not be air-tight. With that out of the way, this latest challenge was added to his final show at the Majestic on Friday night, January 14. If the theater was not already sold out for the performance, this guaranteed a capacity crowd wanting to see how he handled this test of his escape artistry. Would the master prevail yet again? Or would the local challengers show him up? It's impossible to know whether the audience that night was rooting for the champ or for the local challenger. No surprise, the champ answered the challenge with another amazing demonstration. Then he was off to Dallas and another pre-arranged challenge, this one to the Dallas Police Department. (He won that one, too.)[4]

Houdini was such a hit in Fort Worth he came to Cowtown again in 1924, this time as a guest of the Ku Klux Klan. The "Man of Mystery" played Klan Hall on North Main on Saturday night, October 18. At this late stage in his career—he was fifty years old—he was less the escape artist than the lecturer, dedicated to debunking all the "mediums" and spiritualists. Spiritualism had been all the rage in America ever since 1848 when the Fox sisters, Maggie and Kate, had claimed to be able to communicate with the spirit world. Their fame grew over the following decades until they ultimately confessed to being frauds, but spiritualism itself would not die and got a boost with "spirit photography." In the aftermath of World War I, with so many families longing to contact their dearly departed, spiritualism got a second life, appealing to the same sort who embraced clairvoyance, palm reading, and telepathy, and just as phony. Houdini, the peerless illusionist, dedicated himself to exposing the fakirs who preyed on the gullible through spirit readings and spirit photographs. He found a ready ally in the popular magazine *Scientific American*, which promised a prize to anyone who produced a "spirit manifestation" that could not be duplicated by deception. It was this crusade that brought Houdini to Fort Worth in 1924—that and the promise of a nice payday.[5]

Fort Worthers were as fascinated by spiritualism as anyone, and the name "Houdini" was still a major draw in the heartland. One of the most popular novels of the time, Robert W. Chambers' *The Slayer of Souls*, was being serialized at the time in the *Star-Telegram*. Debunking spiritualists was the second act in Harry Houdini's illustrious career though he continued to bill himself as "the world-famous magician." Upon his arrival he announced that he would not be doing his popular vaudeville act, but instead he would be lecturing on "Can the dead speak to the living?" Of course, people still expected to see him perform magic, so the advance advertising promised "30 minutes of inexplicable feats of magic" before the star launched into his expose of spiritualist frauds. The venue was not particularly significant. Houdini was no Klansman, but Klan Hall was an affordable venue that could seat more than 2,000, and The Great Houdini could still attract a big crowd.[6]

Tickets were $1, $1.50, and $2.50 in advance at Renfro's Drug Store. While Houdini's crusade against charlatans was sincere, the master showman was not above arranging a publicity stunt on the side to generate a few more headlines. There is no way to prove it, but one of those attending the lecture that night was Dr. Howard R. Whiteside, the famed spiritualist and president of Whiteside University in Los Angeles. He came to

Fort Worth to defend his cause and specifically to take up Houdini's standing "challenge" to pay $6,000 to any spiritualist who could do any feat on stage that Houdini could not duplicate. The arrangements committee announced that Whiteside would be joining Houdini on the Klan stage the very next night.[7]

At eight PM Saturday night the show began with every seat filled. After the preliminaries Whiteside joined Houdini on stage and the two began to verbally spar. Whiteside refused to make contact with the spirit world on stage, but they agreed to a compromise that would also just happen to stretch out interest in Houdini's visit to town. The challenged (Whiteside) would produce irrefutable evidence that it was possible to contact the spirit world with a demonstration of spirit photography at a neutral site under strictly monitored conditions. Spirit photography reportedly could produce images on film of persons in the next world using an ordinary camera. The site of their "experiment" would be the Hotel Texas. It would be the greatest test of faith since Elijah challenged the priests of Baal in the Old Testament![8]

Each of the principals brought along a camera and a roll of film, which a local photographer loaded into the cameras while closely observed by two newspaper reporters. The photographer then took a series of pictures in a darkened room pointed toward a green curtain while Houdini and Whiteside looked on. Afterwards he developed both rolls and displayed the prints for all to see. As Houdini had predicted, no ghostly images were present. Whiteside protested that all the "skepticism and hostility" in the room had made conditions unfavorable for the spirits to appear. Houdini crowed that he had exposed another fraud, and both men left town.[9]

Whiteside's career suffered no ill effects from his setback. In 1927 he spoke in Dallas, telling his audience that "motion pictures of heaven" would be coming soon. A couple of years later in Eastland, Texas, he was called by the defense in an insanity case as an "expert who understands the human mind." After his testimony his so-called expertise was debunked by the judge who declared he was "not qualified as either an expert or non-expert witness."[10]

As for Houdini, he never returned to Fort Worth. Two years after his 1924 visit he was dead from a ruptured appendix suffered after he accepted a challenge to test the vaunted strength of his abdominal muscles by letting a man strike him in the stomach with all his might. He died on Halloween night 1926. Ironically, the man who spent his later years debunking spiritualists had made a secret pact with his wife that he would communicate with her from the next world. She faithfully conducted seances on Halloween night for the next ten years but never succeeded in reaching across the void to contact her dearly departed. Harry Houdini has not publicly appeared in Fort Worth or anywhere else since his death.[11]

Chapter 25

When Gutzon Borglum Came to Fort Worth and Robert E. Lee Almost Did

There is an oft-told myth that Robert E. Lee, posted to Texas before the Civil War, once stood on the bluff where the 1849 fort was placed and announced he could hear "the footsteps of oncoming millions" of settlers headed for the Lone Star State. It never happened. But a larger-than-life version of Lee almost wound up on that same bluff over the Trinity River some 70 years later, the creation of sculptor Gutzon Borglum.[1]

Borglum, better known for carving massive sculptures on Stone Mountain, Georgia, and Mount Rushmore, South Dakota, was of Czech heritage, born in 1867 in Idaho to a Mormon family though he himself was never a particularly religious man. He learned art at the California School of Design and the Académie Julian in Paris, France, concentrating on sculpture. He exhibited his work at the Metropolitan Museum of Art before helping organize the history-making New York Armory Show in 1913. However, he fell out with the other organizers and moved to Stamford, Connecticut. In 1915 he fell out with the patrons of the Stone Mountain project, destroyed all his models and left the state in the dark of night. He subsequently turned up in Dallas where the mercurial sculptor told a newspaper reporter that he planned to make his home in Texas "where people would really understand him." As a high-ranking member of the revived Ku Klux Klan, he would have felt right at home in a town where the Klan ruled, and the Lost Cause was still alive.[2]

In 1925 Borglum moved to San Antonio to work full-time on his Texas projects. He found Texans congenial on the whole and a receptive audience for his kind of heroic-sized sculpture. His biggest commission was from the Trail Drivers' Association to sculpt a massive monument to the long-drive era in state history. He took up residence in the equally historic Menger Hotel while completing the "Trail Drivers" sculpture for the city that considered itself the starting point for the Chisholm Trail. Never content with a single piece, he sculpted two cowboys on horseback leading their herd north. The thirty-three-foot clay model was ready for casting by early January 1926, and he hit the road with a maquette (model), measuring two inches to the foot and accurate in every detail. He visited Dallas in January and Fort Worth in February. His tour coincided with the Trail Drivers' Association's drive to raise the $150,000 it would take to have the bronze casting done in Europe.[3]

His visit to Fort Worth was perfectly timed to coincide with the 1926 Fat Stock Show, a golden opportunity to appeal to those who most appreciated the state's cattle heritage. The traveling model was displayed in the lobby of the Hotel Texas for the duration of the Fat Stock Show, and the Trail Drivers' Association came to town for their annual convention that year. Borglum stayed in town a few days, making speeches to raise money for the monument fund. Of course, he also had a personal interest in seeing the monument completed. If it were not cast, he would make little or nothing on the clay model he had created.[4]

Borglum fit right in with Fort Worth audiences, not just in the Western attire he adopted, but as a big thinker and flag-waving patriot who believed larger-than-life monuments

Gutzon Borglum's magnificent Trail Drivers statue, San Antonio, TX. Author's collection.

to famous historic figures were memorials to American civilization. His previous works honored Gen. Philip Sheridan, Pres. Abraham Lincoln, and the Puritans. Fort Worthers were so smitten with him, the local chapter of the United Daughters of the Confederacy (UDC) approached him about creating a

Gutzon Borglum as a guest of the Fort Worth Fat Stock Show. Courtesy Amon Carter Museum of American Art, Fort Worth, TX.

heroic-sized memorial to the Southern Confederacy. The subject they had in mind was no less than Gen. Robert E. Lee. Borglum was still bitter over the abrupt end of his Stone Mountain dream before completion. His "moment of greatest triumph" on the project had come on January 19, 1924, when the face of General Lee had been unveiled while the sculpture and a group of UDC ladies looked on from half a mile away. He had started sculpting the massive tableau of 1,200 figures on the granite mountain in 1915. Lee's head alone was 20-feet high. The unveiling in 1924 was the first time Borglum had seen his handiwork from an appreciative distance. Not long after that he was fired from the project when costs soared. Now the UDC of Fort Worth was giving him a second chance to realize his vision of a larger-than-life General Lee. He told them he had a business meeting in New York but promised to come back and start the work before the end of April. Meanwhile, other Fort Worthers were more interested in snatching the Trail Drivers monument from San Antonio and giving it a home where it really belonged.[5]

Borglum's other obligations kept him from getting back to Texas until July. There was the dedication in Newark, New Jersey of "The Wars of America" memorial, not only a personal masterpiece but at the time the largest bronze anywhere in the world. He also accepted commissions to execute a statue of Alexander Stephens, vice president of the Confederacy (1861–65) for the state of Georgia, to go into Statuary Hall in Washington, D.C., and to carve a "colossal natural granite monument" about some aspect of American history under Congressional authorization, to go on the side of a 1,000-foot mountain in South Dakota. The commission for the South Dakota project alone was $447,000.[6]

Borglum's simplistic view of life influenced both his art and his view of history. He believed it was the larger-than-life heroes who advanced civilization. Like Greek mythology, godlike heroes determined the course of events, sometimes working on concert, sometimes at odds with each other. He once said, "If Abraham Lincoln and Robert E. Lee could have gotten together in an intimate conference at the outset of the Civil War, they would have settled their sectional differences as only strong, noble men can." The preposterousness of an elected president and a U.S. Army colonel sitting down as equals and solving the sectional crisis was lost on the unsophisticated sculptor.[7]

The members of Fort Worth's Julia Jackson Chapter of the UDC may not have known how many commissions he was juggling when they agreed to pay him $50,000 for General Lee. He told them he would be occupied with the Trail Drivers' memorial until the end of the year, but he promised as soon as he wrapped that up, he would be in Fort Worth to start work on the UDC commission. As it turned out, he was still working on the Trail Drivers monument in the middle of 1927 and with no end in sight. All he could say in June of 1927 was that the work was "progressing satisfactorily." In fact, the casting of the massive bronze was held up by lack of money until 1940, and when finally cast it was only one-quarter its planned size.[8]

Problems with the Trail Drivers monument, however, did not prevent Borglum from trying to keep the General Lee project on track. In early 1927, he made several trips to Fort Worth to confer with his UDC patrons. Somewhere in the planning the projected cost of the work tripled from $50,000 to $150,000. Cost overrun was a problem that plagued every Borglum commission. To their credit, the ladies of the Julia Jackson chapter did not blink. They were determined that Fort Worth would have its Lee statue, and a little thing like money was not going to deter them. In April Borglum brought four different Lee maquettes to Fort Worth for the ladies to choose from. One went on display in the Carnegie Public Library where viewers were asked to envision the model as a forty-foot equestrian statue (not counting the base) with Lee on horseback flanked by five other "prominent" Confederates (unnamed), just as Hercules or Ulysses in Greek sculpture had been flanked by their "companions." Another of the models had Lee on horseback flanked by just two worshipful soldiers. The final work would be mounted on a four-sided granite base with a bas-relief panel on each side depicting Lee's great battlefield victories. The whole thing was a cut-down version of Borglum's Stone Mountain vision. When completed it was to be placed on Bluff Park, AKA the "north terrace" of the Courthouse where it would majestically overlook the Trinity River. This particular piece of land had only recently opened up after the old 1884 county jail was demolished and the ground repurposed as a public park. The Paddock Viaduct would be like a promenade leading up to the site. The UDC hoped to have an elaborate unveiling ceremony in the late fall of 1927.[9]

When the sculptor's work was done, the bronze casting would be done in Europe where all the best statues were cast.

But things were a long way from that stage. In early June Borglum announced that he had "completed plans for the beginning of the work" and that "every factor" in the project from the form the work would take to where it would be placed was being "coordinated" with the city of Fort Worth and his patrons. Truth be told, the only involvement of the city came because as caretakers of Bluff Park they had the final say in allowing the statue to be placed there. City fathers had no intention of putting any money into something like this. The only funding besides what the Julia Jackson chapter could raise was what the Sons of Confederate Veterans pitched in. Borglum kept local interest burning bright by promising that his Lee statue would be "the largest equestrian statue in the United States," even larger than his General Sheridan statue (1908) in Sheridan Circle, Washington, D.C. Perhaps Bluff Park would be renamed "General Lee Park" in honor of the work? Borglum for all his grandiose promises was seemingly distancing himself from his Fort Worth commission. Before departing for South Dakota, he announced he had "completed plans for the beginning of the [Fort Worth] work," which was a long way from turning a clay maquette into a full-size bronze sculpture. And there was no way it would be ready for casting by the fall, not even working day and night, if he was climbing all over Mount Rushmore.

As reality set in, the dream got smaller. The latest figure on the cost that summer was $130,000 although it was unclear whether that amount included the base or just the sculpture. It was obvious to anyone following developments that the base was not going to have bas-relief carvings around it. Some sort of a stair-stepped plaza was about as elaborate as it was going to get. The revised cost estimate also reflected the fact that Borglum was now talking about a thirty-foot sculpture, not the original forty-foot version. However, he assured his patrons, it would still be visible "for a great distance." Just before leaving for South Dakota, he promised to spend "a large part of the summer" working on the Lee commission. He made that promise in early June.[10]

After June of 1927, Gutzon Borglum was rarely seen in Fort Worth, and that was on the train through from Dallas to San Antonio where he was still an artist-in-residence and a popular public speaker. His favorite topics nowadays were the Stone Mountain and Mount Rushmore projects, defending his role in the former and promising the sky with the latter. He vowed Mount Rushmore would be the grandest and most unique sculpture in the entire world. Since Borglum could never turn down a big, fat commission, the little Fort Worth project for which funding was still being raised ceased to hold his interest. His instincts were right. The Julia Jackson chapter and their SCV brothers were unable to raise the necessary money to pay the sculptor or cast the bronze. The rest of the citizenry, while proud of their Southern heritage, were not willing to dig deep to pay for yet another grand vision. The maquette on display in the library was quietly taken down and disappeared, never to be seen again. Perhaps Borglum reclaimed it, or maybe it was thrown out when the city tore down the old building, replacing it with a new library on the site in 1939.[11]

If General Lee was not going to reside in Fort Worth, there was still plenty of sentiment for a Lee statue in Dallas where love of the Lost Cause was just as strong if not stronger. In 1929, the Southern Memorial Association (SMA), a thinly veiled Lost Cause group, launched a memorial project to "the South's greatest hero," which could only mean General Robert E. Lee. The ladies of the SMA wanted to find some budding "Paganini of the chisel" to make their vision a reality. An editorial in the *Dallas Morning News* lamented, "There is so little good public sculpture in our American cities, particularly those of the Southwest," and urged the SMA to correct that deficiency. Sculpture "builds ideals … celebrates truth … [and] wins men's hearts through the eye, singing the praise of great lives that have been lived."[12]

They rejected Borglum's portrayal of General Lee as an action equestrian figure in favor of a "quiet, dignified portrayal" of the great man sitting erect on Traveler gazing serenely upon the modern world. To realize that vision, they sought a "great" artist who possessed "the polish of academic culture" and a visionary personal philosophy that he could translate into stone. A spokesman sniffed that they wanted an "artist" not just a "stone-cutter." They eventually settled on A. Phimister Proctor of New York as the artist with the necessary vision. Whether they considered Borglum, or he was even interested is not revealed in the record. By the 1930s he was hard at work on Mount Rushmore.[13]

The SMA began soliciting donations, getting the ball rolling with a $1,000 gift from Mrs. Henry Exall, Sr. As the price mounted, eventually quintupling, they tapped federal funds (Works Progress Administration) for the $15,000 base of the statue. The $40,000 for the memorial was still trickling in in 1933. Before getting the WPA to fund the base, the Association likely appealed to another New Deal agency, the Civil Works Administration (CWA), to back the project. Ironically, in 1933 Gutzon Borglum was head of the CWA in Texas, in which position he was busy promoting civic "beautification programs" with a "modernist" emphasis. He was not interested in putting money into things as quaintly old-fashioned as equestrian statues. He did not see his own involvement in a similar statue in Fort Worth just a few years before as contradictory. His most ambitious project as head of the CWA was re-developing the Corpus Christi waterfront. Never one to bite his tongue, Borglum offered some unsolicited criticism of Texas public art in general: "vulgar" and "frightful." Proctor's Lee memorial, costing less than half of Borglum's imagined work, consisted of a mounted General Lee trailed by a mounted orderly riding bravely into History. It was impressive, but it was no Stone Mountain or Mount Rushmore.[14]

Presumably there were no hard feelings on Fort Worth's part because in January 1934 Borglum was back to pass judgment on a $500,000 countywide beautification program. He used the occasion to announce the creation of an annual prize to go to the Texas city that made the best use of CWA money to beautify itself. The prize would come with a silver punch bowl designed by Borglum himself. He expressed the hope that the annual competition would create a competitive spirit like baseball championships and predicted unofficially that Fort Worth would be the first city to win the silver bowl, but there was no subsequent announcement that Fort Worth won the prize. Instead, the Silver Bowl Championship was laughed to death by public officials and artists alike.[15]

On March 6, 1941, Gutzon Borglum died of coronary sclerosis in Chicago, leaving his son, Lincoln, to finish his Mount Rushmore masterpiece. He claimed to have lived in Texas for fifteen years, which number is not supported by the facts as he moved to California in 1937, but he always thought of himself as a Texan at heart. All true Texans were not as kindly disposed toward the mercurial, arrogant, judgmental artist who had adopted their state. Still, there is no denying his influence on Texas, starting with the 32-foot statue of "Christ the Man" that he created for Corpus Christi, the Robert E. Lee statue that almost came to Fort Worth but went to Dallas instead, and the trail drivers monument that stands in front the Witte Museum in San Antonio.[16]

It is impossible to know what would have transpired if the Gutzon Borglum statue of Robert E. Lee had been erected in Fort Worth. Judging by the unveiling of the Proctor memorial in Dallas in 1936, it would have been the occasion for a presidential visit. What has always been known as Paddock Park might have been renamed Lee Park in honor of its massive occupant, as Oak Lawn Park in Dallas was renamed Lee Park. It would also have wound up at the center of a fierce public debate about its appropriateness that eventually led to the Dallas statue being removed from its proud place in Lee Park and put in storage in 2017. Instead, the only memorial occupying Paddock Park to date was an eight-foot statue of businessman Charles Tandy by sculptor Jim Reno. It was removed to the TCU campus without fanfare in 2009. Since then, that spectacular spot overlooking the Trinity River has remained empty, waiting for a suitable monument.[17]

Chapter 26

Goodbye, Fort Worth, "Hello, Sucker!"

Two of the biggest names in the New York social scene in the 1920s wore their Texas origins proudly: Tex Rickard and Texas Guinan. Since both were larger than life, the "Texas" appellation fit them.

George Lewis "Tex" Rickard (1870-1929) was the biggest promoter of his day, who got his nickname while working as a town marshal in Henrietta, Texas. Mary Louise Cecilia "Texas" Guinan (1884–1933) was a stage and film star from Waco, Texas, who told a newspaper reporter "Texas" was her birth name. But her real claim to fame was as "Queen of the Nightclubs," the legendary speakeasy hostess who greeted her customers with the famous catchphrase, "Hello Sucker!" After she became famous, she regularly instructed reporters and fans how to pronounce her last name: "with a long 'i' and the 'u' silent and the accent on the first syllable."[1]

Guinan never forgot her Texas roots. She learned roping and riding as a girl on her father's ranch before getting a scholarship to the American Conservatory of Music in Chicago in 1898. She exhibited genuine vocal talent to go along with her chutzpah and after graduating from the Conservatory she joined a touring Wild West show. She settled down to married life in 1904 but that lasted only two years before her restless yearning led her to divorce John Moynahan and head for the bright lights of New York. She quickly found work in vaudeville, starting in the chorus line before stepping up to the front of the stage. It is believed she adopted the name "Texas" to give her an edge getting hired in the highly competitive world of vaudeville.[2]

Guinan was a big girl, and her weight eventually got her banished from the chorus line and then excluded from ingenue dramatic roles. She tried to cash in on her lifelong battle with her weight by becoming a spokesperson for a weight-loss company. Their advertising campaign turned out to be a swindle, which drove her from the New York stage. She turned to the vaudeville circuit in the heartland, which is how she came to Fort Worth in 1917. These years, 1915–1920 are what her biographer calls "the most elusive" period in her life because while performing on the stage she was also launching a film career in California, and claiming to have gone to France during World War I to entertain the troops for which she claimed to have been decorated by the French government. While the latter claims are patently false, it is indeed true that she managed to juggle a stage and film career for several years.[3]

Her movies were short two-reelers that promoted her as a Western gun-totin' gal, Texas-born, of course. They called her the "female Tom Mix," and she incorporated that image into her stage performances. After churning out nearly three dozen pictures for others she formed her own production company in 1921 and made three more films where she called the shots. She eventually found her way back to the New York vaudeville stage before starting her legendary nightclub career in 1923, first as a singer then as the hostess/emcee. It was here she coined her most famous catchphrases, "Hello, Sucker!" and "Give the little lady a great big hand." She took her schtick from the same playbook as her contemporary Mae West, mixing glamour with witty, sarcastic patter that customers ate up. She once summarized her likes and dislikes thusly:

> I like noise, rhinestone heels, customers, plenty of attention, and red-velvet bathing suits. I smoke like a five-alarm fire; I eat an aspirin every night before I go to bed; I call every man I don't know "Fred," and they love it; I have six uncles; I sleep on my right side; and I like carrots; I eat a dozen oranges every day; and I once took off thirty-five pounds in two weeks. I guess that settles my personality.[4]

During the so-called "elusive" stage of her life, she played Fort Worth and Dallas stages a few times but was better known through her films. She first appeared locally on the Majestic stage in Dallas in 1917, with Billy Dixon in a short sketch, "Honk, Honk Maybe!" She and Dixon were the top billing in a seven-act show that ran for three weeks in Dallas before moving to Fort Worth's Majestic theater (Tenth and Commerce), an equally classy venue with an ornate marble lobby and red velvet seats. The *Star-Telegram* heavily flogged the show before it opened on this side of the Trinity, promising "Big Time Vaudeville" and "a riot of fun." Management counted on Guinan and Dixon both being both well-known names, but also reminded the public that Guinan was "Texas' Own Daughter." The show opened in Fort Worth with a matinee on Friday, February 16 followed by an evening show that same night. Tickets were 25¢ for adults. Vaudeville was a punishing life, requiring two shows a day for six or seven days a week, and that was the plan. But management miscalculated this time. The "comic story of a temperamental car" occupied by its two stars had been a huge hit with Dallas audiences, but not so much on this side of the Trinity. The two stars' frantic song-and-humorous-patter act "fell flat," which in vaudeville usually meant an act was dropped down

The second Majestic Theater (Commerce at Tenth) where Texas Guinan appeared on the vaudeville stage and in the movies. Described in 1914 as "the finest theater building in the Southwest." Author's collection.

to the bottom of the program, replaced at the top of the program by a more popular act.[5]

Guinan's vaudeville act may have fallen flat in Fort Worth, but her movies could still pull 'em in. In January 1918, only a year after her disappointing stage debut in Fort Worth, the Hippodrome movie house booked *The Gun Woman* for three days. Guinan was the big draw in a film promising "a tremendously stirring story with touches of human interest." It was a silent movie, of course, but Guinan could emote "romance and thrills" with the best of them. It was her third film for the Triangle Film Corporation, but "her first stellar screen role," making it must-see entertainment for the movie-going public. In the years that followed her movies continued to play well in Fort Worth, including her self-produced films with her own company in 1921. One, *The Hermit,* which played in Fort Worth in its first-run release, is not even listed in her filmography.[6]

She did not come back to north Texas in person again until 1922. For her return, she was booked by Dallas's Majestic theater for a week with a mixed-medium show of film and live performance. She was the headliner naturally. The film was her own production, a two-reel oater titled *The Spitfire,* written especially for her by "well-known vaudeville author" Jack Lait. It had Guinan in the same sort of Western derring-do role that audiences ate up, playing a "hard-riding, fast-acting heroine" of the Western frontier. The ticket-buying public was reminded that the star was a "Waco girl" and "extremely versatile in 'Western scenes,'" adding, "Wherever film flickers she is known." Movie ticket prices at 10¢ and 15¢ for adults were typically cheaper than vaudeville tickets, but this show with both a moving picture and a live performance headlined by Texas Guinan was in another category. Ticket prices were 25¢ and 35¢ for adults. Guinan and "her company" still had to be on the stage twice a day for the matinee and the evening performance. After the film finished, the star rode out on the stage on a horse accompanied by her four supporting actors, all still in character. One critic commented that as pretty as she looked in her "riding costume" on the screen, she looked even more fetching in the bright red dress she changed into for the second part of the show. The most significant thing about the show, however, was the mixing of film and live performance, which at least to Texas audiences was something entirely new. After 1920 vaudeville was dying a slow death while moving pictures were becoming the big draw. Offering the best of both worlds was a brilliant idea whether it was original with Texas Guinan or not.[7]

After the first show she gave the obligatory interview to the press, which in this case meant the *Dallas Morning News* and *Dallas Times-Herald.* She said she was pleased to be back "in the State for which [I am] named." She added, however, that she was not too fond of the August weather in Texas. She said everyone who ever knew her in her early days in Waco seemed to have moved to Dallas. It was for them that she hosted a swanky reception at the Adolphus Hotel, squeezed in somehow between shows. She also opined that Dallas would be a great place to make moving pictures, wondering why the city had not jumped on the Hollywood bandwagon. This show did not go to Fort Worth. After it closed in Dallas the star was off to Mexico to make another Western. It must have been a very short production schedule because by mid-December she was back in New York City hosting a farewell party for fellow actress Pearl White of "Perils of Pauline" fame.[8]

Interested in leaving the touring life behind and making more money, in 1923 she started her nightclub career in New York as a singer at the Beaux Arts club. It was Prohibition and all the nightclubs were really speakeasies where the show came with exorbitantly priced (illegal) liquor. Texas' singing talents were okay, but it was her witty, sarcastic repartee with customers that made the Beaux Arts the in place to go for New York society. She soon had her own floor show where her principal job was to introduce the performers in her inimitable way, which included "Let's have a big hand for the little lady." She moved on to her own place, Texas Guinan's Club until police shut it down then on to the 300 Club until federal agents raided it and charged her with violating the Volstead Act. She was acquitted in 1929 and found that her brush with the law made her too hot to go back on the speakeasy circuit, a fate that had earlier befallen comedian Fatty Arbuckle. Undaunted, she put together a revue that did not run from but capitalized on her racy reputation, "Too Hot for Paris." She took it on the road and showed skeptical booking agents that she still had it.

In September 1933 rumors circulated in Dallas, encouraged by State Fair management, that she was coming to Dallas that year as part of the annual State Fair extravaganza (October 7–22, 1933). Reportedly she was going to appear at the Majestic to introduce her latest film, *Broadway Through a Keyhole,* written as a vehicle for her by newspaper columnist and radio broadcaster Walter Winchell. To spice up the program she was going to bring along "her girls" from her touring show. The rumors turned out to be false, but the Majestic did book her and her revue for an engagement starting on November 25. Like Sally Rand later, Texas Guinan's name on a show came with the promise of scantily clad girls and risqué patter, strictly for adults. It never happened because two weeks earlier on November 5, the same day her New York office signed the Dallas papers, she died in British Columbia where she was wrapping up her tour. She had come down with amoebic dysentery while in Chicago but pressed on to the last engagement on the schedule.[9]

Fort Worth's last taste of Texas Guinan while she was alive had come nine months earlier, in February 1933. Her short film, *Texas Guinan Down Memory Lane* played in a double bill at the Palace theater with "State Fair" with Janet Gaynor and Will Rogers. At 25¢ the tickets were too pricey for the short film alone but paired with a newsreel and feature film it was a good deal. The film is so obscure today it is not even listed on Guinan's filmography.[10]

No one can say Texas Guinan put Fort Worth on the entertainment map, nor did she get her big break in Fort Worth. But like Buffalo Bill, Will Rogers, Sally Rand, and other big-name stars of their day, Fort Worth was not too small or too "hick" for her to play either. It was just another stop on the theater circuit back when big stars played small towns and gave the local yokels a show to remember.

Belatedly, Guinan received the Hollywood treatment in the 1945 Paramount musical, *Incendiary Blonde,* with glamorous Betty Hutton of *Annie Get Your Gun* in the star role. The movie has about as much connection to the subject's real life as Guinan's

Celebrity Texas Guinan never forgot her roots. Here seen with her mother, 1931. Author's collection.

stage act had to performing art. Today it is viewed by some film buffs as a female-empowerment movie, which is closer to the truth than the script ever was.

Texas Guinan returned to Fort Worth in spirit in 1969 with the world premiere of *Hello, Sucker!*, a musical by Casa Mañana director Robert Turoff with Ruta Lee in the comedic role of Guinan. It was reportedly "Broadway-bound," and Lee's flamboyant costumes sparked discussion in the fashion pages of the *Star-Telegram*. Sadly, not even Ruta Lee's star power could save the show from obscurity after a two-week run.[11]

Chapter 27

Public Enemy No. 1 Nabbed in Fort Worth

No one remembers Raymond Hamilton today though they remember his pals, Bonnie Parker and Clyde Barrow. A two-year crime spree (1932-34) that covered several states landed them on the FBI's "Most Wanted" list. Bonnie and Clyde were the fatalistic romantic couple with delusions of being modern-day Robin Hoods. There was nothing either romantic or appealing about Ray Hamilton, their sidekick. He was rail-thin with sharp features and wispy blond hair. He had a hair-trigger temper, was impulsive and a bundle of nerves.[1]

Hamilton's criminal career began modestly enough as a juvenile bootlegger in Wichita Falls, Texas, before graduating to boosting cars in Dallas in July 1931. Caught by Dallas police he was given a three-year suspended sentence. Rearrested for the same offense in McKinney and facing serious time, he sawed his way out of his cell in January 1932 and escaped under cover of darkness.[2]

He hooked up with Bonnie and Clyde soon after that, still just nineteen years old when they embarked on a spree of robberies and car thefts. Raymond's role in the "Barrow gang" was stealing cars. He was a whiz at it. He could pick out a good getaway car and hot-wire it in a matter of seconds. Clyde was the designated driver. What Ray was not particularly good with was guns and keeping his cool in tight situations. Clyde and Ray hit the big time in April when they robbed a mom-and-pop store outside of Hillsboro, Texas, and Raymond shot and killed the owner. It was not cold-blooded murder, just a case of nerves making his trigger finger twitch, but John Bucher was just as dead. For a while the three were virtually inseparable, but according to one source, sexual tensions split them up. Ray was sleeping with both Bonnie and Clyde, and there was no way that *menage à trois* could last.[3]

In August Clyde and Ray engaged in a shootout with Oklahoma officers that left a sheriff severely wounded and his deputy dead. The two now made a death pact never to be captured alive. Ray went to Michigan that winter to see his father and got arrested while he was there and extradited back to Texas to stand trial for the Bucher murder. In May he was transferred to LaGrange, Texas to stand trial for a November 1932 bank robbery. He was found guilty and sentenced to life in prison. In June he was tried for the Bucher murder and got another life sentence. Texas authorities sent him to the Eastham prison farm to serve his time. On January 15, 1934, Clyde and an accomplice broke Hamilton and four others out of prison, including Joe Palmer, serving time for bank robbery. Palmer and Hamilton were uncomfortable members of the Barrow gang thereafter although they could not stand each other. All they ever had in common was serving time in Eastham and being freed by Clyde Barrow in the murderous 1934 breakout, which was ironic considering their ultimate fate.[4]

Reunited, the gang robbed a Lancaster bank at the end of February 1934 but broke up soon thereafter in a dispute over splitting the take. Raymond and girlfriend Mary O'Dare went their own way, heading to New Orleans to lay low and spend their loot. When Clyde and another accomplice gunned down a couple of Oklahoma lawmen, Ray sent a letter to his own Dallas attorney disclaiming any involvement in the latest Barrow gang homicides. Ray and Mary returned to Texas and at the end of March he robbed a bank at West, Texas, then Ray found another partner and in April they robbed a bank at Lewisville in Denton County, twenty-five miles north of Dallas. Their getaway was cut short when police caught up with them near Sherman. They gave up without a fight, with Ray telling officers, "Don't shoot, boys. I'm fresh out of guns, ammo, whiskey and women." Once again, he was behind bars.[5]

Clyde playfully sent him a message at the Dallas jail, saying he and Bonnie were sorry to hear of him being captured but expressing no sympathy because he had "offered no resistance." Clyde closed the letter by calling him "a boastful punk." Dallas transferred him to the Denton jail to answer for the Lewisville robbery.[6]

While Hamilton was in jail, Bonnie and Clyde's reign of terror ended on May 23, 1934, in an ambush near Arcadia, Louisiana. Reporters interviewed Ray in his Denton jail cell, asking him about his reaction to the news. He lamented the death of his "good friend" and denied that they had ever been at odds.[7]

Ray was returned to the Texas prison system to face a total of 462 years in stacked sentences. While he was in Huntsville, another jury gave him the death sentence for killing the Eastham prison guard when he broke out. There were also federal charges pending against him for breaking into National Guard armories and stealing heavy weapons. But if Hamilton had learned nothing else from his one-time pal, he had learned that Texas prisons were easy enough to break out of for a determined man. On July 22, 1934, he and five pals shot their way out of the death house using guns smuggled in to them by friends on the outside. It was his fourth jailbreak and the "most sensational escape" in the history of the Huntsville penitentiary. He returned to Dallas for a time hiding out at brother Floyd's house until police found out and set another ambush like the one that had brought down Bonnie and Clyde eight months earlier. The two brothers escaped the trap in a blaze of gunfire and fled Dallas. Raymond headed for Mississippi to continue his crime spree in March 1935 by holding up a bank, taking hostages, and disarming a posse. He managed to elude police roadblocks and picking up a couple of companions slipped back into Texas hoping to stay out of sight. The FBI and authorities in several states were now looking for the man dubbed "the blond bandit from West Dallas."[8]

The newspapers that kept track of such things called him an escape artist and "probably the most daring bank robber the State has ever produced" as if there were a competition in such matters. The *Star-Telegram* anointed him the successor to Clyde Barrow as "Texas' most-sought desperado," while other reporters went even further, crowning him "Public Enemy No. 1." J. Edgar Hoover who had originally created that list to win public attention for the FBI, neither confirmed nor denied the title for the twenty-three-year-old career criminal.[9]

He could not go back to Dallas since everyone with a badge and a gun was on the lookout for him there. He was a fugitive on the run now with few friends outside his immediate family. The days of racing around the country with Bonnie and Clyde in stolen Fords, knocking over small-town banks and filling stations were over. He came into Fort Worth on April 4 on a freight train from Oklahoma City and jumped off in the rail yards. He was accompanied by two companions, an illiterate Mississippi youth named Nolan Allred and an older man they'd picked up in Illinois, Glen Allen. The formerly dapper outlaw was wearing grimy overalls and scuffed brogans. He had no desire to stay in Fort Worth, but he needed traveling money and some new clothes. Those would have to come from family in Dallas.[10]

The manhunt for Raymond Hamilton ended in that rail yard the next day. He had sent a couple of notes by Allred to his sister in Dallas asking for help. On the second trip Allred was caught by Dallas Deputy Sheriff Bill Decker who was watching the sister's house. He gave up Hamilton under questioning. Hamilton and Allen were holed up in the Rock Island rail yards just east of downtown. Deputy Decker and Sheriff R.A. "Smoot" Schmid rounded up three more deputies and called Fort Worth authorities to enlist their assistance. Then they drove to Fort Worth where they were joined by Fort Worth Detective Chester Reagan and Tarrant County Deputy Sheriff Carl Harmon. They entered the rail yards near the Belknap St. bridge while other officers set up roadblocks at both ends of the bridge then began a sweep of the yards with guns drawn, moving south from the bridge checking empty boxcars and hobo campsites. They came upon Hamilton and Allen some fifty feet north of the East First St. overpass "sprawled on the tracks" almost indistinguishable from "six or seven other bums" nearby except for the two .45s Hamilton had on him and a suitcase full of brand-new clothes. Bill Decker walked up to him and covered him with his pistol and said, "Hoist 'em, Ray, before I cut you in two." At least that was the way he told it later. Hamilton's decision was made easier because he was surrounded by officers with drawn guns. He meekly surrendered. When asked later why he had not gone out in a blaze of glory like Bonnie and Clyde, he replied it was because he knew Decker would give him a "square deal." The other officers quickly closed in with guns drawn. They handcuffed him, threw him into a car, and roared off to Dallas. The next morning a *Dallas Morning News* headline credited a "Dallas posse" with Hamilton's capture. Pictures in the *Star-Telegram* told a different story, showing the sad-sack fugitive standing meekly between Fort Worth Detective Reagan and Dallas Sheriff Schmid immediately after being captured, suggesting that the credit should have been shared.[11]

Subsequent investigation revealed that Hamilton had been hiding out in the rail yard for about twenty-four hours. When detectives showed his photo around, they learned he had eaten at the Round House Café (507 Diamond) and had a few beers at Choate's Famous BBQ stand (1415 Peach). Neither the owners nor the regular customers took any notice of the slight newcomer since working men and hoboes both were a familiar sight in the area. He apparently slept in a "toolhouse" under the East First St. overpass. The foreman of the yards had noticed him hanging around the area but did not bother him. "He was very polite," recalled Tom Stanfield. Other employees thought Hamilton was "just another tramp" among many who passed through the rail yards riding the rails or looking for work. (The police apparently did not inquire about Hamilton's two traveling companions.) One of the men in on the finale for Hamilton was Dallas Deputy Sheriff Ted Hinton who had also been part of the ambush that put an end to Bonnie and Clyde.[12]

Though he could not hold a candle to other well-known gangsters of his era like John Dillinger or Pretty Boy Floyd, Ray Hamilton was the biggest "public enemy" ever captured in the Fort Worth-Dallas area. He was a celebrity in an era that liked its criminals bigger than life. Taken back to Dallas, Hamilton' presence drew more than 500 curiosity-seekers to the courthouse hoping to get a look at him. It was reported that "parents brought their babes in arms, and youngsters … rubbed elbows with women in formal dress and men in overalls." Meanwhile, the sheriff's office got calls from as far away as New York trying to confirm the report of his capture that had gone out over the wire.[13]

Truth be told, Raymond Hamilton was no steely-eyed gangster in the mode of Dillinger, sneering in the face of death.

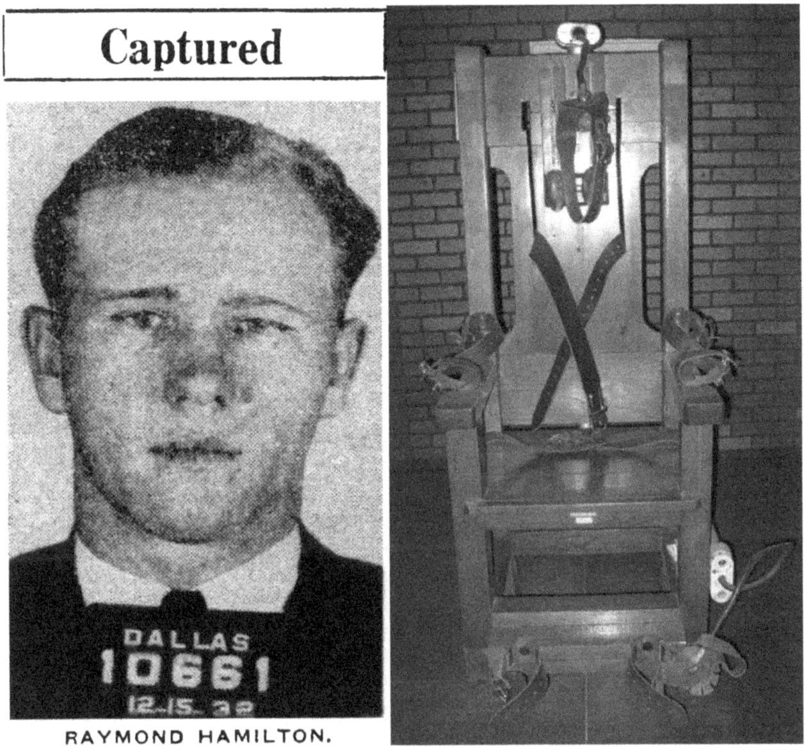

(a) Fort Worth police used Ray Hamilton's 1932 Dallas mug shot to identify their man. (b) Huntsville's "Old Sparky," the last sight Ray Hamilton ever saw. Both from author's collection.

The androgynous one-man crime wave had always played second banana to Clyde Barrow. Attempts to inflate his criminal record in the press could not hide the fact that he was a two-bit hoodlum, not a daring outlaw. He and Joe Palmer shared a date with the electric chair on May 10, 1935, just after midnight. When the time came, Hamilton's nerve failed him, and he persuaded Palmer, whom he had always considered soft and never liked, to go first. By the time it was Ray's turn, he was composed enough to walk steadily into the chamber and even speak to the prison chaplain before they strapped him into the chair.[14]

Chapter 28

The *Green Book* Guide to Fort Worth

Before Supreme Court decisions and legislation and the mass movement known as "civil rights," there were two Americas, one white and one black. Whites ruled, and blacks got along the best they could as second-class citizens. This was true not just in the South but all over. The *Negro Motorist Green Book* (usually referred to simply as the *Green Book*) was a practical expression of that time.

Hardly anyone remembered the *Green Book* until the 2019, Oscar-winning movie of the same name brought it alive. *Green Book* (the movie) was based on the inexpensive guidebook for black motorists traveling through the United States during the Jim Crow era of racially segregated accommodations, eating places, etc. It was the brainchild of Harlem mail carrier Victor Hugo Green in 1936. It began as a modest effort to help blacks navigate the diverse boroughs of New York City, but in the years that followed it expanded to cover neighboring states, then the South and eventually the Far West. The *Green Book* listed hotels, roadhouses, restaurants, even gas stations that welcomed African-American business. It promised to make the user's journey "more enjoyable" if not perfectly safe by putting in print what had been passed along by word of mouth for years. It also marked the dawn of a new age when blacks were not limited to traveling by segregated trains and interstate buses. The automobile gave African Americans the freedom to travel the open road. but it did not answer the question of where to stay, eat, and gas up. Victor Green's little booklet did. It carried this simple warning on the cover: "Carry your *Green Book* with you. You may need it!"[1]

The 1939 edition was the first to include Fort Worth. The modest local offerings reflected just how deep segregation ran in north Texas and how small the African-American business community was. It listed just two hotels, the Del Rey at 901 Jones St. and the Jim at 413–15 E. Fifth, both on the eastern edge of downtown, and one service station (970 E. Humboldt). In all of Fort Worth's four or five identifiable black neighborhoods these were the only public accommodations where black travelers could be guaranteed a friendly welcome. Of course, they had to find all three places, which in the days before GPS technology meant stopping and asking for directions. An earlier hotel, The Main Hotel on Rusk across from the Majestic Theater, had closed by the time the *Green Book* came out. Public accommodations were so sparse not just because few blacks traveled far from home but because the tradition in the black community was for black visitors to stay in the homes of friends or relatives or mom-and-pop places known as "tourist homes." This was what opera star Marian Anderson did when she came to town in 1939 and 1941, and what Martin Luther King did in 1959.[2]

The Jim was run like a real hotel even if it looked like large house, not a commercial establishment: fifty rooms, a front desk, room service, a beauty shop, and a dining room. It was built by William "Gooseneck Bill" McDonald in the late 1920s, named for his second wife, Jimmie Strickland McDonald. McDonald was a banker, not a hotelier. He sold the Jim to Oscar and Levi

Cooper in 1934 who added a twenty-five- room annex with a space for private parties and a nightclub that proved to be the most memorable part of the operation. In the years following, the "Varsity Club" became an important stop on the "chittlin' circuit" and a hotbed of black musical culture in north Texas. Aaron "T-Bone" Walker, Fats Waller, Louis Armstrong, Count Basie, and countless other African-American greats played there, attracting both black and white audiences. Walker led the house band, achieving recognition far beyond Fort Worth. In 1953 it became the New Jim Hotel whose name belied its downhill slide. The place finally fell to the wrecking ball in 1964 after desegregation opened up other, nicer accommodations. Today the site is a parking lot in back of the old *Fort Worth Press* building at Fourth and Jones, currently a Fort Worth police substation.[3]

Oscar Cooper also operated the Green Leaf Restaurant originally at 315 E. Ninth, the only all-night eatery for blacks in Fort Worth. It was a gathering place for locals who came for the

The Jim Hotel, named for Bill McDonald's wife at the time. Nice accommodations, great nightclub scene! Author's collection.

home-style cooking and for travelers who found it a welcome oasis on long road trips. All-night diners were an urban fixture for white travelers; a novelty for black travelers.[4]

In subsequent editions of the *Green Book* the list of Fort Worth accommodations expanded, reflecting both the growth of tourism among African Americans and the opening of more places catering to black travelers. In 1947, two restaurants and another service station were added to the list. One of the restaurants was part of the three-story Negro YMCA at 1604 Jones. The property had been donated in 1939 by Bill McDonald in honor of his son, Bill McDonald, Jr. who died in 1920. The service station at 1151 New York St. was further recognition that black motorists also had to gas up their cars on road trips.[5]

In 1956 the Clover and Mohawk hotels joined the listings. The Clover (1901 E. Fourth) was in the Rock Island Bottom, a mixed business and residential district in the Trinity River bottoms just east of town. The Mohawk (217 E. Fifteenth), like most other black businesses of the era, was in the original black business district on the eastern edge of downtown, an area stretching from Sixth to Sixteenth streets and Calhoun to Jones.

In 1957 and '58, new additions to the listings included the Monterey Hotel and Rose Cliff restaurant, both in the Terrell Heights neighborhood on the near South Side. This was Fort Worth's first middle-class black neighborhood, located on the axis of Rosedale and Terrell streets.

The 1966 edition included the familiar names from earlier books. But the times were "a-changing," as Bob Dylan sang. It was two years after the Civil Rights Act had decreed an end to segregated public accommodations. Leonard's Dept. Store was in the forefront, taking down its "Whites Only" signage starting in 1962. Construction of the North-South Freeway and Tarrant County Convention Center had wiped out many black businesses and residences, and what had once been a thriving black business district on Calhoun and Jones had been largely taken over by industrial properties and parking lots.

The book evolved over the years. The title went from *The Negro Motorist Green Book* to *The Negro Travelers' Green Book*, and price creeped up to $1.25 by the 1950s. With a rising black middle class hitting the road, the book became not just a travelers' guide, but a guide to "vacation spots." Vacations were something relatively new in the black community. Ever the optimist, Victor Green predicted in the 1948 edition that the day was coming when such a guidebook would no longer be needed because, "We as a race will have equal opportunities and privileges in the United States." Then, "We can go wherever we please, and without embarrassment." In 1966 for the first time the *Green Book* made no reference on the cover to color and used an illustration of a racially vague person. Presumably, it was now for all travelers who desired a "vacation without

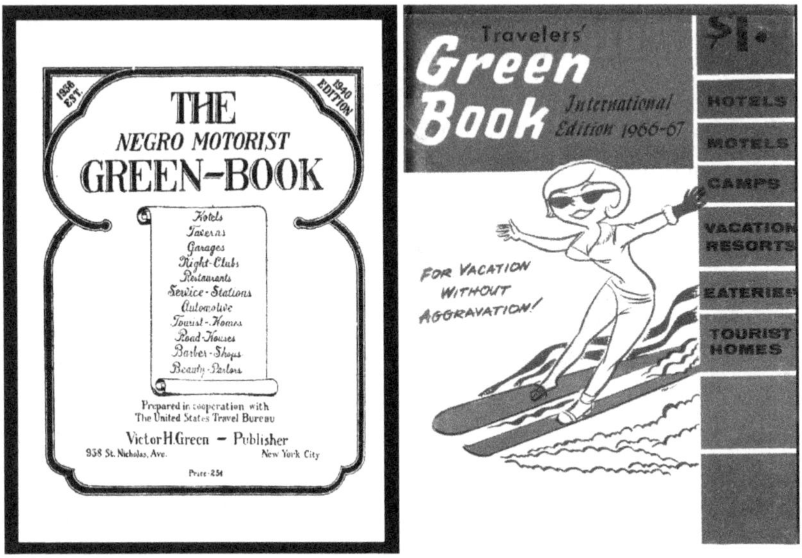

Front covers of 1940 and 1966 editions of *The Green Books*. Hugo Green was aiming for a wider audience by 1966. Author's collection.

aggravation." Black readers understood what "aggravation" meant. All the book's listings were still for the comfort and convenience of black travelers. It was the last year the *Green Book* was published.[6]

Its demise reflected the changing times. At least legally, blacks could now eat and stay anywhere they wanted. The downside of the new freedom was that many of the familiar black establishments went out of business, unable to compete with more genteel white establishments. It was only race loyalty and habit that kept some of them open. The writing was on the wall when the Clover Motel sold in 1963, advertised at the time as "Colored property" with "great potential." It was finally erased from history with the completion of the North-South Freeway (I-35W) through the heart of the Rock Island Bottom.[7]

Today, the *Green Book* is just a movie, but in its day it was the field guide of the African-American traveler. One of its last vestiges of that era was Green Acre Courts in Dallas, in the 1940s and '50s the premier "motor lodge" for black travelers on the east side of the Trinity looking for an air-conditioned room and a hot shower. Long after it closed, amidst some talk of trying to save the place as a historic landmark, it was demolished in 2017. By putting a spotlight on the book, the movie made it a collectors' item. In 2019 a well-worn copy of the 1958 edition sold for $27,500 at auction. A pristine copy of one of the early editions sells for many times that amount if one can even be found.[8]

Chapter 29

Dark Days on Both Sides of the Trinity

It was the summer of 1950, and the modern civil rights movement was still four or five years in the future. Sad events on both sides of the Trinity River offered a foreshadowing of what was to come in a fateful conjoining of news stories that the white press took no notice of. But the *Dallas Express*, a black-owned newspaper, did. On page 1, right below a headline about the bombing of homes in Dallas's black neighborhoods, was a headline about the "massive crowd attend[ing] rites for Gooseneck."[1]

William Madison McDonald passed away in Fort Worth on Tuesday, July 11 at the age of eighty-four. Better known to whites and blacks alike as "Gooseneck Bill," he had been an African-American leader in social, political, educational, and fraternal circles for more than sixty years. Reportedly, he was the first black millionaire in Texas and certainly one of the first in the nation. He first came to Fort Worth about 1908, and with other Prince Hall Masons organized the Fraternal Bank & Trust, the first black-owned bank in Texas. For years it was the only bank in Fort Worth that would loan money to blacks.

McDonald was a leader in the Republican coalition of blacks and whites known as the "Black and Tan Alliance," having a voice in national conventions. It was at one of those conventions in 1896 that he was given the name "Gooseneck Bill" by a *Dallas Morning News* reporter. The name stuck and followed him the rest of his life. It was so accepted even the *Dallas Express* felt comfortable calling him that. The party elected him chairman of its state committee in 1904, a singular honor since he got both black and white votes. He was a spellbinding platform speaker, giving public speeches until four years before his death when he took ill. One of his last was at I.M. Terrell High School. As "kingmaker" of the black (Prince Hall) Texas masons, he exerted enormous influence and made a lot of money. Part of his legend is that when all the Fort Worth white banks were going bust in the Depression, they came to McDonald's Fraternal Bank & Trust to borrow money.[2]

In his last years McDonald lived with his fifth wife in a magnificent home in Terrell Heights. After standing-room-only funeral services at Mount Pisgah Baptist Church on July 16, 1950, he was buried in the (segregated) Trinity section of Oakwood Cemetery.

His death left a huge hole in the leadership of the black community, not just in Fort Worth but in all of Texas. He was the rare black man able to sit down and talk with white leaders, working out compromises that kept the peace and helped keep blacks safe in their neighborhoods. It was not equality, but it was better than the alternative. The peaceful relations he oversaw in Fort Worth for so many years would carry over after his death, paving the way for Martin Luther King Jr.'s historic visit in 1959 and school desegregation in the 1960s.

On the other side of the Trinity, even as the *Dallas Express* mourned the passing of McDonald, the newspaper expressed outrage over a recent series of bombings of African-American residences in south Dallas, aimed at keeping black home-owners

William M. "Gooseneck Bill" McDonald in his office at the Fraternal Bank & Trust. Author's collection.

out of white neighborhoods. Six houses had been dynamited in the previous six months, the most recent on Friday night, July 7. This brought the total number of bombings to twenty-five since they started in 1941, and to date, Dallas police had not made a single arrest. Thankfully, no one had been killed. The police investigation was literally clueless. The Texas Rangers had declined repeated requests to come to town to "assist" the police, saying local law enforcement had things under control and besides, local authorities had not invited them in. The local chapter of the NAACP begged Governor Allan Shivers to do something, and he flatly refused to even so much as offer a reward. It was Dallas's problem, he said. The *Dallas Express* warned ominously, "If Dallas authorities don't stop these bombings, we'll awake one morning with one of the worst kind of riots.... There will be killing."[3]

Fort Worth had experienced its own bombings of black homes on the Near South Side in 1925. That was just five years after the lynching of Fred Rouse by unnamed white night riders. This series of dynamite bombings was unrelated to Rouse's murder. In response, police promised to protect black residents from "dynamiters and night riders." They found no motives for the series of five bombings in nine months except the rapid transformation of the neighborhood from white to black and had no suspects. The bombings continued into 1926, and the city even offered a reward for information leading to the apprehension of the bomber(s), but that also produced no results. Fortunately, no one was killed, which may or may not have been what the bombers desired. By the 1930s peace reigned once again in the neighborhood now known as Terrell Heights (for black educator I.M. Terrell), and everyone was hoping it stayed that way. In 1950 Fort Worth leaders could pat themselves on the back that their city had enjoyed racial peace for twenty years.[4]

The Dallas epidemic of bombings from 1941-1950 ceased as mysteriously as it had begun, too, and peace returned to south Dallas. The authorities breathed a sigh of relief, probably glad that they had not been forced to make any arrests. Trying to prosecute white suspects would have provoked an ugly situation on both sides of the racial divide. Better that the crisis fizzled out of its own accord. Racial violence was averted in both Fort Worth and Dallas for a few more years. But as Bob Dylan would sing in the next decade, "The times they are a-changin'." The nation was four years from the *Brown* Supreme Court decision (ordering the desegregation of public schools) and five years from the Montgomery, Alabama, bus boycott. If Bill McDonald had lived so long, we can only wonder at what he would have thought of events and what he could have done. This was the same man who had once led the "Black and Tan Alliance" in the Republican Party, but whose message to his own people had always been to pull themselves up by their bootstraps without looking for help from whites or the government.[5]

Chapter 30

A Tale of Two Ritzes

Fort Worth has always been racially segregated since the beginning, but the lines became hard and fast with the arrival of Jim Crow toward the end of the 19th century. Jim Crow is the descriptive term for the patchwork of laws and ordinances that aimed to separate the races in everyday life despite constitutional protections guaranteeing equality. Local custom proved as effective as statutory law in maintaining separate facilities. For instance, Fort Worth had a White Elephant Saloon uptown and a Black Elephant Saloon in Hell's Half-acre whose names said all that needed to be said.[1]

Strict racial lines were drawn at all public venues. At theaters, for instance, it was not a matter of blacks being allowed to sit in the balcony or at the back; they were not admitted at all. In February 1911 a riot erupted at the Dixie Theater in the 1100 block of Main after the owner decided to start catering to black customers after white business fell off. On February 27, 1911, a mob of white men and boys who took exception to the new policy gathered in front of the theater to express their displeasure. After breaking out the windows and sending the

Seventh Street's "Show Row" at night. Courtesy Scott and Linda Jo Barker.

employees running for their lives, they turned their anger on the nearby black neighborhood centered on E. Ninth, rampaging for hours. The white police force did not interfere.[2]

Black and white theaters were still segregated by the 1920s when a wave of new theaters opened offering both vaudeville and silent films on the playbill. One of the most popular names for the new theaters was "the Ritz" because the name conveyed a sense of opulence. Ritz theaters opened all over Texas, in Dallas, Houston, Corpus Christi, Amarillo, and San Angelo, to name the most prominent.[3]

The Ritz name first appeared in Fort Worth in 1924 as a vaudeville venue whose opening act from September 3–6 was a musical revue by the University Club. That was followed on September 7 by "Adam and Eva" by the Ritz Stock Company in a two-week run. The theater was located at Tenth and Commerce,

Fort Worth's first Ritz Theater under construction, 1924. Newspaper clipping from author's collection.

which was called by the *Star-Telegram*, "the heart of the city's theatrical district" because seven vaudeville theaters and moving picture shows were within a block and a half. Ironically, this same area used to be the heart of Hell's Half-acre and even now marked the western edge of "Little Africa."[4]

Constructed of brick over a steel framework, the three-story structure cost $150,000 and boasted of being the city's "most modern show house with every comfort and convenience, including a pipe organ." It was also the largest with seating for 1,561 between the orchestra, family circle, and balcony, having a spacious ten inches between seats. The manager was Sam Bullmann, hired away from a Dallas theater to bring his "wide experience" to the new place. A program of plays for the coming season was published that included Broadway touring companies as well as popular standards.[5]

Everything about the place was first-class, which meant blacks not allowed. The only black person on the premises was the "negro porter" Henry Bragg who would have remained forever anonymous had he not been severely burned in a boiler-room explosion two months after the Ritz opened. The damage was slight, and the show was resumed an hour and a half later, but Henry was not so fortunate. Since he himself had no insurance, and the theater did not carry coverage, he was out of a job.[6]

The Ritz never lived up to expectations due to falling interest in vaudeville and the high costs of maintaining a resident stock company while also bringing in big-time traveling acts. Less than two years after the Ritz opened, Sam Bullmann and the Ritz Players gave up on Fort Worth and headed to Dallas where they went separate ways. The Ritz Players took up residence at the Circle Theater, and Bullmann found another employer, not the New Ritz Theater which opened as a "second-run" movie house on Elm St. in October 1928.[7]

In Fort Worth, the "Ritz" name was briefly appropriated by the Chamber of Commerce for their auditorium in 1926 before again falling into disuse. Meanwhile, Tenth St. between Main and Commerce remained a popular spot for theaters, including the Pantages (102 E. Tenth) which opened in 1921 and booked both vaudeville and films for the rest of the decade. In 1929 the chain of theaters bearing the Pantages name was bought by RKO, and Fort Worth's Pantages was renamed the New Liberty Theater. As the area around it declined, so did the theaters in the neighborhood, which coincided with a shift in clientele toward people unwelcome in the movie palaces uptown.[8]

The "Ritz" name was rescued from obscurity in 1940 for a black movie house at 911 Calhoun. This was not a problem legally because no one had the name copyrighted, and the Ritz theaters had never been a chain, just a popular name for theaters. What had changed was the surrounding neighborhood. What had formerly been "the heart of the theater district" was now the heart of the city's black business district. White folks did not venture into this area much anymore. Next door to the new Ritz at 915 Calhoun was the Gilton Building, named for its owner Robert Gilton, an African-American dentist.

While white audiences took their business to the trio of first-run theaters on Seventh St.—the Hollywood, Worth, or Palace—to see Hollywood blockbusters like *Gone with the Wind*, African Americans went to the Ritz Theater to see low-budget black films like *Marching On*, *Hi De Ho*, and *Stormy Weather.* And if white kids did not want to go downtown to one of the big three movie palaces, they could go to one of the neighborhood theaters like the Tower, Parkway, or Isis. Black Fort Worthers had no such choices. The Calhoun St. Ritz did not advertise in either of the city's two dailies. It stuck to the Como newspaper and word of mouth. This second Ritz theater closed in 1968 only to reopen in the next couple of years as the XXX-rated *Finne* [*sic*] Arts Theater, which never attracted sizable audiences because of its sexploitation film fare and dicey location. [9]

Unofficially, black movie patrons could sit upstairs at the Hollywood, Worth, Palace, and Majestic theaters, but they were not really welcome even there. The Majestic (Tenth and Commerce), the last respectable venue in the old neighborhood, was so down-at-the-heels by 1958 that management rented out the entire place for an appearance by Martin Luther King, Jr. (his only visit to Fort Worth). By the mid-1970s all the downtown theaters were closed. Ironically, the last to close, the Hollywood, in its final years hung on by catering to black audiences, showing such "blaxploitation" films as *Blacula*, *Super Fly*, and *Foxy Brown*.

The transformation of the "Ritz" from a name promising high-class entertainment to a name synonymous with low-rent movies, plebian patrons, and shabby surroundings was Jim Crow in a nutshell. In its first incarnation, the Ritz did not allow blacks in the door. In its second incarnation, whites avoided the place like the plague. The name on the marquee had not changed, only what it signified.

Chapter 31

Fort Worth Gets Air-Conditioned

Air conditioning came to Texas in the 1920s. One of the greatest inventions of the 20th century is as Texan as Dr. Pepper and Blue Bell ice cream. And like ice-cold Dr. Pepper and Blue Bell ice cream, it makes Texas livable in the summer. Without the luxury of air conditioning in our homes, our cars, and our workplaces, Texas would still be a big, empty state.[1]

Before we began calling it "air conditioning" it was known as "refrigeration" or "washed air cooling." "Washed air cooling" was the preferred term until the mid-20th century. It was a gift from the gods. Before air conditioning, Texans had to find other ways to cool off in the summer. Sleeping porches and slow-turning ceiling fans were about the only ways to fight the Texas heat. One of the main reasons to have a porch on your house was to set up your bed there at night to catch whatever cooling breeze there was. Ceiling fans were mostly good for moving the hot air around; they did not really do much to cool. Before air conditioning, state-of-the-art buildings boasted of steam heat, elevators, and hot-and-cold running water on every floor. Summer heat is one reason why

Southerners ate their big meal of the day in the cooler evening hours. The wealthy had slaves/servants to stand around the room with large fans to fan the diners.

Conventions in Fort Worth in the summer could be miserable. In 1916, when the state Constables' Association came to town in August for their annual convention, they first met in the Chamber of Commerce auditorium. The second day they moved their sessions from the Chamber of Commerce auditorium to the Courthouse "where it is cooler," and still adjourned their daily sessions after that from 11:00 AM to 2:00 PM "because of the heat." Where attendees went during those three hours to find relief is anyone's guess. At best, they might find a quiet bar where they could have a cool brew or two.[2]

The wealthy enjoyed a primitive form of air conditioning that kept their homes pleasant on all but the hottest days. It consisted of blowing air over large blocks of ice through ducts that carried the cooled air throughout the house. Of course, the house had to be constructed with the necessary ductwork for this to work, such as the palatial home of Tom and Electra Waggoner on 1200 Summit, built in 1913.[3]

Things started looking up for ordinary folks when Willis Carrier came along. Carrier, a New Yorker, invented the modern air-conditioning unit in 1902 by reversing the traditional heating process—blowing air through hot coils—to blow air through coils filled with cold water. By cooling the air, his invention could also control humidity, an important consideration in southern climes. Invented as a manufacturing process, the Carrier air conditioner would go on to revolutionize living conditions for the masses. He formed the Carrier Air Conditioning Company of America to meet the demand for his invention. It took Stuart W. Cramer of Charlotte, North Carolina to coin the term "air conditioning" when he patented a process for adding moisture to the air, but as far as Texans are concerned, Willis Carrier is the hero of the story.

Air conditioning first made an impact on the theater business. Whether vaudeville or movie houses, trying to keep hundreds if not a thousand or more people comfortable for two or more hours caused most venues to close for the summer months or at least cut back to evening hours only. The fluttering of fans and handkerchiefs during a show was a familiar distraction to audiences. A stuffy theater was especially tough in an era when both sexes routinely dressed to the nines when going out in public, no shorts and T-shirts.

The history of air conditioning is usually dated from 1924 when Willis Carrier tested an improved air conditioning system in three Texas theaters owned by Will Horowitz, Jr., one in Dallas and two in Houston. Between June and August that year, he installed his "centrifugal refrigerating apparatus" in Dallas's Palace theater, proclaiming it the first theater in the country to have the system. The Palace advertised that its interior "weather" was "cool and clear," terms that were new to theater goers. As an added benefit, the system was so easy to operate, the janitor could run it.[4]

Despite Carrier's claim to be the father of air conditioning, Texas theaters had already invested in other systems. In 1921 the new Pantages vaudeville theater in Fort Worth (Tenth St. between Main and Commerce) boasted of every seat being "upholstered in leather." It was a good thing the theater was also "cooled by an elaborate system of air washing, giving it an even temperature the year round" because otherwise the prospect of sitting among 2,599 other patrons on leather seats in July and August was enough to kill attendance during the summer months. In 1922 a "washed air cooling system" was installed in Dallas's new Capitol theater (1521 Elm). The installation was done by the Hosch Rotary Air Conditioning Co. There is no record of how much it cost or how well it worked, but since the Capitol opened in December it had several months to work out the kinks before the summer arrived. The theater seated 1,200 persons, which was a daunting challenge to an untried technology. It must have performed up to expectations because in June 1925 the Capitol was able to boast that the temperature inside was "at all times as cool and breezy as a mountain top." By then it had been joined by Dallas's Majestic Theater, which boasted of being "the coolest spot in town" with "cool, clean, pure air in constant circulation."[5]

In the 1920s, Karl Hoblitzelle's Interstate Theater chain (vaudeville) pioneered the use of air conditioning in Texas to keep its theaters open year-round. Hoblitzelle was a modern-thinking theater operator in more ways than one. He was also the first in the Southwest to install sound systems in his theaters. He owned the Majestic in Fort Worth just as he owned the Majestic in Dallas, which explains why the same acts were booked successively into both houses.[6]

In another twenty years, portable "washed air cooling units" were available for home use for only about $120. Inclusion of central air conditioning in new-home plans was still a few years away.[7]

The new movie palaces naturally followed the lead of their vaudeville predecessors. The Worth Theater set the standard for entertainment luxury when it opened in 1927, boasting of being "cooled by Fort Worth's finest refrigeration system." In fact, it was the first Fort Worth building designed with a central air-conditioning system. No surprise, it was the most popular vaudeville stage and movie palace, more popular than the Majestic, the Hollywood, or the Palace theaters because it was the first. The Hollywood opened one block away in April 1930 with central air conditioning. The Majestic and the Palace had to be retrofitted to compete with the newer show palaces.[8]

Other Fort Worth buildings took their cue from the theaters, but it took time to incorporate air conditioning into design plans and budget for it. The 18-story Medical Arts Building (1927) was not air conditioned, nor was the 19-story Electric Building above the ground floor, opening two years later. The ground floor of the Electric Building was occupied by the Hollywood theater. Office workers above had to swelter. Even the 21-story Blackstone "luxury hotel" that opened in 1929 and the 16-story Aviation Building that opened in 1930 (Main and Seventh) relied on ceiling fans and exterior windows. The design of buildings with windows that opened and closed continued for many years, even after central air conditioning became standard, showing that design lagged far behind technology. The beautiful Aviation Building, which stood until 1978, tried to catch up with the times in later years with window units hung from the windows, aesthetics be damned. The historic moment for Fort Worth office buildings and their perspiring workers came with the opening of the Sinclair Building in 1930. It was touted by its builders as "the very last word in a modern office

(a) Willis Carrier, the father of air conditioning. Author's collection.
(b) Moviegoers to the Worth in 1932 could watch *Tarzan* in air-conditioned comfort. Courtesy Dalton Hoffman.

building." In addition to automatic, high-speed elevators and a marble lobby, it was "cooled by refrigeration" – at least the first two floors were. On floors three through sixteen, employees of Sinclair Oil, Cantey & Hanger law firm, and others, all of them wearing standard business attire of the day, had to sweat. They also had to fight the dust and insects that came in through open windows.[9]

After Seventh Street's "Show Row" set the standard, air conditioning became virtually a requirement for any theater that wanted to compete. The New Isis, which opened on North Main in 1936, boasted of being "cooled by refrigeration" as well as showing color films, another novelty at the time. It was the first neighborhood theater in Fort Worth to offer such luxury. The demand for air conditioning only grew. When it opened in 1941, the Motor Inn on U.S. Highway 80 (5200 Camp Bowie) boasted of being the city's first "modern suburban tourist hotel" in order to coax travelers away from the big downtown hotels. It was air conditioned besides having a restaurant and telephones in all fifty rooms, all for $2.50 a night double occupancy. The Motor Inn was also victimized by bad timing. World War II and rationing came along a only few months after it opened, severely cutting into the tourist trade that it hoped to attract.[10]

In 1934 under Gov. Miriam "Ma" Ferguson, Texas mounted a public-funded "campaign" to introduce air conditioning statewide. The state was mired in the Depression and officials were desperate to attract convention business. The campaign was more than a public relations gimmick. The new air-conditioning industry was eager to install the expensive equipment and considered Texas a prime market for its product. Industry-produced surveys showed that theaters, hotels, restaurants, barber shops, banks, and retail stores would all see a big boost in business. Officials still shuddered when they remembered the 1928 Democratic National Convention in Houston where delegates had to swelter through triple-digit temperatures and Gulf Coast humidity. Industry promoters claimed the equipment was being installed by restaurants at such a pace that even those places with no lack of business were being forced to air condition just to keep up with their competitors. Air conditioning was both practical and the latest thing, like the automobile and home appliances before it.[11]

Still, central air conditioning remained a luxury for the privileged few for many years, long after the mechanical kinks had been worked out of the technology. Koslow's, the Fort Worth business where fashionable ladies stored their furs during the warm months of the year, installed "below-freezing storage vaults" in 1945. They also advertised their retail sales by boasting, "Our show rooms are refrigerated air-conditioned," confusing redundancy with repetition. Elected officials had to be more cost-conscious when putting up public buildings. Fort Worth's City Hall was not air conditioned when it was built in 1938. Decades later those working there still had to settle for outside window units to get a little relief from summer heat. Likewise, county employees who worked in the 1895 courthouse had to rely on small units until central air was installed as part of the building's renovation in 1982-83. The noisy units were a jarring sight hanging from outside windows and in transoms in inside hallways. Fortunately, for those with business in county and district courts, the courtrooms got central air in 1959 when Porter Engineering Co. put condensers on the roof and "air handlers" in every courtroom. Fort Worth public schools remained sweat boxes for their students and teachers through the 1960s while principals and their staffs were blessed with air conditioning. Getting sent to the office was almost a joy. One of the big attractions when Fort Worth Country Day and Trinity Valley prep schools opened in 1963 and 1959 respectively, besides the all-white student body and top-drawer academics, was air-conditioned classrooms.[12]

Air conditioning fundamentally changed daily life in Texas though it took decades. Like other new technology, it was adopted from the top down, first by high-end businesses and wealthy homeowners before eventually becoming available to the masses. This author remembers growing up in the Oakhurst neighborhood in the 1950s. We got air conditioning when my father put a window unit in the master bedroom. When our parents were not at home, my sister and I would sneak into their bedroom and plop ourselves down in front of the cold air. It ranked right up there with television as the greatest inventions ever.

Chapter 32

Those Old Neighborhood Theaters Bring Back Memories

Fort Worth got its first purpose-built movie house in 1910, the Odeon at 1004 Main showing silent one-reelers. Admission was a nickel. Within a few short years there were five movie houses downtown, including the Odeon. In those days going to the movies meant dressing up and going downtown. There were small houses off the main drag, then came the big movie palaces on Seventh St. in the 1920s, the Palace (1919), the Worth (1927), and the Hollywood (1930). As the city grew outward and new neighborhoods were planted, people no longer wanted to have to go downtown to see a movie. Thus, the neighborhood theater was born.[1]

Neighborhood theaters served a different audience, younger, more casually dressed, with less money in their pocket, willing to pay to see second-run features and B-studio releases. They had to eschew certain amenities offered by the downtown houses in the early years, such as a "fully staffed nursery" and a squad of ushers patrolling the auditorium with flashlights. Every theater was a single-screen theater in those days. The big movie palaces had bigger screens and better sound systems. The neighborhood houses did their best business on weekends when the kids were out of school. For those of a certain age (baby-boomers) who grew up in Fort Worth in the 1950s and early '60s, there was no better way to spend a Saturday afternoon than sitting in a darkened movie theater watching a double-feature. This was before Six Flags and water parks seduced us outdoors during those long, hot summers. There was always a neighborhood theater close enough to walk to, admission was pocket change, and our parents were glad to get us out of the house for a few hours. No one worried about the bogey man lurking in a darkened theater.[2]

The names of those old neighborhood theaters still reverberate in our memories. For baby-boomers their names evoke the smell of fresh popcorn and big-screen action. Depending on where you lived you could never forget the Tower, Parkway, New Isis, Bowie, 7th Street, Heights, Grand, Poly, Varsity, and Tivoli, just to name the most prominent. Every neighborhood had at least one. You did not need to trek all the way downtown to the Hollywood, Worth, or Palace on "Show Row." These little local venues had everything a kid wanted. Sure, they showed B-movies and second-run features, but who cared? Plus, there was almost always a cartoon or two.

Fort Worth's first neighborhood theater predated by many years double features, Bugs Bunny and Roadrunner, too. It was the Isis Theater on North Main, which opened about 1915 to serve the North Side. It was a movie theater from the beginning, not a vaudeville house, reportedly selling as many as 3,200 tickets (all showings) on a typical Sunday. And that was the problem; being open on Sunday violated the Sunday Closing Law. The Isis was the first movie theater convicted of violating a law that originally targeted saloons and dance halls, bringing a fine of $50 in corporation court. Less than a year later city fathers decided that seeing a movie did not violate the Sabbath after all like, say, going to a saloon, and called off the dogs.

They probably also noticed that the movie theaters provided a healthy boost to business on what had always been the slowest day of the week.[3]

In the 1920s most Fort Worthers still preferred to go downtown to see a movie. The Isis remained the city's only neighborhood theater. The 1930s changed all that, and that decade and the '40s saw a wave of neighborhood theater construction not equaled since. The Great Depression and World War II intensified people's desire to escape into the fantasy world of the movies. Vaudeville was virtually dead before the 1930s was half over, opening the door for small movie houses to fill the entertainment void. It did not hurt that it cost a lot less to run a movie theater than a vaudeville house because management did not have to book live acts. Then during the war gasoline and tires were rationed so it was nice to have a theater within walking distance. Most of the movie houses that went up in those years were part of the Interstate Theater circuit of Dallas, but a few were independently owned and operated.

When the New Tivoli on Magnolia opened in the summer of 1935, it was "the first deluxe neighborhood theater." Its success led to the White Theater (Hemphill) in 1940; the Rosen (Lake Worth) in 1941; the Bowie (Camp Bowie), and the Tower (Six Points in Riverside), all in 1942. The New Isis on North Main opened on March 27, 1936. (The original, 1914 Isis burned to the ground in 1935.) As new suburban communities grew to maturity, they built their own theaters, like Poly, Haltom City and River Oaks. Having a movie house was a sign that a neighborhood had arrived. Among all these houses was not a single hole-in-the wall joint. They all had marquees and box offices out front and well-stocked snack bars inside. Typically, they seated upwards of 700 with the New Tivoli seating 1,000 (240 in the balcony), and the Tower having "more neon out front than any other Fort Worth playhouse." They typically cost under $100,000 to construct and were run on the cheap using high school kids behind the concession stand and taking tickets. The Tower and Parkway were part of the 150-theater, state-spanning Interstate chain. The TCU on University Dr. was independent from the day it opened until it was demolished in the name of urban progress in 2006. The best kind of opening was to book a "Hollywood premier," but that was almost impossible for a small, neighborhood theater. Hollywood premiers tended to play the big downtown palaces.[4]

Their bread and butter were second-run films that had already played the downtown houses, foreign imports, and poverty-row releases from studios like Republic and Monogram. Many programs were aimed at the youth audience, which meant a lot of Italian sword-and-sandal epics with second-tier stars like Richard Egan, Rory Calhoun, and Steve Reeves. Who could ever forget *Hercules Unchained* or *The Colossus of Rhodes,* both 1960? Monster movies like American International's *Attack of the Crab Monsters* (1956) and Japanese releases like *Rodan* (1956) and *The Mysterians* (1957) were also big draws. Many of these were double features. *Attack of the Crab Monsters* was on the same bill as *Not of This Earth.* Two for the price of one! What kid could not get excited about that?

Each theater catered to its particular neighborhood. The Berry on Hemphill (formerly the White, named for its owners, not its admission policy) played Spanish-language films exclusively after 1961. Ditto for the Rose Marine Theater on North Main, which opened in 1943 to cater to its heavily Hispanic North Fort Worth neighborhood.[5] The New Isis, another North Side movie house within smelling distance of the Stockyards, catered to a tough crowd that liked violent films and slapstick comedies. At one point in the 1970s it ran nothing but kung fu films. The Grand Theater on Fabons had an exclusively black audience from nearby Terrell Heights and showed a lot of old "Negro cinema" features that would never play the white houses. The TCU Theater on University (1946–2006) mixed classy second-run features (*To Kill a Mockingbird* in 1964) with more “artsy” bookings (*Far from the Madding Crowd*), both aimed at the nearby university crowd. University students did not necessarily have more money in their pocket, but they had more refined tastes in film fare.

This writer’s personal favorite was the Tower at the intersection of Race, Riverside Dr., and Belknap. It was only 15 minutes (10 minutes by car) from our house in Oakhurst, and I was looking forward to the day I could ride my bicycle there when we moved across town after the third grade at Oakhurst Elementary. Now that I was a west-sider, the closest neighborhood theaters besides the TCU were the Bowie and the Ridglea. The latter was too big and fancy to qualify as a neighborhood theater. It ran first-run and “road show” features, which meant higher ticket prices and concessions. After all, they had to pay for all the fancy artwork in the lobby, too.

By the end of the 1960s, malls and multiplex theaters were driving the little neighborhood, single-screen theaters out of business. They died one-by-one, although the New Isis managed to hang on into the early 1980s. The obituaries for others, like the Interstate’s Parkway (Eighth Ave.) in 1964, said they were victims of “the city’s growth patterns.” Even the Big Three downtown show palaces, the Hollywood, Worth, and Palace, died before the 1970s were half over. Today, movie houses have ten or more different screens, reclining seats, and Dolby Surround Sound, and you can buy your ticket online. They also have concessions that cost more than a full meal at a nice restaurant used to cost. What they do not have is the magic of those old neighborhood theaters where you slapped down your quarter at the box office out front, bought your popcorn for 10¢ or maybe 15¢ (large with butter) then plopped down for three hours of air-conditioned thrills.

A handful of those old neighborhood theaters have been repurposed, none as theaters because they cannot compete with

(a) The Parkway Theater, undergoing remodeling, 1948. Courtesy Fort Worth Star-Telegram Collection, Special Collections, University of Texas at Arlington Library, Arlington, TX. (b) The old Berry neighborhood theater as it looks today, forty years after showing its last movie. Author's collection.

the multiplexes or giant screens and Dolby sound systems of the new auditoriums. The old Bowie Theater has been recycled as a bank, and the old Haltom Theater, which opened on December 28, 1941, is trying to make it as an art gallery. Rose Marine Theater is a live performance venue now. The rest are all gone or sit empty and crumbling, recalling an era that was magic to a kid with 25¢ in his pocket.[6]

Endnotes

Introduction

1. Knight's book was written from the material he gathered for the *Fort Worth Star-Telegram* Centennial Edition, October 1949, on which he served as editor.
2. *Fort Worth Star-Telegram*, June 16, 1909; and March 29, 1915. B.B. Paddock, ed., *History and Biographical Record of North and West Texas* (Chicago: Lewis Publishing Co., 1906), Vol. 1, p. 87.
3. *Fort Worth Morning Register*, September 8, 1901.
4. B.B. Paddock, ed., *History of Texas: Fort Worth and the Texas Northwest Edition* (Chicago: Lewis Pub., Co., 1922), Vol. 2, p. 871. This story became part of local lore thanks solely to Paddock. It is retold in Mack and Madeline Williams, eds., *In Old Fort Worth*, Texas Centennial Ed., Collected columns of the *Fort Worth News-Tribune* (Fort Worth: privately printed, 1986). See also Chapter 29 in this book for the story of the Spring Palace fire.
5. Fort Worth, the military post, closed in 1853, three years before Peak was born. *Fort Worth Morning Register*, July 19, 1899. *Fort Worth Star-Telegram*, June 8, 1922; and March 5, 1939 (obituary).

Chapter 1

1. Obituary, *Dallas Morning News*, March 4, 1939. *Fort Worth Morning Register*, July 19, 1899. *Fort Worth Star-Telegram*, March 5, 1939.
2. Howard W. Peak, *A Ranger of Commerce OR 52 Years on the Road* (San Antonio: Naylor Printing Co., 1929), pp. 164–65.
3. Peak, pp. 166–67.
4. Peak, pp. 168–69.
5. Peak, p. 169.
6. Peak, p. 169.
7. For Harris, see B.B. Paddock, ed., *History and Biographical Record of North and West Texas* (Chicago: Lewis Pub. Co., 1906), Vol. 1, p. 87. *Fort Worth Morning Register*, "Historical Edition," reprinting the reminiscences of Dr. C.M. Peak, no date, files of Ruby Schmidt, Tarrant County Archives.

8. Clay Perkins, *The Fort in Fort Worth* (Keller, TX: Cross-Timbers Heritage Publishing Co., 2001), pp. 147–48. For Jim Ned, see James Pratt, *Sabotaged* (Lincoln: University of Nebraska Press, 2020), p. 75.
9. Freeman's report and Merrill's letter are both reproduced in M.L. Crimmins, "Fort Worth Was an Early Army Post," *Frontier Times* 16, no. 4 (January 1939): 139–141.
10. Paddock, *History and Biographical Record of North Texas*, Vol. 1, pp. 87–88.
11. B.B. Paddock, *History of Texas: Fort Worth and the Texas Northwest Edition* (Chicago: Lewis Pub., Co. 1922), Vol. 2, pp. 877–78.
12. For Daggett, see *Fort Worth Record*, September 4, 1913. For Holloway, see interview with Donna Roberts in *Fort Worth Record*, undated (*ca.* 1913) in vertical files of Fort Worth Library, Local History, Genealogy and Archives Unit; and *Fort Worth Star-Telegram*, May 29, 1921.
13. A fuller version of this story can be found in Richard Selcer, "Phantom Raiders on the Trinity," *Wild West Magazine* 26, no. 3 (October 2013): 54–60.

Chapter 2

1. The principal biographies of Courtright in order of importance are F. Stanley, *Longhair Jim Courtright: Two-gun Marshal of Fort Worth* (Denver, CO: World Press, 1957); Robert K. DeArment, *Jim Courtright of Fort Worth: His Life and Legend* (Fort Worth: TCU Press, 2004); and Richard F. Selcer, *Fort Worth Characters*, "Legendary Marshal Timothy Isaiah Courtright" (Denton: University of North Texas Press, 2009).
2. *Fort Worth Gazette*, February 2, 1886. *Dallas Morning News*, March 4, 1886; and February 9, 1887.
3. *Fort Worth Gazette*, April 2, 1886.
4. *Fort Worth Daily Gazette*, April 2 and 6, 1886.
5. *Fort Worth Daily Gazette*, April 2, 1886. *Dallas Morning News*, April 4, 1886. For the best account of the Buttermilk Junction shootout, see Richard F. Selcer and Kevin Foster, *Written in Blood: The History of Fort Worth's Fallen Lawmen, Vol. 1* (Denton: University of North Texas Press, 2010), pp. 88–115 (Chap. 5).
6. *Dallas Morning News*, April 24, 1886. *Fort Worth Gazette*, April 10, 1886.

7. *Fort Worth Daily Gazette*, May 7, 1886. *Dallas Morning News*, May 7, 1886.
8. *Dallas Morning News*, May 7, 1886.
9. *Dallas Morning News*, April 22 and 29, 1886; April 19, 1889.
10. *Dallas Morning News*, January 18, 1887.
11. *Dallas Morning News*, June 25 and December 22, 1887.
12. *Dallas Morning News*, February 9, 1887; and April 17, 1891.

Chapter 3

1. J.C. Terrell, *Reminiscences of the Early Days of Fort Worth* (Fort Worth: Texas Printing Co., 1906), p. 7. Gavin Wright, *Old South, New South* (New York: Basic Books, 1986), p. 35 (table 2.5).
2. I.C. Terry, "Reminiscences of Fort Worth Fifty Years Ago," 1929 unpublished MS, p. 1, Fort Worth Library, Central Branch, Local History, Genealogy and Archives Unit. Oliver Knight, *Fort Worth: Outpost on the Trinity* (Norman: University of Oklahoma Press, 1953), p. 116.
3. *Fort Worth Daily Gazette*, September 19 and 25, 1885. *Fort Worth Press*, May 4, 1944.
4. Janet Schmelzer, *Where the West Begins* (Northridge, CA: Windsor Publications, 1985), pp. 54–55. Bill Fairley, "Fiery Preacher Scoured Hell's Half-acre," *Fort Worth Star-Telegram*, June 25, 1997.
5. Howard W. Peak, *My Recollections of Fort Worth* (Fort Worth: privately printed, 1922), and serialized in the *Fort Worth Star-Telegram*.
6. *Fort Worth Star-Telegram*, January 28, 1973; February 12, 1989.
7. Daniel Vaughn, "The History of the Pig Stands," *Texas Monthly Magazine*, February 18, 2015.
8. *Fort Worth Star-Telegram*, October 21 and 28, 1995; January 19, 1996; April 12, 1997.
9. *Fort Worth Star-Telegram*, January 27, 2010.

Chapter 4

1. *Dallas Weekly Herald*, July 21, 1881.
2. *Fort Worth Star-Telegram*, January 17, 1915.
3. *Fort Worth Star-Telegram*, May 21, 1911; February 27, 1912; and January 22, 1915. *Fort Worth Daily Gazette*, May 22, 1885.

4. *Fort Worth Daily Gazette*, March 30, April 27 and October 4, 1884; July 1, 1889. Cissy Stewart Lale, *Sweetie Ladd's Historic Fort Worth* (Fort Worth: TCU Press, 1999), p. 20.
5. *Fort Worth Morning Register*, July 6, 1899. *Fort Worth Daily Gazette*, June 1, 1890; and June 26, 1893. Stewart Lale, p. 20. Mike Nichols, *Lost Fort Worth* (Charleston, SC: The History Press, 2014), pp. 113–15.
6. *Fort Worth Star-Telegram*, January 12, 1915. For Hogsett, see Ann Arnold, *History of the Fort Worth Legal Community* (Austin, TX: Eakin Press, 2000), pp. 8–9
7. *Fort Worth Star-Telegram*, January 15, 1915.
8. *Fort Worth Star-Telegram*, March 2, 1911.
9. *Fort Worth Star-Telegram*, August 25, 1912.

Chapter 5

1. *Fort Worth City Directory*, 1882, p. 9 (on microfiche and digitized, Fort Worth Library). The Quanah newspaper is quoted in the *Fort Worth Gazette*, June 23, 1887, the *Houston Post* in Ibid., December 7, 1888.
2. *Fort Worth Weekly Gazette*, June 26, 1890. For Will Rogers, see *Fort Worth Star-Telegram*, December 7, 1982. Rogers was speaking in 1936 about the construction of what became Will Rogers Memorial Coliseum. For Howard Peak, see Ibid., July 18, 1926.
3. Unnamed Texas editor in 1893, cited in Dee Brown, *Wondrous Times on the Frontier* (New York: Harper Perennial, 1992), p. 148. For Bolen, see *Fort Worth Star-Telegram*, December 10, 2006. Michael Q. Hooks, "The Role of Promoters in Urban Rivalry: The Dallas-Fort Worth Experience, 1870–1910," *Red River Valley Historical Review* 7, no. 2 (Spring 1982): 4–9.
4. Mack Williams, "Trunk Full of Gold from California," part of "In Old Fort Worth" series, [Fort Worth] *News-Tribune*, July 2–4, 1976, p. 22.
5. *Fort Worth City Directory*, 1882. *Fort Worth Morning Register*, June 14, 1902. Julia K. Garrett, *Fort Worth, A Frontier Triumph* (Fort Worth: TCU Press, 1996 reprint), p. 158.
6. *Fort Worth Daily Democrat*, September 25, 1880; June 5, 1881. *Dallas Daily Herald*, June 1, 1881; June 29, 1883. B.B. Paddock, History of Texas: *Fort Worth and the Texas Northwest Edition* (Chicago: Lewis Publishing Co., 1922), Vol. 2, pp. 508, 613. For Gulf, Colorado & Santa Fe, see *Galveston Daily News*, December 29, 1880; also cited in Harold Rich, *Fort Worth: Outpost, Cowtown, Boomtown* (Norman:

University of Oklahoma Press, 2014), p. 17. For Fort Worth & Rio Grande, see Ibid., p. 18; and *Fort Worth Daily Gazette*, February 5, 1889. Sandra Myres, ed., *Force without Fanfare: The Autobiography of K.M. Van Zandt* (Fort Worth: Texas Christian University Press, 1968), pp. 159–172 ("Steel Rails and Trolley Cars"). For Chamber of Commerce review of amounts paid, see *Fort Worth Star-Telegram*, January 9, 1917. Note: the exact amounts shelled out to the various railroads is not consistent in every source. *Cf. Fort Worth City Directory*, 1882, p. 9 (on microfiche and digital, Fort Worth Library). For Hovey, see *Makers of Fort Worth*(Fort Worth:Fort Worth Newspaper Artists' Association, privately printed, 1914;rare book collection, Fort Worth Library).

7. *Fort Worth Star-Telegram*, October 30, 1949, p. 2 "Our Growth" section.
8. *Fort Worth Gazette*, June 28, 1891. *Fort Worth Telegram*, November 7, 1902.
9. *Fort Worth Daily Gazette*, November 23, 1890. *Dallas Herald* quoted in Nancy Katherine Summers, "Struggle for Existence: Fort Worth, 1870–1876" (Master of Arts thesis, History Dept., Texas Christian University, 1968), p. 32.
10. Rod Evans, *Palaces on the Prairie* (Fargo, ND: North Dakota Institute for Regional Studies, North Dakota State University, 2009), pp. 179–180. For Peak, see *Fort Worth Star-Telegram*, August 13, 1922.
11. *Fort Worth Daily Gazette*, January 18 and 23 and February 3, 5, 10, and 19, 1889. *Fort Worth Weekly Gazette*, January 25 and February 1, 1889. *Dallas Morning News*, February 10, 1889.
12. Rich, pp. 57–59 and 69–79. *Fort Worth Weekly Gazette*, June 26, 1890. *Fort Worth Daily Gazette*, January 31, 1889.
13. For "faith in the city," see *Fort Worth Weekly Gazette*, July 4, 1889. Kennedy's comment was in the impromptu speech he made to a crowd in front of the Texas Hotel on the morning of November 22, 1963.
14. There is some dispute over exactly how much the memorial cost. A few years later the *Telegram* put the cost at $2,500. Surviving records, however, show a more realistic cost of $1,437. *Fort Worth Telegram*, April 8, 1905. *Cf. Fort Worth Star-Telegram*, May 25, 2008 (Metro section).
15. *Fort Worth City Directory*, 1882. *Fort Worth Star-Telegram*, January 13, 1922. For Paddock, see Rich, p. 91. For Swift and Armour, see Ibid., pp. 105–06.
16. Rich, pp. 105–06. *Fort Worth Register*, October 8, 1901.
17. Bud Kennedy, "A Blockbuster for Fort Worth Was Almost a Bankbuster," *Fort Worth Star-Telegram*, September 26, 2010.

18. For waterworks and streets, see Rich, pp. 37–39.
19. Contract between the Fort Worth Chamber of Commerce and the United States Army, National Archives Record Group 92, Records of the Office of the Quartermaster General, Entry 1998, No. 601.53. *Fort Worth Star-Telegram*, January 22, August 7, and December 16, 1917; December 7, 1982.
20. *Fort Worth Star-Telegram*, September 28, 1918.
21. Amon Carter had to sell off some of his oil properties in west Texas to pay off his part of the debt. Jim Gatewood, *J. Frank Norris, Top O'Hill Casino, Lew Jenkins, and the Texas Oil Rich* (Garland: Mullaney Corp. 2006), p. 133.
22. Harvey J. Graff, *The Dallas Myth* (Minneapolis: University of Minnesota Press, 2008), pp. 92–93, 125, and 129. Jack Z. Smith, "The City That Runs on Pro Bono," *Fort Worth Star-Telegram*, October 25, 1999; and Smith, "We've Taken It to the Limit in Fort Worth," Ibid., November 8, 1999.

Chapter 6

1. *Dallas Morning News*, May 31, 1890. *Cf.* reminiscences of Fort Worth resident Howard Peak, *Fort Worth Star-Telegram*, August 13, 1922, which differs in significant details. Sketches of the Spring Palace show the two staircases on the rear (south side) of the building, nothing on the east or west side.
2. B.B. Paddock created the myth that Hayne leaped from a second-story window, breaking both his ankles. B.B. Paddock, *History of Texas: Fort Worth and the Texas Northwest Edition* (Chicago: Lewis Pub., Co. 1922). It was perpetrated by Amos Melton in "Fire Hero Is Without Statue," *Fort Worth Star-Telegram*, March 30, 1930. For short biography of Hayne, see Richard F. Selcer, *Fort Worth Characters* (Denton: University of North Texas Press, 2009), pp. 88–106 (Chap. 5).
3. "Williams, J.," Tenth Census of the United States (1880), Tarrant County, Fort Worth, Enumerator District 89, sheet 6B, line 22.
4. *Fort Worth Daily Gazette*, June 4, 1890.
5. *Fort Worth Daily Gazette*, June 5, 1890. The Dallas newspapers did not mention Jesse.
6. *Dallas Morning News*, May 31, 1890. *Fort Worth Daily Gazette*, June 4, 1890. For other (white) heroes of the fire, see *Dallas Weekly Times Herald*, May 31, 1890. For number of injured, see "Federal Writers' Project," Research Data: Fort Worth and Tarrant County, Texas, Series I (Fort Worth Public Library Unit, 1941), Vol. 11, p. 4089.

7. The *Gazette* mentions "different theories" without blaming anyone in particular. *Fort Worth Daily Gazette*, June 4 and 5, 1890. *Cf.* the recollections of Clay Sandidge, a volunteer fireman interviewed by reporter Mack Williams for the *Fort Worth Press* many years later, and an account of the fire by *Star-Telegram* columnist Amos Melton also many years later. *Fort Worth Star-Telegram*, March 30, 1930. *Fort Worth Press*, May 27, 1957.
8. *Fort Worth Gazette*, June 3, 4, 5, and 6 1890. Selcer, *A History of Fort Worth in Black & White*, p. 128, fnt. 59.
9. *Fort Worth Telegram*, April 8, 1905. *Fort Worth Star-Telegram*, June 4, 1950 (AM ed.); March 30, 1930. *Fort Worth Press*, May 27, 1957.

Chapter 7

1. Erik Larson, *The Devil in the White City* (New York: Crown Publishers, 2003).
2. Adam Selzer, *H.H. Holmes: The True History of the White City Devil* (New York: Skyhorse Publishing, 2017), pp. 17–18, 21. Personal description of Holmes comes from A.E. Allen who spent time in jail with him, cited in *Dallas Morning News*, August 1, 1895.
3. Selzer, pp. 27–29.
4. Selzer, pp. 375–381.
5. Selzer, pp. 68–73, 147. For Massie, see Ibid., pp. 70–71.
6. "The Williams Girls," *Galveston Daily News*, December 6, 1895. Selzer, pp. 76–77, 145–46.
7. Selzer, pp. 86–90, 175.
8. *Galveston Daily News*, August 5, 1895. Selzer, pp. 92–96, 254–5. For Oak Cliff property, see Ibid., p. 99. For property's value, see Ibid., 113, 146.
9. Selzer, p. 95.
10. Selzer, pp. 95–96, 280.
11. *Dallas Morning News*, August 6, 1895.
12. *Fort Worth Daily Gazette*, November 21, 1894. Selzer, pp. 95–96.
13. Selzer, pp. 97–99.
14. "Built for Murder," *Dallas Morning News*, August 2, 1895.
15. Selzer, pp. 146–48.
16. *Fort Worth Daily Gazette*, August 1 and 29, 1895. William Capps was one-half the firm of Capps and Cantey, later to become the premier law firm of Capps, Cantey, Hanger & Short. He was also editor of the *Fort*

Worth Record in later years. In 1910 he purchased a mansion on "Quality Hill" (1120 Penn St.) that is still there today. *Galveston Daily News*, December 24, 1894; and August 22, 1895. Selzer, pp. 210–11, 265.

17. *Dallas Morning News*, August 1 and 2, 1895. *Galveston Daily News*, August 5, 1895.
18. Selzer, p. 290.
19. Skip Hollandsworth, *The Midnight Assassin* (New York: Henry Holt & Co., 2015), pp. 3–4 *ff*. "An American Ripper," *The History Channel Magazine*, 2018, pp. 71–79.
20. Joseph C. Terrell, *Reminiscences of the Early Days of Fort Worth* (Fort Worth: Texas Printing Co., 1906), p. 11.
21. *Fort Worth Morning Register*, February 14, 1897; October 10, 1900. *Fort Worth Telegram*, April 5, 1905; February 17, 1907.
22. *Fort Worth Morning Register*, June 20, 1897; November 15 and December 3, 1900. *Dallas Morning News*, November 5, 1900. *Fort Worth Telegram*, February 17, 1907. *Fort Worth Star-Telegram*, April 28, 1918. For Cromer, see Ibid., April 23, 1980.

Chapter 8

1. As in so many cases, judging by the record, he settled out of court. *Dallas Morning News*, January 12, 1890.
2. Retrospective in *Cleburne Times-Review*, February 24, 1929. For other encounters between people, animals and the Interurban, see *Fort Worth Morning Register*, November 27, 1900; and *Dallas Morning News*, July 29, 1900. For "Tom Powell," see Kevin Foster, "A Little Bit of FWPD History," *SIGNAL 50*: The Newsletter of the Fort Worth Police Officers Association (4th Quarter, August 2013): 36.
3. For bell, see *Dallas Morning News*, May 16, 1894 (re: W.F. Lake's accident). For track conditions, see *Fort Worth Telegram*, December 6, 1908. For Chicago study, see *Fort Worth Star-Telegram*, June 3, 1910. For Jim Crow protocol, see *Fort Worth Telegram*, July 29, 1907.
4. *Fort Worth Star-Telegram*, February 26, 1915.
5. *Dallas Morning News*, January 12, 1890.
6. For use of these strategies in the case of recent train accidents, see *Dallas Times Herald*, November 16, 1890.
7. *Fort Worth Star-Telegram*, February 26, 1915. *Fort Worth Gazette*, April 30, 1895.

8. For New York case, see *Fort Worth Telegram*, March 21, 1906.
9. *Fort Worth Star-Telegram*, April 14, 1912; and April 11, 1910. For the dangers of horse-drawn vehicles vs. streetcars, see *Dallas Morning News*, May 23, 1900; and *Fort Worth Star-Telegram*, April 11, 1910. For inquests, see, for example, *Fort Worth Telegram*, April 19, 1907. For box scores, see, for example, *Fort Worth Star-Telegram*, July 31, 1910.
10. *Fort Worth Gazette*, April 30, 1895.
11. *Fort Worth Telegram*, July 29, 1907. *Fort Worth Star-Telegram*, December 17 and 20, 1909; April 14, 1912.
12. *Fort Worth Star-Telegram*, January 18, 1920.
13. *Fort Worth Star-Telegram*, June 23 and December 5, 1918.
14. By 1907, most write-ups used the term "streetcar" instead of the more old-fashioned "trolley." Generally, only writers trying to sound high-brow still used the older term. *Fort Worth Telegram*, November 29, 1907.
15. For Doughty, see *Dallas Morning News*, March 10, 1918. For Shiel, see Ibid., July 20, 1906. For Warren, see *Fort Worth Star-Telegram*, May 7 and 8, 1919; and *Dallas Morning News*, May 18, 1919. For Shiel, see Ibid., July 20, 1906. For "three officers," see *Fort Worth Star-Telegram*, August 9, 1920.
16. Bill Fairley, "Waples Left Business, Civic Legacy," *Fort Worth Star-Telegram*, May 11, 2005.
17. *Fort Worth Star-Telegram*, June 23, 1918.
18. For Dial, see *Dallas Morning News*, March 31, 1890. For Edrington, see *Fort Worth Star-Telegram*, May 7, 1915. *Weatherford Daily Herald*, May 7, 1915.
19. *Dallas Morning News*, November 17, 1913, pages 2 and 11.
20. *Fort Worth Evening Telegram*, February 1, 1905. *Fort Worth Star-Telegram*, June 28, 1912; and July 27, 1915.
21. *Dallas Morning News*, April 12, 1890.
22. *Fort Worth Star-Telegram*, February 13, 15, and 28, 1912. *Dallas Morning News*, February 28, 1912.
23. *Dallas Morning News*, May 16, 1894. *Fort Worth Star-Telegram*, July 11, 1917.
24. *Fort Worth Telegram*, July 5, 1905.
25. Charles Swartz was buried in Oakwood Cemetery but whatever marker was placed on the grave had long since disappeared before a new granite marker was installed in

2013. Richard F. Selcer, *Photographing Texas: The Swartz Brothers, 1880–1918* (College Station: Texas A&M University Press, 2019), pp. 30–31.

26. *Fort Worth Star-Telegram*, April 25, 1916. Mike Nichols, "James F. Moore House: A Quality Hill Survivor," Hometown by Handlebar website, https://hometownbyhandlebar.com, posted February 7, 2020.
27. *Fort Worth Star-Telegram*, June 2, 1911.

Chapter 9

1. Desirable attributes comes from a column in the *Pittsburgh Dispatch*, 1881, quoted in Brooke Kroeger, *Nellie Bly: Daredevil, Reporter, Feminist* (New York: Times Books, 1994).
2. *Weekly Houston Telegraph & Texas Register*, January 27, 1838.
3. Lt. Sam Starr to wife, January 6, 1850, Richard Selcer, *The Fort That Became a City* (Fort Worth: Texas Christian University Press, 1995), p. 94.
4. John Jay Good Papers, University of Texas at Arlington Special Collections, cited in *Fort Worth Star-Telegram*, October 21, 2019.
5. Florence Peak to Kitty Barry, *Fort Worth Star-Telegram*, June 6, 1912.
6. The *Denver Republican* story was reprinted in the *Fort Worth Gazette*, January 1, 1889.
7. *Fort Worth Gazette*, September 16, 1894.
8. The *Journal*'s research said nothing about teaching. *Fort Worth Daily Gazette*, September 11, 1883. (The *Journal of Commerce* was out of St. Louis, MO.)
9. *Fort Worth Morning Register*, June 29, 1902.
10. *Fort Worth Telegram*, October 27, 1907.
11. *Fort Worth Star-Telegram*, July 9, 1909.
12. *Fort Worth Star-Telegram*, October 30, 1916.

Chapter 10

1. *Fort Worth Star-Telegram*, April 24, 1960.
2. George W. Engelhardt, *The City of Fort Worth and the State of Texas* (Fort Worth: Geo. W. Engelhardt & Co., 1890), p. 97. *Dallas Morning News*, May 7, 1889. *Fort Worth Morning Register*, August 4, 1901.

3. See Davidson's obituary, *Fort Worth Star-Telegram*, October 27, 1924.
4. *Fort Worth Telegram*, September 27, 1905; August 24 and September 25, 1906.
5. *Fort Worth Telegram*, March 4, 1909. *Fort Worth Star-Telegram*, April 17 and August 27, 1913; June 23, 1915; January 20, 1921; April 24 and December 5, 1922.
6. *Fort Worth Star-Telegram*, April 17, 1913. For slogan, see Ibid., May 29, 1921.
7. *Fort Worth Telegram*, March 11, 1906. *Fort Worth Star-Telegram*, April 17, 1913; February 22, 1916.
8. *Fort Worth Star-Telegram*, November 21, 1915 (pp. 24 and 35).
9. For description of Ragtime Chocolates, see *Dallas Morning News*, February 11, 1962. For description of Millionaires, see *Fort Worth Star-Telegram*, February 8, 2016.
10. *Fort Worth Star-Telegram*, June 11, 1922; December 27, 1925. Camp Bowie info comes from Jim Atkinson, a former officer of Pangburn's. Atkinson to Jack White, June 7, 2010.
11. *Fort Worth Star-Telegram*, May 6, 2002. *Chamber of Commerce Magazine*, April 1947, p. 15.
12. *Fort Worth Star-Telegram*, May 23, 1913; December 22, 1916; February 18 and October 26, 1919; November 1, 1920; and December 19, 1942. Carol Roark, "Early Greek Residents of City Were Thankful Americans," *Fort Worth Star-Telegram*, Nov. 24, 2019. Additional information by email from Roark, December 31, 2019.
13. *Fort Worth Star-Telegram*, June 23, 1915. *Dallas Morning News*, August 11, 1948 (John King's obituary). The decline and fall of Pangburn's can be followed in the newspaper. *Fort Worth Star-Telegram*, February 2 and 21, 1999. For bacterial contamination, see Ibid., March 31, 1978.

Chapter 11

1. "The Rest Is History," Fort Worth Star-Telegram, December 7, 1982. Michael Collins, Those Daring Young Men: A History of the Automobile Pioneers in Fort Worth, 1902–1940 (Fort Worth: Frank D. Kent and The Fort Worth News-Tribune, 1985), pp. 6–7. Fort Worth Telegram, June 8, 1904.

2. Fort Worth Telegram, March 12, 1905. Dallas Morning News, October 10 and 25, 1906; and May 2, 1907. Makers of Fort Worth , (Fort Worth: Fort Worth Newspaper Artists' Association, privately printed, 1914; rare book collection, Fort Worth Library).
3. Dallas Morning News, January 26, 1907. For first speeder, see Ibid., October 10, 1948. Fort Worth Telegram, May 28, 1907. Collins, p. 12.
4. Fort Worth Star-Telegram, December 8, 1909; and July 27, 1911. For Sanguinet, see Fort Worth Telegram, July 11, 1904.
5. Collins, p. 12. Fort Worth Star-Telegram, June 17 and October 12, 1909. For Vernon, see Ed Wallace, "Frontier Motorists," Ibid., February 10, 2013, p. 1H.
6. Fort Worth Star-Telegram, August 24 and September 20, 1911.
7. Collins, p. 12.
8. Fort Worth Star-Telegram, March 16, 1910. Samuel E. Kinch, "Amon Carter: Publisher-Salesman" (Master of Arts thesis presented to Journalism Dept., University of Texas, 1965), pp. 86–87.
9. Dallas Morning News, July 10, 1909. Fort Worth Record, June 19, 1919. Fort Worth Star-Telegram, July 24, 1919.

Chapter 12

1. *Fort Worth Daily Gazette*, September 14, 1893.
2. *Fort Worth Gazette*, April 10, 1891; and January 31, 1892.
3. *Fort Worth Gazette*, September 14 and December 7, 1893.
4. *Fort Worth Gazette*, December 7, 1893.
5. *Fort Worth Morning Register*, August 14, 1897. For peddler problem, see *Fort Worth Telegram*, April 4, 1906.
6. *Fort Worth Morning Register*, August 14, 1897. *Fort Worth Telegram*, April 4, 1906.
7. *Fort Worth Telegram*, April 4, 1906.
8. For tree, see *Fort Worth Star-Telegram*, September 6, 1912.
9. *Fort Worth Star-Telegram*, April 30, and September 6 and 8, 1912; October 17, 1916.
10. *Fort Worth Star-Telegram*, September 8, 1912; January 22, 1917.
11. Carol Roark, ed., *Fort Worth & Tarrant County, An Historical Guide* (Fort Worth: Texas Christian University Press, 2003), p. 64.

Chapter 13

1. *Fort Worth Telegram*, December 28, 1904. The *Star* and the *Telegram* were separate newspapers until 1909. Oliver Knight, *Fort Worth, Outpost on the Trinity* (Norman: University of Oklahoma Press, 1953), p. 172.
2. Roze McCoy Porter, *Thistle Hill: The Cattle Baron's Legacy* (Dallas: Taylor Publishing Co., 1980), pp. 83, 130. For Electra's relationship with working-class girls, see Ibid., p. 99.
3. *Fort Worth Telegram*, December 20, 1906. *Dallas Morning News*, December 22, 1906. Porter, pp. 93 and 95.
4. *Fort Worth Telegram*, December 20 and 21, 1906. *Dallas Morning News*, December 20, 1906. For the ever-changing value of the jewels, see *Fort Worth Telegram*, December 20 (pp. 2 and 7), 31, 1906; and April 7, 1907; and *Dallas Morning News*, January 1, 1907.
5. *Fort Worth Telegram*, December 23, 1906.
6. *Fort Worth Telegram*, December 31, 1906. *Dallas Morning News*, January 1, 1907. For "sweating," see *Fort Worth Star-Telegram*, April 24, 1907.
7. *Fort Worth Telegram*, December 31, 1906 (p. 8, 2nd of two stories). *Dallas Morning News*, January 1, 1907.
8. *Fort Worth Telegram*, January 2, 1907.
9. *Fort Worth Telegram*, February 4, 1907.
10. *Fort Worth Telegram*, April 17, 1907. For failure to seek an indictment, see *Fort Worth Telegram*, November 5, 1907.
11. *Fort Worth Telegram*, April 24 and November 5, 1907.
12. *Fort Worth Telegram*, November 5 and 13, 1907. For Mabel Palmer, madam, see *Fort Worth Star-Telegram*, July 20, 1915; and March 22, 1917.
13. *Fort Worth Telegram*, November 16, 1907. See also Chap. 12, "When Harry Houdini Appeared in Fort Worth."
14. *Fort Worth Telegram*, March 10, 1905; and April 6, 1910. The theory that Maddox's "inside job" was the Whartons themselves falls into the category of pure speculation.
15. Mr. Bencini also won a lawsuit against his insurance company over the value of the never-recovered jewels, setting their value at $6,600. *Fort Worth Star-Telegram*, September 28, 1914; December 13, 1915; and January 8, 1916.
16. *Fort Worth Telegram*, September 6, 7, and 9, 1909; October 26, 1910.

17. For the sale, see Porter, pp. 104, 111, and 122. The closing was not until March 1, 1911.
18. *Fort Worth Star-Telegram*, February 16, 1911.

Chapter 14

1. The slogan first appears on the August 15, 1923, edition of the newspaper. At the time, Carter was vice president and general manager of the *Star-Telegram*. He later bought it.
2. *Fort Worth Star-Telegram*, March 11, 1910; and August 5, 1915. *Fort Worth Record*, August 8, 1915.
3. In 1893 young Wisconsin history professor Turner delivered an address at the Chicago World's Fair entitled, "The Significance of the Frontier in American History" that said the frontier had for all practical purposes "closed" in 1890. His thesis set the template for all discussion of the American West thereafter.
4. *Dallas Morning News*, July 12, 1902.
5. For a fuller account of the case, see Richard Selcer and Kevin Foster, *Written in Blood, Vol. 1* (Denton: University of North Texas Press, 2010), pp. 173–186 (Chap. 7).
6. *Fort Worth Star-Telegram*, April 27, 1908.
7. For a full account of Ike Knight's case, see Selcer and Foster, *Written in Blood, Vol. 1,* pp. 227–259 (Chap. 10).
8. *Fort Worth Record*, December 22, 1920.
9. For a fuller account of the case, see Richard Selcer and Kevin Foster, *Written in Blood, Vol. 2* (Denton: University of North Texas Press, 2011), pp. 261–288 (Chap. 9).

Chapter 15

1. M.L. Crimmins, "Elliott Roosevelt's Visit to Texas in 1876–1877," *Texas State Historical Quarterly* 48, no. 2 (October 1944): 186. Crimmins references J. Bony Moore as being a part of that first Roosevelt hunt in Texas. Cf. "Teddy's Wolf Hunt Recalled," *Fort Worth Star-Telegram*, May 24, 1936. For Rough Riders, see H.W. Brands, *T.R., the Last Romantic* (New York: Basic Books, 1997), pp. 339–343. Edward Hake Phillips, "Teddy Roosevelt in Texas, 1905," *West Texas Historical Year Book* [*sic*] 51 (1980): 58–67.

2. *Fort Worth Telegram*, April 2, 3, 6, and 7, 1905.
3. *Fort Worth Telegram*, April 2 and 8, 1905. *Cf.* Dallas which gave him a first-class welcome but otherwise showed little interest in his trip. See "Jim Hog, Dallas," Ibid., April 8, 1905; and *Dallas Morning News*, April 3, 1905.
4. *Fort Worth Telegram*, April 2 and 8, 1905. It is some of Stohmeyer's photos that are in the Library of Congress today. For sectional tolerance, see Phillips, "Teddy Roosevelt in Texas," p. 59.
5. *Fort Worth Telegram*, April 8, 1905. For surrey and trotters, see Victor Petta's recollections in William E. Jary, ed., *Camp Bowie, Fort Worth, 1917–1918* (Fort Worth: B.B. Maxfield Foundation, 1975), p, 46. The story of the black children is in a sidebar on p. 1.
6. *Dallas Morning News*, April 6, 1905. *Fort Worth Telegram*, April 6 and 7, 1905. For Weatherford numbers, see *Dallas Morning News*, April 12, 1905. For crowd size, see *Fort Worth Telegram*, April 8, 1905.
7. President Roosevelt's Open Letter to U.S. Schoolchildren on the occasion of Arbor Day, April 15, 1907.
8. *Fort Worth Telegram*, April 8, 1905.
9. Joseph Bucklin Bishop, *Theodore Roosevelt's Letters to His Children* (New York: Charles Scribner's Sons, 1919), pp. 114 ff.
10. *Fort Worth Telegram*, April 2 and 10, 1905.
11. *Fort Worth Star-Telegram*, April 14; May 19 and 30; October 19; and November 24, 1905.
12. Will Rogers tree story comes from Mack Williams, "Thousands Turned Out to Welcome Teddy Roosevelt, FDR and Truman," *Fort Worth Star-Telegram*, October 30, 1949, Centennial Ed., p. 36 Merchandising section. Reporter John Henry perpetuates the story in "Teddy Roosevelt Visited Show in 1911," Ibid., February 1, 2012.
13. *Fort Worth Star-Telegram*, February 1, 2012.
14. *Fort Worth Star-Telegram*, March 8, 1919.

Chapter 16

1. Ann Arnold, *A History of the Fort Worth Medical Community* (Arlington, TX: Landa Press, 2002), pp. 18–20 (St. Joseph's), 81–82 (All Saints), 29–30, 34 (Medical School).
2. For costs, see Arnold, p. 19; and Mack Williams, *The News-Tribune*, July 204, 1976, p. 25.
3. *Fort Worth Morning Register*, May 26, 1901.

4. *Fort Worth Telegram*, May 29, 1904. Ad in *Fort Worth City Directory*, 1902.
5. *Fort Worth Star-Telegram*, May 26, 1901. Ad in *Fort Worth City Directory*, 1902.
6. *Fort Worth Star-Telegram*, May 21, 1903.
7. *Dallas Morning News*, April 4, 1909.

Chapter 17

1. A&M took over the program but refused to recognize the Wesleyan law school graduates who came before as A&M alumni with all rights and privileges. The backlash from that decision included a lawsuit by disgruntled Wesleyan graduates. *Fort Worth Star-Telegram*, August 14, 2015; November 13, 2017.
2. *Fort Worth Star-Telegram*, September 29, 1911; June 12, 1912; and September 21, 1913.
3. *Fort Worth Star-Telegram*, June 12, 1912; and May 7, 1915. *Dallas Morning News*, November 14, 1911; and May 28, 1912.
4. *Fort Worth Star-Telegram*, December 9, 1914.
5. *Fort Worth Star-Telegram*, November 16, 1912; September 16 and December 9, 1914. *Fort Worth Record*, September 26 and October 26, 1915; October 28, 1916; and November 18, 1921.
6. *Fort Worth Star-Telegram*, October 14, 1914.
7. For Moser, see *Dallas Morning News*, July 15, 1935.
8. *Fort Worth Star-Telegram*, October 14, 1914.
9. *Fort Worth Star-Telegram*, October 14, 1914.
10. TCU was not young historically, dating back to 1873, but it was young to Fort Worth, having returned to the city only in 1911. *Fort Worth Star-Telegram*, December 9, 1914.
11. *Fort Worth Star-Telegram*, May 21, 1920.

Chapter 18

1. Mack and Madeline Williams, eds, *In Old Fort Worth*, Texas Centennial Ed., Collected columns of the *Fort Worth News-Tribune* (Fort Worth: privately printed, 1986), p, 77. Bill Fairley, "In a Lurid Light," *Fort Worth Star-Telegram*, May 28, 1997. Simone C. De Santiago Ramos,

Fort Worth's Historic Hotels, Images of America series (Charleston, SC: Arcadia Publishing, 2013), pp. 27–28.

2. *Fort Worth Telegram*, January 11, 1903.
3. *Fort Worth Star-Telegram*, August 25, 1904.
4. *Dallas Morning News*, September 15, 1912. The full story of the Boyce-Sneed love triangle is told in Bill Neal, *Vengeance Is Mine* (Denton: University of North Texas Press, 2011).
5. *Fort Worth Star-Telegram*, October 11, 1913.
6. *Fort Worth Star-Telegram*, November 15, 1921.
7. *Fort Worth Star-Telegram*, December 9 and 10, 1922; January 31, 1923. *Dallas Morning News*, December 10, 1922.
8. *Fort Worth Star-Telegram*, March 15, 1932. *Dallas Morning News*, March 16, 1932.
9. *Fort Worth Star-Telegram*, March 29, 1932; March 5, 1936. *Dallas Morning News*, May 4 and September 16, 1932; May 25, 1933.
10. Blanton claimed self-defense, and a jury agreed at his trial three months later. *Fort Worth Star-Telegram*, January 22, 23, and 24, and April 27 and 29, 1910. *Dallas Morning News*, January 22, 23, 27, and 29, 1910.
11. *Fort Worth Star-Telegram*, November 28, 1922.

Chapter 19

1. Eva Bloore who goes on to become Tarrant County Judge Eva Barnes. Ann Arnold, *History of the Fort Worth Legal Community* (Austin, TX: Eakin Press, 2000), pp. 46047,
2. Fortunately for McLean's future political ambitions, the Fort Worth newspapers did not print his radical proposal. *Dallas Morning News*, February 23, 1900.
3. The sheriffs' resolution came on the occasion of their annual convention in Fort Worth. *Fort Worth Telegram*, July 20, 1904.
4. Juliet George, *Fort Worth's Arlington Heights* (Charleston, SC: Arcadia Publishing, 2010), p. 38.
5. Marsha Brown, "Weatherford Princess: The Mary Couts Burnett Story," *Parker County Today: Our County Magazine*, June 2013, pp. 81, 83. Several official website sources state incorrectly that she was committed in 1920.
6. "Mrs. Burnett's Mind Held Sound," *Fort Worth Star-Telegram*, July 5, 1922, p. 2. Burnett's family challenged the probated will that favored Mary, resurrecting the original verdict

of insanity. The family and TCU settled out of court. Brown, "Weatherford Princess," p. 85. Colby D. Hall, *History of Texas Christian University* (Fort Worth: Texas Christian University Press, 1947), pp. 185–86. Bill Neal, *From Guns to Gavels: How Justice Grew Up in the Outlaw West* (Lubbock: Texas Tech University Press, 2008), pp. 119–120. For Harris, see *Fort Worth Star-Telegram,* January 23, 1920; and July 4, 1942. For Slay, see Ibid., December 25, 1955 (obituary).

7. *Fort Worth Star-Telegram,* July 25, 1912.
8. *Fort Worth Star-Telegram,* July 25, 1912.
9. *Fort Worth Star-Telegram*, December 31, 1911; January 5, and February 6 and 7, 1912, *Dallas Morning News*, January 20, February 10, and November 26, 1912; February 26, 1913.
10. Fort Worth Star-Telegram, March 3, 12, and 14, 1912.
11. *Fort Worth Star-Telegram*, March 18, 1912.
12. *Fort Worth Star-Telegram*, September 15 and November 10, 1912.

Chapter 20

1. Vincent Giardino, *A Century of Seeking Justice* (Fort Worth: privately printed, 2019), p. 31.
2. Giardino, p. 30.
3. *Fort Worth Star-Telegram*, September 26, 1920.
4. Giardino, pp. 30–31.
5. *Fort Worth Star-Telegram*, December 5 and 18, 1902.
6. *Fort Worth Star-Telegram*, December 18, 1902.
7. *Fort Worth Star-Telegram*, November 8, 1915. Betty Trapp Chapman, *Rough Road to Justice* (Austin: State Bar of Texas, 2008), p. 12. For Mansfield, see address by Kerr County Court at Law Judge Susan Harris, quoted in *Kerrville Daily Times*, August 28, 2015.
8. *Fort Worth Star-Telegram*, January 5, 1915. For Swayne, see Richard Selcer, *Fort Worth Characters* (Denton: University of North Texas Press, 2009), pp. 220–235 (Chap. 12: "James W. Swayne, Straight-arrow Judge").
9. Chapman, p. 13.
10. Chapman, p. 43.
11. *Dallas Morning News*, August 10, 1948.

Chapter 21

1. Marsha Brown, "A British Castle in North Texas," *North Texas Star Storyteller & Rambler*, June 2009, p. 4.
2. Brown, pp. 7,8, 11.
3. Vernon received his pilot's license from the Aero Club of America on February 3, 1916. *Fort Worth Star-Telegram*, February 15, 1918. The newspaper says he purchased a Franklin roadster while he was in Fort Worth. Ibid., February 17, 1918.
4. The Westbrook roof garden was successor to the Wheat Building roof garden (1902–03) as the in-place to spend warm summer nights high above the city. *Fort Worth Star-Telegram*, July 26, 1911. For dance fads, see David Nasaw, *Going Out* (Cambridge, MA: Harvard University Press, 1993), p. 106. For black night clubs, see *Fort Worth Record*, June 24, 1913.
5. For "Westerners" see Eve Golden, *Vernon and Irene Castle's Ragtime Revolution* (Lexington: The University Press of Kentucky, 2007), p. 186. For court martial, see Commandants' Correspondence files, Carruthers Field, 1917, Dept. of the Army, Records of the Adj. General's Office, 1917 *ff.*, Record Group 407, National Archives and Record Administration.
6. Golden, pp. 184–85, 188.
7. Golden, p. 187. *Fort Worth Star-Telegram*, February 15 and 16, 1918. *Dallas Morning News*, February 16, 1918. Bill Fairley, "No pilot more dashing than Castle in WW I," *Fort Worth Star-Telegram*, May 21, 1997.
8. *Fort Worth Star-Telegram*, February 15 and 17 and March 1, 1918. *Dallas Morning News*, February 17, 1918.
9. Vernon Castle Blvd. was eventually renamed Vernon Castle Ave., which seemed more fitting for the little 14-block stretch that its namesake never set foot on, and his widow turned her nose up at. Irene died in 1969. Golden, pp. 226–27. Brown, pp. 12 and 14.

Chapter 22

1. Charles R. Perkins, "History of Fort Worth Lodge No. 148, A.F.&A.M, 1855–1955" (Thesis submitted to History Dept., Texas Christian University, in partial fulfillment of the requirements for the degree of Master of Arts, 1957). "First Masonic Hall in Fort Worth," *Fort Worth*

Star-Telegram, August 27, 1922. *Fort Worth Press*, February 25, 1973. Richard Selcer, "Fort Worth's First Masonic Hall, 1857–1878," Texas Historic Marker application, Tarrant County Archives. Joseph C. Terrell, *Reminiscences of the Early Days of Fort Worth* (Fort Worth: Texas Printing Co., 1906), p. 92.

2. Carter told his own story in one of the very few pieces he ever wrote, in response to a *Time Magazine* article about him that he took exception to. His lengthy "Letter to the Editor" appeared in the next issue on October 31, 1933.
3. "Amon G. Carter" in *Makers of Fort Worth* (Fort Worth: Fort Worth Newspaper Artists' Association, privately printed, 1914; rare book collection, Fort Worth Library).
4. Louie L. Hulme, ed., *Rotary Club of Fort Worth, 75th Anniversary, 1913–1988* (Fort Worth: privately printed, 1988), pp. 137–38.
5. Ben H. Procter, "Amon G. Carter, Sr.," *The New Handbook of Texas*, Ron Tyler, ed. (Austin: Texas State Historical Association, 1996), Vol. 1, p. 998. The latest biography of Carter is Brian A. Cervantez, *Amon Carter: A Lone Star Life* (Norman: University of Oklahoma Press, 2019).

Chapter 23

1. *Fort Worth Star-Telegram*, May 19, 1924.
2. *Fort Worth Star-Telegram*, November 6, 1924.
3. *Fort Worth Star-Telegram*, May 18 and 19; June 26; and November 6, 1924. For proposed memorial, see Ibid., October 27, 1919.
4. *Dallas Morning News,* July 29, 1924. *Fort Worth Star-Telegram*, October 18, 1924.
5. *Fort Worth Star-Telegram*, November 3, 6, 7, and 8, 1924. For newspaper names, see *Fort Worth Star-Telegram*, October 29, 1924 (Klan) and Ibid., March 23 and September 30, 1922. Norris and the Baptists could not have been unaware of the congruence; it could not have been mere coincidence.
6. *Fort Worth Star-Telegram*, June 5, 1925. For temporary quarters, see Ibid., January 1, February 13, April 17, and May 8, 1925.
7. *Fort Worth Star-Telegram*, October 23, 1925.
8. For sale, see *Dallas Morning News*, February 4, 1927. For name change, see *Fort Worth Star-Telegram*, January 24, 1929.
9. For wrestling, see *Fort Worth Star-Telegram*, January 23, 1934; and January 14, 1940. For Golden Gloves, see Ibid., January 23, 1948.

10. *Fort Worth Star-Telegram*, "Business" section, December 2, 1957; November 5, 1979; October 3, 1991; and July 14, 2000. For a description of working conditions in the pecan business, see Barbara Finlay, "Shell Game," *American History Magazine*, October 2019, p. 60.
11. *Fort Worth Star-Telegram*, April 7, 1924; and September 30, 1962.
12. *Fort Worth Star-Telegram*, July 7, 2020.

Chapter 24

1. *Fort Worth Star-Telegram*, January 9, 1916.
2. *Fort Worth Star-Telegram*, January 9 and 11, 1916.
3. *Fort Worth Star-Telegram*, January 11, 12, and 14, 1916.
4. *Fort Worth Star-Telegram*, January 14 and 15, 1916.
5. For Fox sisters, see Peter Carlson, "Foxy Ladies," *American History Magazine*, April 2019, pp. 20–21.
6. *Fort Worth Star-Telegram*, October 16, 17, and 19, 1924. For Chambers, see Ibid., August 27, 1922.
7. *Fort Worth Star-Telegram*, October 16 and 17, 1924.
8. *Fort Worth Star-Telegram*, October 16, 17, and 19, 1924.
9. *Fort Worth Star-Telegram*, October 19, 1924.
10. *Dallas Morning News*, March 18, 1927. *Fort Worth Star-Telegram*, September 1, 1929
11. *Fort Worth Star-Telegram*, October 28, 2012. A modern spiritualist, Arthur Moses of Fort Worth, claims to still be trying to contact Houdini today.

Chapter 25

1. The story says that Lee and an unnamed companion were gazing out over "the boundless plains of West Texas" when the companion asked Lee, "What do you see?" Lee replied illogically, "I am listening to the footsteps of oncoming millions." The story has been placed at various frontier posts in Texas sometime between 1856 and 1859, including in addition to Fort Worth, Ringgold Barracks, and Camp Cooper. The earliest known version was part of a "Tribute to Texas" written by famed New York advertising executive Bruce Barton in 1932. *Fort Worth Star-Telegram*, April 18, 1932. See also Ibid., March 18, 1965; and *Dallas Morning News*, January 19, 1943. Significantly, the story is not related

in the standard reference work on Lee's time in Texas, Carl Coke Rister, *Robert E. Lee in Texas* (Norman: University of Oklahoma Press, 1946).

2. *Dallas Morning News*, March 7, 1941. Howard Shaff and Audrey Karl Shaff, *Six Wars at a Time: The Life and Times of Gutzon Borglum, Sculptor of Mount Rushmore* (Sioux Falls, SSD: St. Augustana College, Center for Western Studies, 1985), p. 197.
3. *Dallas Morning News*, January 8 and July 15, 1926. For an account of Borglum's rise and fall with the Stone Mountain project, see Gerald W. Johnson, *The Undefeated* (New York: Minton, Balch Co., 1927).
4. *Dallas Morning News*, March 12, 1926.
5. *Dallas Morning News*, April 6, 1926; and March 7, 1941. Johnson, *The Undefeated.*
6. *Dallas Morning News*, July 15, 1926; and June 5, 1927.
7. Borglum speaking at a Dallas luncheon in 1928. *Dallas Morning News*, May 18. 1928.
8. *Dallas Morning News*, July 15, 1926.
9. *Dallas Morning News*, April 27, 1927.
10. *Dallas Morning News*, June 5, 1927.
11. *Dallas Morning News*, May 18, 1928.
12. *Dallas Morning News*, April 7, 1929.
13. *Dallas Morning News*, April 7, 1929; April 26, 1936.
14. The New Handbook of Texas online; *Dallas Morning News*, December 14, 1933; April 7 and June 11, 1936; and March 7, 1941.
15. *Dallas Morning News*, January 17, 1934.
16. The Corpus Christi statue was modified by Lincoln Borglum and placed on a South Dakota mountaintop.
17. Franklin D. Roosevelt unveiled the Lee statue in Dallas in 1936. *Dallas Morning News*, June 12, 1936. Joseph Connor, "Unforgiven: What We Talk About When We Talk About Robert E. Lee," *American History Magazine*, June 2018, pp. 32–39. For removal of Tandy statue after 28 years, see *Fort Worth Star-Telegram*, July 8, 2009.

Chapter 26

1. [San Francisco] *The Call*, December 11, 1910. The best biography of Guinan is Louise Berliner, *Texas Guinan, Queen of the Nightclubs* (Austin: University of Texas Press, 1993). See also Debbie Mauldin Cottrell, "Mary Louise (Texas) Guinan," *Handbook of Texas Online*, Texas State Historical Association; and Peter Carlson, "'T' for Texas. 'G.' for a Good Time," *American History Magazine*, October 2107,

pp. 18–19. For her name's pronunciation, see *Dallas Morning News*, August 22, 1922.

2. Mona Sizer, "Too Hot for Texas," *Outrageous Texans: Tales of the Rich and Famous* (Lanham, MD: Taylor Trade Publications, 2008), p. 82.
3. Berliner, p. 209.
4. Obituary, *Dallas Morning News*, November 6, 1933.
5. *Dallas Morning News*, January 21, February 11 and 13, 1917. *Fort Worth Star-Telegram*, February 12 and 17, 1917.
6. *Fort Worth Star-Telegram*, January 27, 1918. For "The Hermit," see *Fort Worth Star-Telegram*, December 30, 1921.
7. *Dallas Morning News*, August 20 and 21, 1922. *Fort Worth Star-Telegram*, December 30, 1921; and August 21, 1922.
8. *Dallas Morning News*, August 22, 1922. *Fort Worth Star-Telegram*, December 19, 1922.
9. *Dallas Morning News*, September 2 and 3, and November 6, 1933.
10. *Fort Worth Star-Telegram*, February 25, 1933.
11. *Fort Worth Star-Telegram*, May 18 and 19, 1969.

Chapter 27

1. E.R. Milner, *The Lives of Bonnie & Clyde* (Carbondale: Southern Illinois University Press, 1996), p. 7.
2. *Fort Worth Star-Telegram*, April 6, 1935. *Dallas Morning News*, April 6, 1935.
3. For threesome, see Carl Sifakis, *The Encyclopedia of American Crime* (New York: Facts on File, 1982), p. 310 ("Hamilton, Ray")
4. Milner, p. 43. Guinn, pp. 245–49, and 260–61.
5. Milner, pp. 116, 133. Jeff Guinn, *Go Down Together* (New York: Simon & Schuster, 2009), pp. 301–02.
6. Guinn, p. 302.
7. Milner, p. 146.
8. *Fort Worth Star-Telegram*, April 6, 1935. *Dallas Morning News*, April 6, 1935.
9. *Dallas Morning News*, April 6, 1935. *Fort Worth Star-Telegram*, April 6, 1935.
10. *Dallas Morning News*, April 6, 1935.
11. Jim Gatewood, *J. Frank Norris, Top o' Hill Casino, Lew Jenkins, and the Texas Oil Rich* (Garland: Mullaney Corp. 2006), p.185. *Fort Worth Star-Telegram*, April 6, 1935. *Dallas Morning News*, April 6, 1935.
12. *Dallas Morning News*, April 6, 1935.

13. *Dallas Morning News*, April 6, 1935.
14. Gatewood, p. 185.

Chapter 28

1. For "more enjoyable," see Victor H. Green, *The Negro Motorist Green Book* (New York: privately published, 1936), Introduction.
2. Richard F. Selcer, *A History of Fort Worth in Black & White* (Denton: UNT Press, 2015), pp. 338, 467–69. Mike Nichols, "'Green Book' Just a Movie Now But a Vital Road Map then," "Hometown by Handlebar" website https://hometownbyhandlebar.com, posted February 28, 2019. For The Main Hotel, see Simone C.D. Ramos, *Fort Worth's Historic Hotels* (Charleston, S.C.: Arcadia Publishing, 2013), p. 37.
3. Cheryl L. Simon, "Jim Hotel," Handbook of Texas Online, Texas State Historical Assoc. website https://www.tshaonline.org/handbook/online. Christopher Evans, "The Hot Spot. Fort Worth's Jim Hotel….," *Fort Worth Star-Telegram*, June 30, 1991.
4. Mike Nichols, "Green Book …," "Hometown by Handlebar," February 28, 2019. In the 1962 edition of the *Green Book*, the address of the Green Leaf was given as 915 E. Eighth.
5. "Revival Led to Men's Y," *Fort Worth Star-Telegram*, October 30, 1949.
6. Mike Nichols, "Green Book …," "Hometown by Handlebar," February 28, 2019.
7. Mike Nichols, "Green Book …," "Hometown by Handlebar," February 28, 2019.
8. *Fort Worth Star-Telegram*, September 10, 2017. For auction copy, see "Mosaic" section, *American History Magazine*, August 2019, p. 10.

Chapter 29

1. *The Dallas Express*, July 15, 1950.
2. For a brief overview of McDonald's life, see Selcer, *A History of Fort Worth in Black & White* (Denton: UNT Press, 2015), pp. 300–303.
3. "Carter Wesley, "Current Events" (editorial), *Dallas Express*, July 15, 1950, pp. 1–10.
4. Selcer, *A History of Fort Worth in Black & White*, pp. 146–47.
5. Ibid., p. 303.

Chapter 30

1. The Black Elephant unlike the White Elephant was not even listed in city directories. Customers could only find it by word of mouth. For a good, short history, see C. Vann Woodward, *The Strange Career of Jim Crow* (New York: Oxford University Press, 1974). For background on Jim Crow in Fort Worth, see Richard Selcer, *A History of Fort Worth in Black & White* (Denton, TX: UNT Press, 2015), pp. 133–230.
2. Selcer, *A History of Fort Worth in Black & White*, pp. 283–286.
3. Several of these theaters were remodeled and updated decades later to serve a new generation of movie-goers. *Dallas Morning News*, October 21, 1928. *Houston Chronicle*, January 21, 1988. *Corpus Christi Caller-Times*, October 14, 2005. *Amarillo Globe-News*, July 15, 2007. *San Angelo Standard-Times*, May 29, 2019.
4. *Dallas Morning News*, August 2 and August 21, 1924. *Fort Worth Star-Telegram*, August 31, 1924 (p. 10). For "theater district," see Ibid., April 2, 1920.
5. *Dallas Morning News*, August 21, 1924. *Fort Worth Star-Telegram*, August 31, 1924 (pp. 11 and 35).
6. *Dallas Morning News*, November 16, 1924.
7. *Dallas Morning News*, February 22, 1926; October 21 and 22, 1928.
8. *Dallas Morning News*, February 25, 1927; May 28, 1928; April 18, 1929. *Fort Worth Star-Telegram*, April 11, December 2 and 3, 1920; March 30, 1929.
9. *Fort Worth Star-Telegram*, February 18, 2002 ("Tarrant Business" section).

Chapter 31

1. Raymond Arsenault, "The End of the Long Hot Summer: The Air Conditioner and Southern Culture," *The Journal of Southern History* 50, no. 4 (Nov. 1984): 597–628.
2. *Fort Worth Star-Telegram*, August 8, 1916.
3. Roze McCoy Porter, *Thistle Hill, The Cattle Baron's Legacy* (Dallas: Taylor Publishing Co., 1980), p. 106.
4. Margaret Ingels, *Willis Haviland Carrier, Father of Air Conditioning* (New York: Arno Press, 1972 reprint), p. 65.
5. For the Pantages, the new system was part of their advertising even before opening. *Fort Worth Star-Telegram*, December 2 and 3 and April 11, 1920. The luxurious appointments boosted the cost of constructing the

Pantages to a reported $600,000! For the Capitol, see *Dallas Morning News*, October 2 and December 16, 1922; June 1, 1925.

6. Finding guide, Interstate Theater Collection, Dallas Public Library, Dallas, Texas.
7. *Fort Worth Star-Telegram*, April 29, 1948.
8. *Fort Worth Star-Telegram*, August 25, 1929.
9. *Fort Worth Star-Telegram*, October 10, 1929; November 16, 1930.
10. For New Isis, see *Fort Worth Star-Telegram*, July 14, 1940. For Motor Inn, see Ibid., August 10, 1941.
11. *Dallas Morning News*, September 5, 1934.
12. *Fort Worth Star-Telegram*, April 1, 1945. Information on the courthouse comes from Art Weinman, the architect in charge of multiple renovation projects on the building.

Chapter 32

1. For the Odeon, see *Fort Worth Star-Telegram*, April 12, 1998. Cf. recollections of Barry Burke that Fort Worth's first movie theater was the Imperial, opening in 1925. *Fort Worth Press*, October 8, 1925.
2. For amenities, see 1930 opening of the New Liberty (1107 Main). *Fort Worth Star-Telegram*, August 30, 1930.
3. *Fort Worth Star-Telegram*, March 26, 1915; and March 6, 1916.
4. For New Tivoli, see *Fort Worth Star-Telegram*, July 21, 1935. For Parkway, see Ibid., February 2, 1964. For TCU, see Ibid., March 24, 1946; and August 26, 2006. For Isis, see Art Weinman, "Isis and New Isis Theater History," historic marker application, Tarrant County Archives. For Interstate chain, see www.paramounthistory.org/interstate-theaters-1915–1975 .
5. Richard Gonzales, "Rose Marine Theater Filled a Void…., *Fort Worth Star-Telegram*, October 20, 2019.
6. A drive to reopen the New Isis theater was launched in 2017 by Jeffrey S. Smith with costs estimated to range between five and thirty million dollars. *Fort Worth Star-Telegram*, December 6, 2017.

Bibliography

Unpublished Sources

Camp Bowie lease. July 2, 1917. National Archives Record Group 92. Records of the Office of Quartermaster General. Entry 1998, No. 601.53.

Dept. of the Army. Records of the Adj. General's Office, 1917 *ff.* Record Group 407. National Archives and Records Administration.

Freeman, Maj. William G. Report on the Inspection of Fort Worth, September 7, 1853. Old Army records. See Crimmins, M.L., under magazines below.

Kinch, Samuel E., Jr. "Amon Carter: Publisher-Salesman." Thesis submitted for Master of Arts degree in Journalism Dept., University of Texas, January 1965.

Perkins, Charles R. "History of Fort Worth Lodge No. 148, A.F.&A.M., 1855–1955." Thesis submitted to History Dept., Texas Christian University in partial fulfillment of the requirements for the degree of Master of Arts, 1957.

Selcer, Richard. "Fort Worth's First Masonic Hall, 1857–1878," Texas Historic Marker application. Tarrant County Archives.

Summers, Nancy Katherine. "Struggle for Existence: Fort Worth, 1870–1876." Master of Arts thesis. History Dept. Texas Christian University, 1968.

Terry, I.C. "Reminiscences of Fort Worth Fifty Years Ago." 1929 unpublished MS in collections of Fort Worth Library, Central Branch, Local History, Genealogy & Archives Unit.

Weinman, Art. "Isis and New Isis Theater History." Historic marker application. Tarrant County Archives.

Books

Arnold, Ann. *A History of the Fort Worth Medical Community*. Arlington, TX.: Landa Press, 2002.

———. *The History of Fort Worth's Legal Community* (Austin, TX.: Eakin Press, 2000.

Berliner, Louise. *Texas Guinan, Queen of the Nightclubs*. Austin: University of Texas Press, 1993.

Bishop, Joseph Bucklin. *Theodore Roosevelt's Letters to His Children.* New York: Charles Scribner's Sons, 1919.

Cervantez, Brian. *Amon Carter: A Lone Star Life.* Norman: University of Oklahoma Press, 2019.

Chapman, Betty Trapp. *Rough Road to Justice.* Austin: State Bar of Texas, 2008.

Collins, Michael. *Those Daring Young Men: A History of the Automobile Pioneers in Fort Worth, 1902–1940.* Fort Worth: Frank D. Kent and the *Fort Worth News-Tribune*, 1985.

Cuellar, Carlos E. *Stories from the Barrio: A History of Mexican Fort Worth.* Ft. Worth: Texas Christian University Press, 2003.

DeArment, Robert K. *Jim Courtright of Fort Worth: His Life and Legend.* Fort Worth: TCU Press, 2004.

Engelhardt, George W. *The City of Fort Worth and the State of Texas.* Fort Worth: Geo. W. Engelhardt & Co., 1890. [This is a very rare book in author's personal collection.]

Evans, Rod. *Palaces on the Prairie.* Fargo, ND: North Dakota Institute for Regional Studies and North Dakota State University, 2009.

Fitzgerald, Hugh Nugent, ed. *Texans and Their State: A Newspaper Reference Work.* Fort Worth: Texas Biographical Association, 1918.

Fort Worth City Directories, 1877–1915. Fort Worth Library, Central Branch, Local History, Genealogy & Archives Unit.

Garrett, Julia Kathryn. *Fort Worth: A Frontier Triumph.* Fort Worth: Texas Christian University Press, 1996 (reprint of Encino Press 1972 ed.).

Gatewood, Jim. *J. Frank Norris, Top O' Hill Casino, Lew Jenkins, and the Texas Oil Rich.* Garland, TX: Mullaney Corp. 2006.

George Juliet. *Fort Worth's Arlington Heights.* Images of America Series. Charleston, SC: Arcadia Publishing, 2010.

Giardino, Vincent. *A Century of Seeking Justice: A Brief History of the Tarrant County Criminal District Attorney's Office.* Fort Worth: privately printed, 2019.

Golden, Eve. *Vernon and Irene Castle's Ragtime Revolution.* Lexington: The University Press of Kentucky, 2007.

Graff, Harvey. *The Dallas Myth.* Minneapolis: University of Minnesota Press, 2008.

Greater Fort Worth, Texas, Illustrated. A. Owens Jennings, publisher. Fort Worth: Texas Printing Co., 1907 (Library of Congress).

Guinn, Jeff. *Go Down Together: The True, Untold Story of Bonnie and Clyde.* New York: Simon & Schuster, 2009.

Hall, Colby D. *History of Texas Christian University*. Fort Worth: Texas Christian University Press, 1947.

Hulme, Louie L., ed. *Rotary Club of Fort Worth, 75th Anniversary, 1913–1988*. Fort Worth: privately printed, 1988.

Ingels, Margaret. *Willis Haviland Carrier, Father of Air Conditioning*. New York: Arno Press, 1972 reprint.

Jary, William E., ed. *Camp Bowie, Fort Worth, 1917–1918*. Fort Worth: B.B. Maxfield Foundation, 1975.

Jones, Jan L. *Renegades, Showmen & Angels: A Theatrical History of Fort Worth, 1873–2001*. Fort Worth: Texas Christian University Press, 2006.

Knight, Oliver. *Fort Worth Outpost on the Trinity*. Norman: University of Oklahoma Press, 1953; repr., Texas Christian University Press, 1990.

Kroeger, Brooke. *Nellie Bly: Daredevil, Reporter, Feminist*. New York: Times Books, 1994.

Lale, Cissy Stewart. *Sweetie Ladd's Historic Fort Worth*. Fort Worth: TCU Press, 1999.

Larson, Erik. *The Devil in the White City: Murder, Magic, and Madness at the Fair That Changed America*. New York: Crown Publishers, 2003.

Makers of Fort Worth. No author. Fort Worth: Fort Worth Newspaper Artists Association, 1914. Collections of Fort Worth Library, Central Branch, Local History, Genealogy & Archives Unit.

McClurkin, Brenda S. *Fort Worth's Quality Hill*. Images of America Series. Charleston, SC: Arcadia Publishing, 2014.

McGown, Quentin. *Historic Photos of Fort Worth*. Nashville, TN: Turner Publishing, 2007.

Milner, E.R. *The Lives and Times of Bonnie & Clyde*. Carbondale: Southern Illinois University Press, 1996.

Myres, Sandra, ed. *Force without Fanfare: The Autobiography of K.M. Van Zandt*. Fort Worth: Texas Christian University Press, 1968.

Nasaw, David. *Going Out: The Rise and Fall of Public Amusements*. Cambridge, MA: Harvard University Press, 1993.

Neal, Bill. *From Guns to Gavels: How Justice Grew up in the Outlaw West*. Lubbock: Texas Tech University Press, 2008.

Nichols, Mike. *Lost Fort Worth*. Charleston, SC: The History Press, 2014.

Oates, Paula, ed. *Celebrating 150 Years: The Pictorial History of Fort Worth, Texas, 1849–1999*. Fort Worth: Landmark Publishing 1999.

Paddock, B.B. *A Twentieth Century History and Biographical Record of North and West Texas*. Chicago: Lewis Publishing Co., 1906.

Paddock, B.B. *History of Texas: Fort Worth and the Texas Northwest Edition*. Chicago: Lewis Publishing Co., 1922.

Pate, J'Nell. *Livestock Legacy: The Fort Worth Stockyards, 1887–1987*. College Station: Texas A&M University Press, 1988.

———. *North of the River: A Brief History of North Fort Worth*. Fort Worth: Texas Christian University Press, 1994.

Peak, Howard W. *A Ranger of Commerce Or 52 years on the Road*. San Antonio: Naylor Printing Co., 1929.

———. *My Recollections of Fort Worth*. Fort Worth: privately published, 1922.

Perkins, Clay. *The Fort in Fort Worth*. Keller, TX: Cross-Timbers Publishing, 2001.

Pratt, James. *Sabotaged: Dreams of Utopia in Texas*. Lincoln: University of Nebraska Press, 2020.

Ramos, Simone C.D. *Fort Worth's Historic Hotels*. Charleston, SC: Arcadia Publishing, 2013.

Rich, Harold. *Fort Worth: Outpost, Cowtown, Boomtown*. Norman: University of Oklahoma Press, 2014.

Rister, Carl Coke. *Robert E. Lee in Texas*. Norman: University of Oklahoma Press, 1946.

Roark, Carol. *Fort Worth Then and Now*. Fort Worth: Texas Christian University, 2001.

———. and Byrd Williams. *Fort Worth's Legendary Landmarks*. Fort Worth: Texas Christian University Press, 1995.

Sanders, Leonard. *How Fort Worth Became the Texasmost City*. Fort Worth: Amon Carter Museum of Western Art, 1973.

Selcer, Richard F. *Fort Worth Characters*. Denton: University of North Texas Press, 2009.

———. *Photographing Texas: The Swartz Brothers, 1880–1918*. College Station: TX. A&M University Press, 2019.

Selcer, Richard F, and Kevin Foster. *Written in Blood: The History of Fort Worth's Fallen Lawmen, Vol. 1, 1861–1909*. Denton: University of North Texas Press, 2010

———. *Written in Blood: The History of Fort Worth's Fallen Lawmen, Vol. 2, 1910–1928*. Denton: University of North Texas Press, 2011.

Selzer, Adam. *H.H. Holmes: The True History of the White City Devil*. New York: Skyhorse Publishing, 2017.

Shaff, Howard, and Audrey Karl Shaff. *Six Wars at a Time: The Life and Times of Gutzon Borglum, Sculptor of Mount Rushmore*. Sioux Falls, SD: St. Augustana College, Center for Western Studies, 1985.

Sherrod, Katie, ed. *Grace & Gumption: Stories of Fort Worth Women*. Fort Worth: Texas Christian University Press, 2007.

Sifakis, Carl. *The Encyclopedia of American Crime*. New York: Facts on File, 1982.

Stanley, F. (Father Stanley Crocchiola). *Longhair Jim Courtright: Two-gun Marshal of Fort Worth*. Denver, CO: World Press, 1957.

Talbert, Robert Harris. *Cowtown Metropolis: Case Study of a City's Growth and Structure*. Fort Worth: Leo Potishman Foundation. Fort Worth: Fort Worth National Bank, n.d.

Terrell, Joseph C. *Reminiscences of the Early Days of Fort Worth*. Fort Worth: Texas Printing Co., 1906.

Williams, Mack, ed. *In Old Fort Worth: The Story of a City and Its People as Published in the News-Tribune in 1976 and 1977*. Fort Worth: Tribune Publishing Co., 1977.

Woodward, C. Vann. *The Strange Career of Jim Crow*. New York: Oxford University Press, 1974.

Wright, Gavin. *Old South, New South: Revolutions in the Southern Economy Since the Civil War*. New York: Basic Books, 1986.

Youngblood, Dawn. *Fort Worth*. Images of America series. Charleston, SC: Arcadia Publishing, 2019.

Magazines, Journals and Newspaper Stories

Arsenault, Raymond. "The End of the Long Hot Summer: The Air Conditioner and Southern Culture." *The Journal of Southern History* 50, no. 4 (November 1984): 597–628.

Brown, Marsha. "A British Castle in North Texas." *North Texas Star Storyteller & Rambler*. June 2009, pp. 4–8 *ff*.

————. "Weatherford Princess: The Mary Couts Burnett Story." *Parker County Today: Our County Magazine*. June 2013, p. 70–87.

Carlson, Peter. "'T' for Texas. 'G' for a Good Time." *American History Magazine*. October 2017, pp. 18–19.

Chamber of Commerce Magazine (Fort Worth). A complete three-year run, 1947–1950, is in the collections of the Amon Carter Museum of American Art, Fort Worth.

Connor, Joseph. "Unforgiven: What We Talk About When We Talk About Robert E. Lee. *American History Magazine*. June 2018, pp. 32–39.

Crimmins, M.L. "Fort Worth Was an Early Army Post." *Frontier Times* 16, no. 4 (January 1939): 139–141.

Fairley, Bill. "No Pilot More Dashing than Castle in WW I." *Fort Worth Star-Telegram*. May 21, 1997, pp. 8–9 B.

Finlay, Barbara. "Shell Game." *American History Magazine*. October 2019, pp. 56–63.

Hooks, Michael Q. "The Role of Promoters in Urban Rivalry: The Dallas-Fort Worth Experience, 1870–1910." *Red River Valley Historical Review* 7, no. 2 (Spring 1982): 4–16.

Phillips, Edward Hake. "Teddy Roosevelt in Texas, 1905." *West Texas Historical Association Year Book* [*sic*]51 (1980): 58–67.

Selcer, Richard. "Phantom Raiders on the Trinity." *Wild West Magazine* 26, no. 3 (October 2013): 54–60.

SIGNAL 50. The Quarterly Newsletter of the Fort Worth Police Officers Association. Fort Worth. Sgt. Kevin Foster, editor. (on file, Fort Worth Library, Central Branch, Local History, Genealogy & Archives Unit).

Time Magazine. October 31, 1933. Letters to the Editor (Amon Carter).

Vaughn, Daniel. "The History of the Pig Stands: America's Motor Lunch." *Texas Monthly Magazine*. February 18, 2015.

Wallace, Edward S. "William Jenkins Worth and Texas." *Southwestern Historical Quarterly* 42, no. 2 (Oct. 1940): 159–168.

Newspapers

Dallas Herald, 1855–1887 (daily and weekly)

Dallas Morning News, 1885–present.

Dallas Times-Herald, 1888–1895.

Fort Worth Democrat, 1871–1881 (daily and weekly).

Fort Worth Gazette, 1882–1896 (daily and weekly).

Fort Worth Mail-Telegram, 1898–1902.

Fort Worth Morning Register, 1895–1905.

Fort Worth Press, 1921–1975.

Fort Worth Record, 1903–1925.

Fort Worth Record-Telegram, 1925–1931 (morning ed. of the *Star-Telegram*)

Fort Worth Star, 1906–1909 (merged with the *Telegram*)

Fort Worth Star-Telegram, 1909–present.

Fort Worth Telegram, 1902–1908 (formerly the *Mail-Telegram*)

The News-Tribune, 1975–1976.

Online Sources

"Fort Worth … the Way We Were." Jack White's photo collections. www.fortwortharchitecture.com/oldftw/oldftw.htm.

Handbook of Texas Online, http://www.tshaonline.org. Texas State Historical Association.

"Hometown by Handlebar," Mike Nichols' blog. http://hometownbyhandlebar.com.

History of Interstate theater chain. www.paramounthistory.org/interstate-theaters-1915-1975.

Correspondence

Atkinson, Jim. Email to Jack White. June 7, 2010. (He was a former officer of Pangburn's Candy Co.)

Parrent, Ms. Dale Wilson. Email to Richard Selcer. Nov. 11 and 13, 2019 (She was one of the women who led the fight to get the Tarrant County Convention Center theater named for John F. Kennedy).

Index

A

B

C

D

E

F

G

H

I

J

K

L

Q

R

S

T

U

V

W